Art Work

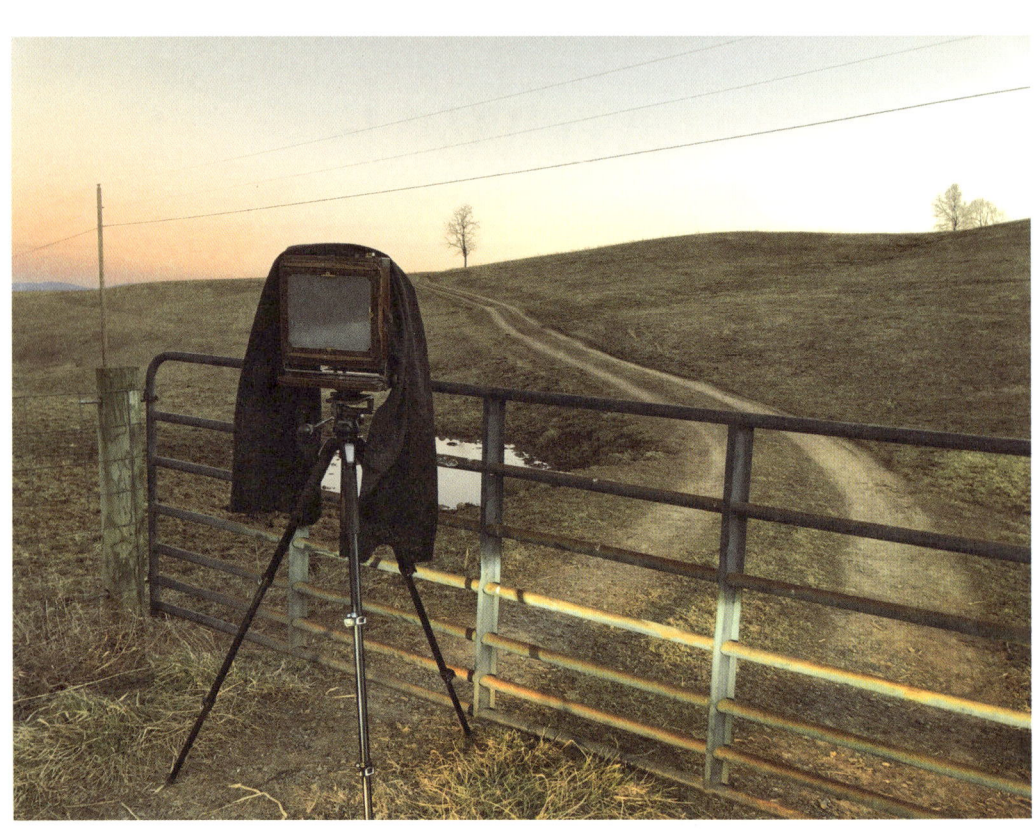

Art Work

On the Creative Life

Sally Mann

Abrams Press, New York

For Emmett
O lost, and by the wind grieved

Library of Congress Control Number: 2025934745

ISBN: 978-1-4197-8071-4
eISBN: 979-8-88707-633-1

Printed and bound in the United States
10 9 8 7 6 5 4 3 2 1

Designed by Laura Lindgren

Abrams books are available at special discounts when purchased in quantity for
premiums and promotions as well as fundraising or educational use. Special editions can
also be created to specification. For details, contact specialsales@abramsbooks.com or
the address below.

Abrams Press® is a registered trademark of Harry N. Abrams, Inc.

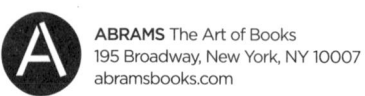

ABRAMS The Art of Books
195 Broadway, New York, NY 10007
abramsbooks.com

Contents

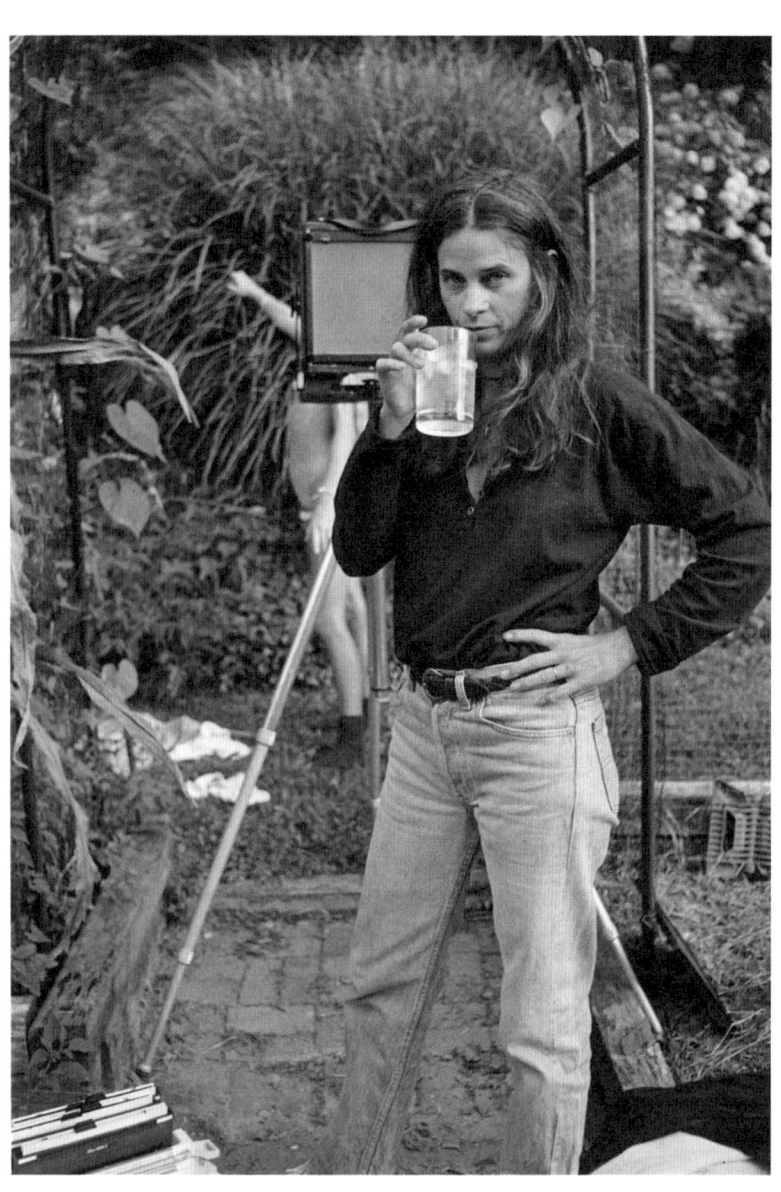

Prologue

Get your work done. If that doesn't work,
shut up and drink your gin.
                              —Ray Bradbury

This is a book about how to get shit done. Or, more particularly, how I got it done. Or didn't. And I guess that's a big part of an artist's life—getting other shit done besides the shit you're supposed to be doing—*the art*, that is.

We should get something straight right off the bat. When I use the word "art" to refer to the stuff I make, there are quotation marks around it in my mind. Other people most assuredly make art, but I have always hesitated to make that claim for myself. Asked by a stranger what I do, I have said, "I'm a photographer," for more than fifty years. Now, I remember to say that I am an artist. For one thing, I don't want to embarrass my highly esteemed gallery, and for another, it saves me from having to decline the well-meaning offers of work photographing weddings or babies. Not that I haven't done those things, and I'm not so proud that I wouldn't do them again if I had to, but explaining the kinds of pictures I take almost always elicits, "Oh, so you're an *artist!*" in a *why didn't you say so* tone of voice, so these days that's what I say.

And why not? Being an artist is not such a big deal. When you get right down to it, art is a job, a profession not unlike being an insurance adjuster or a sportscaster. And it's not all that hard, either. The writer Nell Zink once asserted that you could take the winos off the sidewalk in front of a drugstore and teach them to be poets in half an hour. And I had a friend who quipped that he could strap his iPhone on his cat and have a series of masterpieces by the end of the day. In a similar vein, Veronica Geng once wrote a mordant *New Yorker* piece in which several hostages play "Lifeboat" to pass the time. Whom do you throw off: the nun, the pregnant woman, the majorette, or the artist Helen Frankenthaler? "Throw off Frankenthaler," one of them says. "What's art, anyway? Somebody making some little something."

So, like the drowned woman, I am just somebody making some little something. Many different little somethings. A lot of the time. And how many little somethings I have made over a long, long time perhaps qualifies me to write this book.

———

Sometimes, the process of being an artist—not the satisfaction of splashing paint on canvas or the shutter clicking at what you know is just the right moment, but the rest of what goes into the making of art—can be rightfully called shit. Here I flash back on Cy Twombly, my neighbor in Lexington, Virginia, dusting off his hands in relief as the van door was shut on his paintings, destined for some billionaire's collection, quipping, "Glad to get that shit out of here," before heading out to the benches at the nearby Walmart to relax in the sun. This is the good shit.

But there's the bad shit, too: the rejections, the failures, the cynical strategies of marketing, the perceived necessity for self-promotion, the compromises, the jealousies, the injustices, the dumbass work you thought was good—and, of course, the fear. And sometimes, contrary to the layman's image of the louche life of bohemian disorder we are supposed to be living, the practice of art-making can be lonely and downright cheerless. It's the rare artist who has an army of assistants, lackeys, cooks, asskissers, and lovers, whose indispensable services he rewards by refusing to acknowledge their existence as he gaily carries on in the first-person singular. Although, yes, those artists do exist and often with flamboyant public personae. But few of us have such an army, even the army of one exemplified by Mrs. Tolstoy. The rest of us soldier on alone, navigating into unmapped territory with only our dubiously accurate artistic compass as a guide in which we place an appalling amount of faith—indeed our entire life depends on the accuracy of its frail, quivering needle.

While fervently swearing to anyone who would listen for the last eight years that I'd never write another damn book, I found myself inexplicably jotting down a list of chapter headings, with associated imagery in adjoining folders, for the book I wasn't going to write, and they went like this:

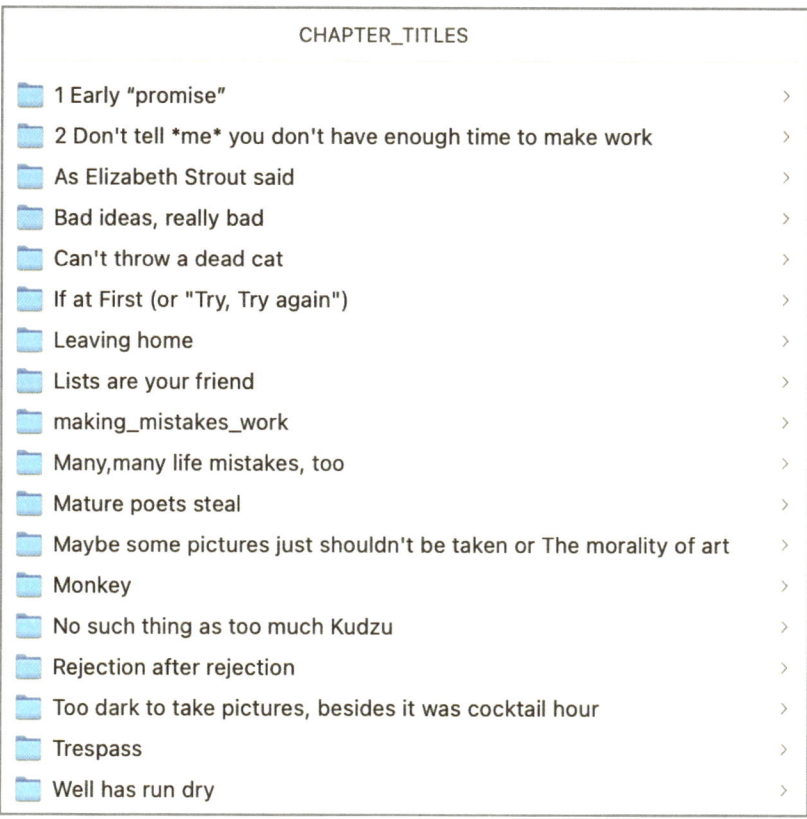

CHAPTER_TITLES

- 1 Early "promise" >
- 2 Don't tell *me* you don't have enough time to make work >
- As Elizabeth Strout said >
- Bad ideas, really bad >
- Can't throw a dead cat >
- If at First (or "Try, Try again") >
- Leaving home >
- Lists are your friend >
- making_mistakes_work >
- Many,many life mistakes, too >
- Mature poets steal >
- Maybe some pictures just shouldn't be taken or The morality of art >
- Monkey >
- No such thing as too much Kudzu >
- Rejection after rejection >
- Too dark to take pictures, besides it was cocktail hour >
- Trespass >
- Well has run dry >

Looking back at it, I think it's still a pretty good start for a book about the creative process, but on the day I sat down and started actually writing the damn book I wasn't going to write, it turned out that what I had to say was about more than just how I made my pictures—it was about all the other things that both buttress the art-making life and hinder it. Like dogs, for instance. Where are dogs on that list? Every artist needs a dog. Every human needs a dog. Rescue a dog right now. But nowhere in the many books I've now read about the creative life does anybody talk about the importance of dogs.

And I probably won't either, but they're right up there with all the other artists' essentials: among them, in my case, an abiding devotion to place, to my "local," to borrow a concept from the poet William Carlos Williams. My particular place has been Virginia, and the South in general, and I have written repeatedly, fulsomely one might say, on the landscape that holds me in its thrall: the collapsing farmhouses, ruinous outbuildings, parishless churches, kudzu-claimed telephone poles, long-forgotten cemeteries, and, all around us, hillsides and mountains greenly serene under our cicada-seething summer sky. This is my landscape, beating inside me like a second heart, and its protection has necessitated activism of various kinds—placing our land in conservation easements, renouncing petrochemical interventions, picking up trash along the roads, writing letters to my representatives, and, of course, making donations, lots of them. Doesn't sound like an artist's life to you? Well, it is. Nowadays, it has to be.

Years ago, my friend Ted Orland (more on Ted soon) used to sign his books "Your Fellow Traveler, Ted," and that phrase was telling. For Ted—and, I hope, my readers—the important thing was that we are all on the same creative road together, however far apart we are in other ways. But we can be brought together by the *how*; how those of us well along in our careers got there, how our lives racked up the miles. It is about more than technique or practice or even, yes, hard work. It is about how you live your life, because the life you lead is your art and the art you make is your life.

My daughter Jessie, a Renaissance woman if ever there was one, proposes that the life suggestions I am making within this book apply not just to artists (of which she is one), but also to scientists (of which she is also one) and to other travelers along many disparate and varied career paths. I hope that may prove to be true, although I can write only from my perspective as an artist and a writer.

And from that vantage, I know the creative life invariably includes a rich, overflowing, varied, and complicated *other* life—not just good ideas, the right equipment, and a Guggenheim grant to buy you time. (Has there ever been a Guggenheim applicant who did not say what they needed was time—and the money to buy that time, of course?) Just look at this journal entry from, if you can believe it, 1970:

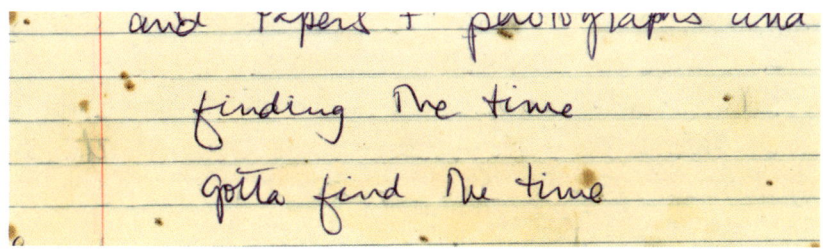

Already worried about not having enough time, and I was nineteen! All I had was time back then. Lots of future, but barely any past; hardly any history, or memories, at that green age. Now, for real, I gotta find the time: At my age, close to handing in my dinner pail, all I have are memories, and hardly any time.

That may not be all bad; it may be that art-making requires not only that you be stressed for time (I found that a full-time job helped with that), but also that you be creative in patching up the crappy equipment you found lying by the dumpster, be as thin-skinned as a naked mole rat, and be convinced that the well has run irreversibly dry and that you will never make another good image or write another good sentence. *Convinced!* Oh, and it never hurts to be impoverished, too. That old parable about the starving artist in the garret? Picasso living in squalor, burning his drawings for heat, Dolly Parton waiting for a sibling to wet the communal bed for a few moments of warmth? There's something to that.

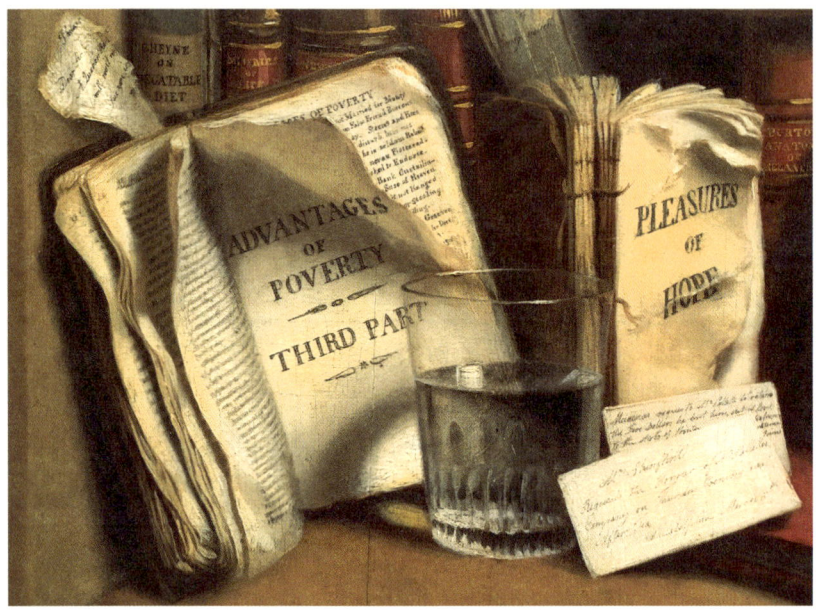

Poor Artist's Cupboard, c. 1815, detail. Painting by Charles Bird King.

I do hope that's gin in the glass.

For years pinned above my desk was a cartoon from *The New Yorker* in which an old man and a young boy are sitting together in what appears to be a city park. The button-nosed boy, whose endearing overbite telegraphs to us his credulity, is earnestly gazing up at the big-bellied, spats-wearing old coot, who imparts this pearl of wisdom: "Always exaggerate. It makes life seem more interesting." I'm with the coot on this one.

So, don't believe everything you read in this book, unless I tell you what I had for lunch fifteen minutes ago. And you shouldn't entirely trust the excerpts from my letters because, as the old man advises, in writing to my distant friends I had to somehow make my life seem more interesting. When we talk about the past, as William Maxwell observed, we lie with every breath we draw. Most of the time, it's not even on purpose; it's just the sanity-imperiling treachery of memory.

Like most everybody, my memories are spotty and whimsical, some elements showing up in vivid detail, others receding, like those tapestries in which certain colors fade over the years, leaving others—often wrongly—predominant. And within that tapestry are great lacunae, gaps in my past where the threads fray and disappear. I take comfort in the late critic Peter Schjeldahl's observation that even my hero Proust had a lousy memory. He points out that there is no "little patch of yellow wall" in Vermeer's *View of Delft*, a memory Proust's character Bergotte conjures just before dropping dead of disappointment or, so he surmised, undercooked potatoes. Proust's memory always appeared to me to be self-sharpening, but perhaps it's as unreliable and mendacious as everyone else's, constantly revised and overwritten.

Even letters, which Janet Malcolm claimed to be the fixative of experience—the fossils of feeling—are not always a conduit to unmediated reality. In reading mine I have occasionally found a gusherful of genuine emotion, usually outrage or regret or, most often, self-doubt so deep it masquerades as swaggering bravado. You won't be fooled; you will see through the bluster and spurious peacockery until you get to the truth. Or something very like the truth, as, winking, a friend's mother once split-haired to us.

To be sure, there has been some drama in my life that even I found unnecessary to enrich with hyperbole, and hilarious coincidences too improbable to be believed in anything but Wolfeian fiction, as well as tragedies too profound to even relate—in other words, I have lived a regular life, like the one you are living right now.

This book is written by an old woman primarily for young artists and writers, with the vain, and vainglorious, hope that some of it will make a difference in the way you organize (yes, I did say organize) your creative practice, or that it might help you avoid some of the pits into which I fell. And fell deeply, I might add, wasting a lot of time—which, in this book, I will try to show isn't maybe all that bad—and also making some piss-poor art, which is not all that bad, either. As long as you know the difference. In the end.

The end is where I am now, and I am studying many of the artistic and life choices I made, scratching my befuddled gray head at why I chose one picture over another or why a picture I now love got tossed in with the losers. And why on earth I would decide to live in Li'l Chickenswitch, as Cy called our sleepy little town, instead of a bustling art metropolis. Why writing weekly letters to a friend three thousand miles away was important. And, speaking of miles away, why would I tear myself from my farm, my darkroom, from my nine dogs for Chrissake, to go across the globe to photograph an alien landscape that I knew absolutely nothing about? And what was I thinking wearing rubber dime-store flip-flops to New York City? Why does a stubborn woman keep taking the same damn picture, a thousand ways? These are some of the mistakes and decisions and questions I will write about here, the answers to which seem obvious to me now, at the end. Or something very like the end.

1

Early Promise

Whom the gods wish to destroy they first call promising.
—Cyril Connolly

As a young woman—girl, actually; I was seventeen when I started taking pictures—it would appear that I didn't have a thing to worry about from the gods. My total lack of promise is exhibit number one in the prosecution of my argument here that it is work, and more work, that makes an artist. Proust became Proust that way, indeed furiously working himself to death. But you don't have to do that—don't kill yourself in your cork-lined room, don't be Mozart dying from exhaustion at thirty-five, just put your head down and steadily, resolutely, pull the load.

I come from good, solid peasant stock; short-waisted, thick-fingered, durable as dirt. I have learned that even if on some uninspired days I can't create, I can always make work. It's hard to shrug on the harness and break the furrow, but once I start, I feel a dray-horse satisfaction that is just a few rows away from something else: call it revelation, creative ecstasy, incipient perfection, serendipity—call it Art.

Not right off the bat, though. In my case, I struggled even to locate the harness, never mind step between the traces and gee-haw my crooked rows. I tried everything—painting, pottery, etching, jewelry-making, poetry, tie-dye—and hardly a glimmer of hope was perceived by anyone. Especially me. And we were right.

If you are so unlucky as to be told you have "promise" by some lying art-room sycophant trying to get into your pants, please for god's sake don't believe it. Instead, allow your malignant insecurities (of course you have them) to kick your lazy ass into gear. I had this figured out in 1969 at age eighteen, writing this in my journal:

> It cannot be a condemnation to trace the creative impulse of the artist to insecurity. And, further, tht that driven impulse should not be denied, for perhaps through creation the artist will find a true security, a true proof of self.
> But does the true artist ever over-come the insecurity that drives him? No — then, definition of artist: one driven by an inner lack of security, certainty of self, to produce proof, tangible, visable, or verbal proof, of that being.

It appears from this that I pragmatically decided that insecurity, with which I still am awash to the front teeth, could be my friend, art-complicit, perhaps even essential for the process. And it also appears that with my profound self-doubt, my overdeveloped sense of independence and old-fashioned cussedness, art might have been the most desirable life path for me. Indeed, maybe the only path.

Basically, from near infancy I wanted to choose, myself, what I was going to do with every aspect of my life, driving my mother to near hysteria by my adamantine refusal to wear clothes. Then, having conceded to underpants, footwear became my Thermopylae: I took my stand and held to it, defeating socks, shoelaces, and the not-infrequent hairbrush to the butt. The despair in my mother's journals of the time helps explain the resultant hands-off approach she adopted for the remaining years spent raising her young porcupine. Nobody was going to boss me around from the first moment I learned I could emit an adult-frazzling shriek.

Short of the loony bin, where can a walking emotional contradiction find a meaningful home? Art, of course. Anybody can do it. It's open admission. Only an artist, I realized as I gazed at the Robert Capa image of Picasso on the beach strutting with the umbrella, can live exactly as she pleases. Only an artist, albeit with a societal eye roll, can get away with idiosyncrasies, sartorial infelicities, with making insulting offers of trades for actual valuable services like medical care, or establishing a circadian clock adjusted to party time. Yes, an artist can live exactly as she pleases, but on the very important condition, of course, that she is willing to practice what my friend Ted calls "financial levitation." More on that later. And maybe we're not "artists"; maybe we are just ordinary people who have chosen to do what we want to do, when we want to do it, and are willing to accept poverty in return.

For sure you don't have to be an egocentric, bossy, pompous, insecurity-riddled asshole to be an artist. In fact, that's unwise for a number of reasons—for one thing, there are only so many Larry Manns that you can find to put up with you. But I am willing to posit that if you possess the stubbornness and defiance that damn near drove my mother over the edge, you can make it work to your advantage in the art-making process. By the age of twenty-one, when I responded to my parents' well-meaning suggestion that I get an actual *paying* job by asserting that I'd sooner eat crabgrass than work at something I didn't love, they had no reason whatsoever to doubt me.

```
.whet ever...
But at that point, I would sooner
eat crab grass than work at something
I didn't lue.
```

And what I loved was taking pictures.

```
    I feel really strong in my photography now, like I don't need a
goddamn BA or anything when I have a handful of my paicture that's
a whole set of BA's and PHD'S put together. So what now?? All I
want to do is work with that goddamn camera..

It's just something that is in my blood so strong now that a day
without doing something with my camera and I am crawing
the walls. I don't know what all this means to you and knowing my
propensity toward hyperbole it probably just beeezez right by
you... "just sally going on about something selse"..but this is
really, really serious.
```

Double "really." My poor parents. At age nineteen, after marrying the first person I had found with the equanimity to put up with me, I was now announcing to them that I was going to quit school, gather up the "handful of my paicture" that were more important than any dumb college degree (and, apparently, than spelling) and be catapulted into success by my passion.

And . . . these important paictures? What did they look like?

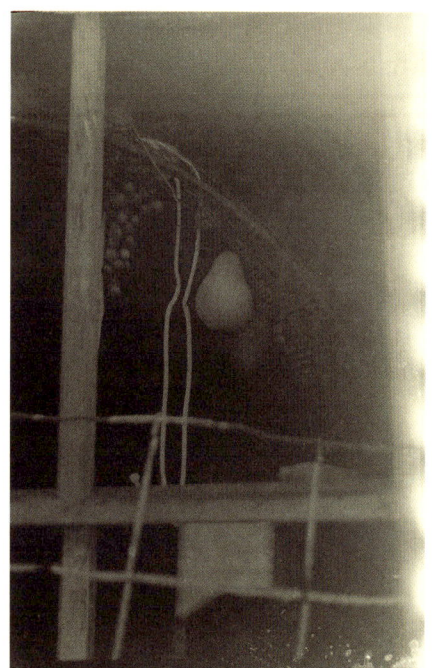
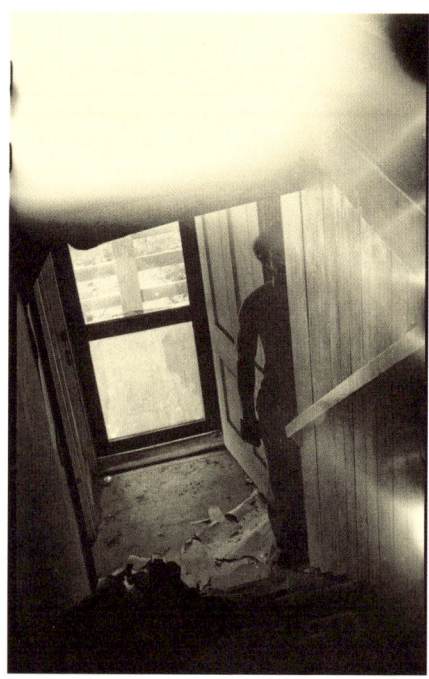

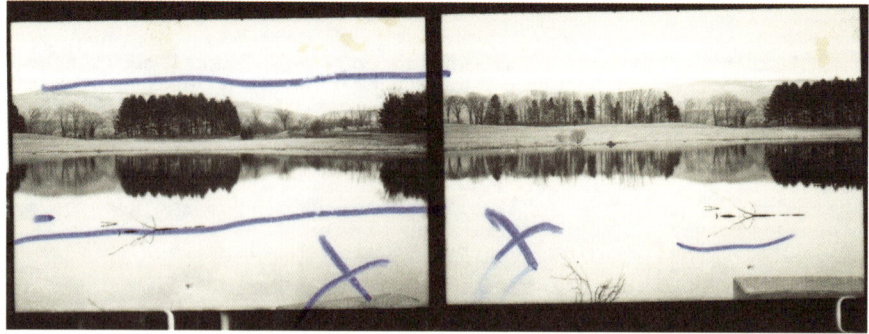

These show you exactly why the gods didn't take the trouble, at that moment, to wipe the ambrosia off their hands and slap the upstart down. There was plenty of time for that, later.

Whether my parents thought it was hyperbole or not, I was indeed "really, really serious." I envisioned myself as an intrepid frigate, magisterially steaming out of port, when in fact I was adrift in a solitary rowboat, taking on water as quickly as I could sluice it out.

How in one short chapter I can employ two metaphors, the agricultural and the nautical, like that, I don't know, but I'm not giving up either one of them. After all, it is the artist's job to facilitate unlikely connections between things, and regardless, you get the point: I was exuberantly hauling ass, I loved what I was doing, and I possessed the kind of naive determination that can alchemically transform crippling insecurity into perfectionism.

I was also lucky.

2

Luck (in Seven Parts)

Luck is not chance—
It's Toil—
Fortune's expensive smile
Is earned—
    —Emily Dickinson

Of course, back in the early 1970s I could barely afford to fly, and the oft-repeated joke that our little regional airplanes were held together with duct tape and chewing gum didn't do anything to encourage me. Sure enough, the one time I did, climbing the aluminum stairs rolled over to the side of the plane, I saw a gob of gum stuck right between the joint of the wing and the spindly braces. Ignoring this portent, I swished on up the steps with the jaunty fatalism of the young, my batik skirt flipping in the June breeze. I remembered to turn and wave to my husband, Larry, standing by the terminal door, before heading down the aisle, scanning the seats for somebody interesting to sit next to. It wasn't hard—about halfway down was a dark-haired, handsome man, a bit older than my twenty-six years, and way better dressed than the average passenger on these tiny planes to New York City. A pocket square; when had I ever seen a man with a pocket square? And a Prince Charlesian double-breasted suit jacket. In this heat!

Back then there were no seat assignments and planes were never filled, so I didn't bother pretending that I was so sorry to require him to gather up his newspaper from the empty seat and make room for me—what with the plane being so crowded and all. Instead, I gave him my most brazen *Hey, it's me* look and plopped right down.

He appeared to be briefly discomfited but courteously shifted the virtually unscuffed sole of his shoe to the other knee. Turning toward me in a disarmingly tentative, even shy fashion, he said, "Hello, my name is Ron."

Sometimes, when you are a young artist, or even a not-so-young artist as I am now, you need plain old luck. I don't think the importance of pure happenstance, of wildly improbable good fortune, of what the poet C. D. Wright once called fuck-me-running coincidence, can be overemphasized in the arc of a career. This is not a thought original to me—indeed many creative people, concerned about that blindfold around Fortuna's eyes, contrive to nudge her rudder a little their way.

For starters, most ambitious young artists and writers put in the obligatory stint in grad school, the more prestigious the better, where they will make friendships and meet the cohort within which they will burst onto the scene, bushy-tailed and sharp-elbowed. To do that, the majority move to a city where they can meet still more artists and writers, but, more importantly, the people who can help them on their quest for attention and success: gallerists, publishers, collectors, and rich, connected people.

This is carefully manufactured luck, not the pure, palm-to-forehead variety, and I see many young artists in happy possession of it. I was not one of those. But consider for a moment what I *did* have: the career-long movement of that rudder at the whim of blind Fortune, and the way it has shifted in salubrious ways to my benefit. From the egg and sperm, I have been lucky to have been born in what was arguably the most prosperous era in human history, and to two beautiful, smart, and financially stable parents. It is not incidental to my success that they were also White.

And despite trying to mess it up at every turn, ungratefully and churlishly, despite taking reckless chances and getting in the kinds of trouble that many other girls, less culturally and genetically blessed, would have paid dearly for, I managed to skate through childhood and early adulthood with very little injury, at least to myself, and shockingly few consequences. Unless, of course, you count the searing guilt and shame-inducing recollections that rise up unbidden nearly every night.

No, you don't want to know. And I sure as shit don't want to tell you, although since we're on the subject, I will say that many of my insomniac nights are spent revisiting the concept of a different kind of luck—that of moral luck. To some extent I have made a career by taking risks and violating societal expectations, and—placed in the most generous light—asking uncomfortable questions. I've long been negotiating my way through heavily mined morality territory.

It was once pointed out by the writer Adam Gopnik that the modern artist, exemplified for him by Gauguin and that carefree man on the beach, Picasso, codified and normalized for all subsequent artists that urge to make a career of shattering norms. Gauguin carried it to such an extreme that he'd elicit a censorious tut-tut from even the most flagrant philanderer (I mean, leaving your wife and kids high and dry; please), but he epitomized the kind of artist that gives us orderly, well-meaning ones a bad name—the kind of bad-boy artist that Gopnik describes as running a red light and flattening the old ladies of custom and convention. And— here's the rub—not only getting away with it, but in doing so, making pedal-to-the-metal almost obligatory for the rest of us.

Because I was a lifelong speeder and a natural rule-breaker, I was a perfect fit to inhabit this paradigm, and even, this is true, once ran over an old woman on Main Street. I wasn't speeding and didn't run any red lights, and she was, after all, jaywalking, so I never even got charged with anything, but seeing her sprawled in the road, her stockings torn at the knees, is a vision that still insistently demands my attention at 2:00 a.m.

That perhaps does not qualify me for the Gopnikian canon of artistic rule-breakers but does remind me of our son Emmett's answer when asked by his driving instructor what the yellow traffic light meant. He replied, "Gun it!" Artistically speaking, gunning it through the yellows is a concept the philosopher Bernard Williams explored in his 1976 essay "Moral

Luck"; The unlucky driver hits the old lady and is morally responsible for doing so, but the other yellow-gunner hits no one—and only chance distinguishes the two. The unlucky driver was just that. This does not, in turn, make the lucky driver morally superior. Gauguin was the lucky driver who enjoyed success and made great, historically significant art that would seem to make the cruel acts of betrayal morally justifiable to modern eyes. But in fact, he's just morally lucky, bathed in the forgiving yellow light of twentieth-century art.

I know I have enjoyed some moral, and perhaps immoral, luck in my time and am occasionally visited in the middle of the night by images of the alternative, the life of the luckless, which I mostly avoided. Miserable in a welter of sheets (my fellow insomniacs will know what I mean), I remind myself that much of my lucky life has been blessed with the plain-old everyday blind kind; sightless Fortuna balanced on her ball, rudder in hand, controlling heredity, the prosperity lottery, the eye averted from the misdemeanor, the lock that held, the forgiving customs agent, that near miss with the chain saw; through all these she has whimsically steered me toward the good work I had absolutely no excuse not to be making. Grabbing the rudder in her off-hours, I have made decisions and taken actions that have occasionally turned out well for me, and in this book, I will try to recommend those that worked and point out those that didn't.

For sure, sitting down next to Ron was one that did. He was a great conversationalist, he knew an *Acer koreana* from a *Chinensis*, he knew the sculptor Kenneth Snelson, to whom I was delivering a 7 × 17 view camera that week, and he modestly confessed he was a rocket scientist. I said, c'mon, what do you really do, and he said, well, I'm kind of a jeweler. My mind skipped briefly to Astor Place in New York's East Village, where folding tables with silver necklaces and rings arranged on them were presided over by their creators, sitting under an umbrella with a half-grown puppy tied next to them.

I accepted a cab ride into the city with Ron and, never one to turn down a free meal, a tuna fish sandwich and a Coke at a coffee shop. Excusing myself, I made a call from the pay phone in the back to confirm that the friend who had distractedly agreed to let me sleep on his couch was still on board with that idea. No answer. More calls—Ron glancing at his watch—still no answer. Another Coke. Finally, Ron gathered up his jacket and newspaper and fished into his pocket and tossed me a set of keys. "Just stay in my place," he said. "I'm headed upstate for the weekend."

I assumed he lived in Greenwich Village—although I speculated that he must have some more casual clothes for his sidewalk sales—but, no, he walked me up Madison to the corner of Seventy-Third Street and pointed west to—good lord—a freaking giant *house*, about halfway down the block toward Fifth Avenue. I began to get a little anxious and said maybe I'd just stay in the lobby until my friend's couch became available and was he sure he wanted to hand over his keys to a stranger and, also, it might be a good idea to get his last name.

"Winston," he said.

Winston. In the jewelry business. No, he wouldn't be swapping his showroom on Fifth Avenue for a folding table, the Pulitzer Mansion on Seventy-Third for a walk-up in Greenwich Village, his bespoke suits for T-shirts and bell-bottoms.

Years later, when I was in the depths of artistic despair, broke and unable to do my work, Ron Winston, through his foundation, came to my rescue with a grant. And even to this day I have a key to his house and feel welcome to crash there. He believed in my work way before I did. This was a chance encounter on a plane, and though I was conspicuously open to it, it was just plain luck.

If chance rewards the prepared mind as, say, your sprouting garden responds to loamy soil, then luck thrives in soil amended with optimism and trace elements of context and contrast. No denying that I have been lucky in many unexpected ways, but much of what gives fortune a nutritive boost is the context in which it takes root. In many cases, what turned out to be a flourishing network of good luck seemed inconsequential at the time; a tiny moment of green success in a very small plot.

I am reminded here of a luncheon with a group of wealthy Texans who were engaged in the vicious final round of the state sport: acreage competition. The losers from the first round remained humbly silent as three elegant ladies produced their property totals, like cardplayers triumphantly slapping down their winning hands. At this level of the competition, each of them boasted big spreads, but one came in at significantly more acres. The victor, her frosted hair French-twisted above a face chalky with powder, resembled nothing so much as a well-dressed iceberg, but she remembered her manners long enough to congratulate the runner-up, who earlier had referred unironically to her father as "Big Daddy" and seemed to be taking this hard. To distract the table from Big Daddy's loser daughter, the winner turned with exaggerated politeness to a florid man across the table and asked, with a poorly disguised air of indifference, how many acres he had.

Shamefaced, he touched his napkin to his lips and ducked his head as he revealed the answer: a mere three hundred acres. Immediately the iceberg floated off to another topic, to avoid further embarrassing their land-poor tablemate. Whose name, it turned out later, was Stemmons. As in Stemmons Freeway, where Kennedy was shot. As in: His three hundred acres were downtown Dallas.

Context matters.

It was a big deal back when I was just starting out for any of us struggling young photographers to score a show, a real show with prints on the walls and all. Sometimes even framed. For people to come and see. Otherwise, nobody would know who you were or what you did. Not like now, when you can put your work on the internet, via any number of platforms, and have thousands or even millions of people see it.

And here, too, context mattered. My first show was on the wall behind the tellers at our local bank (which, in an attempt to disguise the truth, I listed as "Bank Gallery" in my subsequent résumé, as if that was the name of an actual gallery). My second show was in a campus snack bar at, as best I recall, a small state university in North Carolina.

```
All the photographs in this exhibit except No 16 and the
Dream Sequence were taken with a Kodak 5x7 camera, made
of Rosewood around the turn of the century. No. 16 and the
Sequence were taken with a Leica M2.

All photographs are for sale except the last at 30.oo apiece.
Copies are available. Contact: Sally Mann
                              c/o Munger  Rt 3
                              Lexington, Va 463-4293
```

Thumbtacked along with this wall text was a list of the twenty-five silver-gelatin prints. Area codes apparently hadn't been invented then; we were barely past the five-digit party line.

By contrast, Stephen Shore, exactly my contemporary, was also having his first solo show that same year, but his was at the prestigious Light Gallery in New York City, and he was hanging around the Factory with Andy Warhol and Lou Reed. People a lot cooler than anyone I ever knew back then. Or, for that matter, now.

And this is where luck comes in, again. For sure, I didn't have my work in the right context—a snack bar in North Carolina versus the most important gallery in New York—and I wasn't selling prints to MoMA at age fourteen, as Stephen Shore did. But at least I had this: I actually *sold a print*. Off the corkboard of that snack bar wall. It may have been, if memory serves—which she often doesn't—the first print I ever sold.

And who was it standing in line at the snack bar, waiting to pay for her Mr. Pibb? Whose eye was caught by that series of pictures, pushpinned to the wall as she moved in the queue toward the cashier? Who forked out thirty dollars for my print?

Olga Hirshhorn.

I was lucky. Even if that print ended up under a magnet on her refrigerator and not in her eponymous Washington, D.C., museum, I knew exactly how very lucky I was. And while context often moderates luck—I know there is a difference between a refrigerator door and a museum, a corkboard and a gallery wall, or downtown Dallas and a spread of barren Texas backwater—lousy context does not necessarily diminish the inchoate, micro-rhizome-like network of opportunity and hope that swells invisibly just below the skeptical surface.

Invisibly is right. Luck, whimsical by nature, does not bestow abiding confidence; as late as twenty years after what I thought of as a promising start, Eeyore despairingly wrote Ted:

```
I'm circling back to landscapes now, possibly in some
subconscious way to get away from the family pictures and
all their baggage, both good and bad. I am experimenting
with old lenses, daguerrotypean (?) in fact. We'll see
what they produce, although I think I've pretty much shot
my wad, artistically. It's a slow decline from here.
```

It appears that I believed these new (old) lenses were the essential element in the transition from my Family Pictures to a radically different body of work, landscapes, a passion that subsequently occupied me for two decades. Long after the shot wad had fatefully sailed over the horizon, I was still toiling away with the dedication of the peasant—trying to get it right, and, true to form, sure that I never would. But without the timely collusion of foresight and chance, in the form of a generous camera collector recently moved to the area, those landscapes might never have been made.

André Breton, in *L'Amour fou* (*Mad Love*), describes an event in the career of Giacometti in which he also was at an impasse in his work, his own shot-wad moment. At a Parisian flea market, he discovered an enigmatic metal mask, and at the instant of the encounter he knew it offered him a way to move forward from this especially vexatious dead end. For

Giacometti, this mask was a catalyst, a variety of coincidence Breton described as *hasard objectif*—objective chance—a confluence of fortuitous events that somehow, often long after the fact, appear predestined or pre-ordained, possessed of an ineluctable power. As he put it in a 1951 radio interview: "How can phenomena that the human mind perceives only as belonging to separate causal series come so close together that they actually merge into one another . . . ? Why is the glow resulting from such a fusion so bright, albeit so ephemeral?"

As for my own shot-wad deadlock, I found within my dubious depths a luck-welcoming state of grace, "lyric behavior," as Breton called it; a hopeful invitation based on the childlike belief that if you expect the extraordinary, it will manifest. The extraordinary I was seeking was a lens to give me a certain glowy-sky effect but also, below that sky, a sharp area of focus, if only a small one; I wanted a John Beasley Greene desert crispness, but also a refulgent Eugène Atget–in–Versailles mystery. I was certain that it was those nineteenth-century lenses that gave each of these practitioners their distinctive look, but in pre-internet times and stuck in rural Appalachia, how on earth was I supposed to find these lenses that—I was convinced—were imperative to realize my embryonic vision?

By, as usual, blind luck. By discovering that a man with one of the biggest collections of cameras—and especially nineteenth-century lenses—*in the world*, had just alighted sixty miles away. What are the odds?! Upon hearing about him, I was immediately at his door and got the full tour—a state-of-the-art museum tucked away in his sprawling suburban house; temperature and humidity controlled, with custom-built cabinets, whose drawers whispered out to reveal exactly the lenses I coveted. Hundreds of them. I was having trouble describing the effect I was looking for, so, to help me along, he suggested that I show him a picture I particularly admired. I had just seen the Nadar show at the Met in New York, and had brought him the catalog as a gift, so I flipped to plate thirty-four.

"Ah! Baudelaire!" he exclaimed. "Yes, of course, 1855, seated in his mother's chair," and he began to wander distractedly around the room, opening, seemingly at random, drawers and glass-fronted cabinets. After some considerable time, during which he muttered to himself, referring back to a library-style card catalog and appearing to have forgotten I was still there, he triumphantly pounced on an open drawer, fetching from its velvet innards a peculiar brass lens.

"Here it is, I knew I had it! This is the very lens Nadar used to make that picture," he said as he handed it to me with a flourish. "Take it with you and see what you get."

I did and I got plenty. I worked with Nadar's lens for well over a decade.

Looking back, I find so many examples, as though there were a hidden pattern, a matrix of coincidence that invisibly undergirded my life. In the midnineties, I wanted to learn the wet-plate collodion process, and the only two people anywhere in the world, period, who understood the process, Mark and France Osterman, just happened to be teaching at my daughter's boarding school. I mean, really, what are the chances? Years later, again trying to track down a source for wet-plate information, I stopped in Reserve, Louisiana, outside New Orleans, in search of a guy named Claude Levet, about whom I knew nothing except that he photographed Civil War reenactments, was into nineteenth-century photographic processes, and had lived there. Beyond that, nada. Totally quixotic search.

Wet-plate collodion has become so popular these days that you can't throw a dead cat without denting a silver-stained camera bellows, but back then, other than Mark and France, there was hardly anybody doing it. Reserve seemed like a small town, so I figured that I could stop at a filling station and ask, right? A photographer? Big camera, black cloth, stained fingers? Levet? Can't be that common a name.

Wrong. The entire town is full of Levets. The phone book bore that out. Pages and pages of them. So, crap. I decided to just drive around to one of the Levet homes in the phone book, the closest one to the filling station, and ask. I did that. No luck. Did it again with another. A gesture to a small stucco house down the street, maybe that one? Knocked. Nope. Kept driving. Stopped a man walking his dog and asked him if he'd ever heard of a Claude Levet, I mean why not? He was out walking; he might just know. And, I swear, it was Claude Levet himself. He took me to his mother's house, where he still lived, and showed me his wet-plate setup and gave me a glass of brackish Louisiana tap water. For an hour he patiently answered my highly technical questions. I mean, again, what are the odds?

———

You may have noticed that one of the chapter titles I proposed, way back when I was never going to write another book, was "Trespass." Early in my career I took to heart an observation from E. L. Doctorow that suggests that transgression is the life and soul of art-making and to be creative you must be in touch with the forbidden. Perhaps I took it a little too much to heart, but for our purposes here, the notion of trespass is tethered to fortune, because trespass without luck is something altogether different: It's a jail cell.

My luckiest trespassing moment came in Mississippi when I was busted for ignoring prisonlike fortifications and signage in order to get to a ruin of alluring columns—and instead of getting slapped with an arrest warrant, I got an invitation to dinner. Of course, I was not blind to the fact that had my skin been another color or my (practiced) abashment less charmingly convincing, the outcome could have been very different.

Trespass is an undeniable necessity in almost all art forms, and especially the two I have chosen to dabble in—as Czesław Miłosz once remarked, when a writer is born into a family, that family is finished. But equally, when the plein air painter spies just the right mountain view, or the videographer needs a certain light, or the graffiti artist finds a virgin wall, nothing short of razor wire will stop them. And maybe not even that: I once tore a hole in the bellows of my view camera trying to squeeze through aggressive barbed wire fencing designed to keep assholes like me out of a bull pasture. To be an artist means you must declare a loyalty to your art form and your vision that runs deeper than almost any other, even sometimes deeper than blood kinship, and certainly deeper than those trifling laws protecting land ownership.

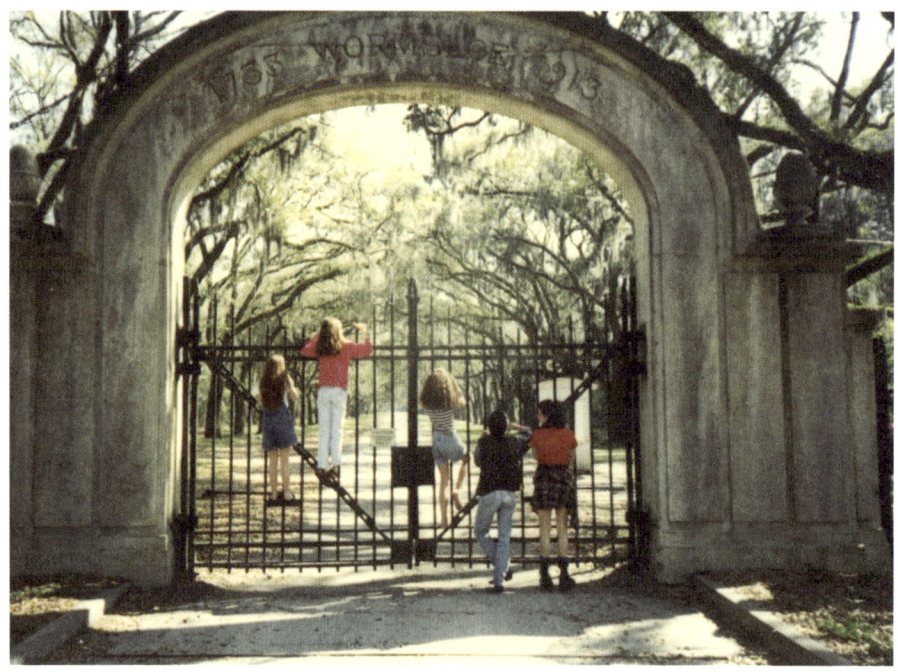

The owners of this plantation house in Georgia probably thought they were doing a great job protecting their land from trespassers—it was sealed tight on all sides. While the girl in the pink shirt was gingerly testing the gate's barbarian-repelling spear tips, Jessie, Virginia, and I were about to concede defeat. As I stood, speculatively examining my eardrum with the stem of my sunglasses and trying to think what to do next, a posse of curious boys wobbled by on bikes, lounging on their banana seats and sneaking sideways glances at us. Hailing them, I asked the biggest one if he knew of any way to get inside the fortifications— because if anyone would, wouldn't it be a neighborhood kid? And again: I was lucky.

He pedaled off and ten minutes later he and the other boys appeared on the other side of the gate and produced a rusted metal pin, which they had fished out of a hiding place in a hollow oak. They fiddled around for a while and then told us to push. The giant gates creaked open and in we sailed; the big, boaty Suburban, packed with my kids and their friends, plus all my camera stuff, with an accompanying flotilla of neighborhood boys buzzing around on their bikes.

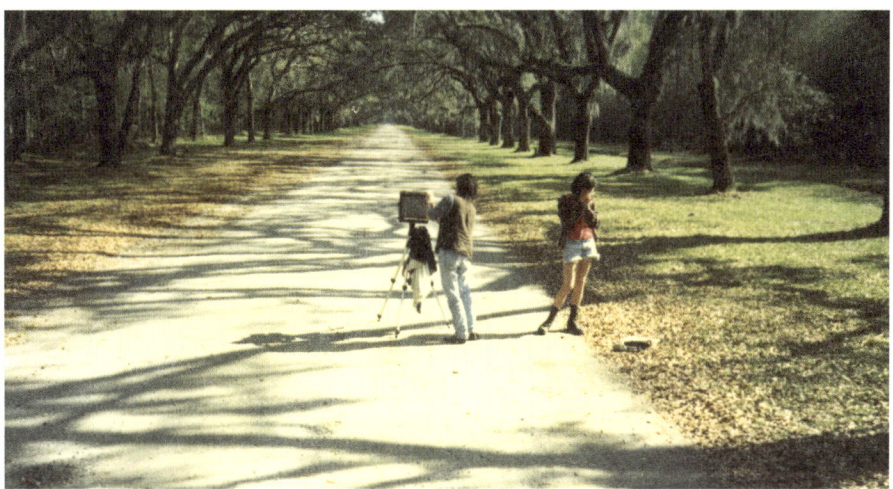

Jessie is here expressing the proper degree of anxiety and embarrassment, awaiting the authorities to come sirening in, while I work with unconcerned sangfroid, convinced my luck would hold. It did.

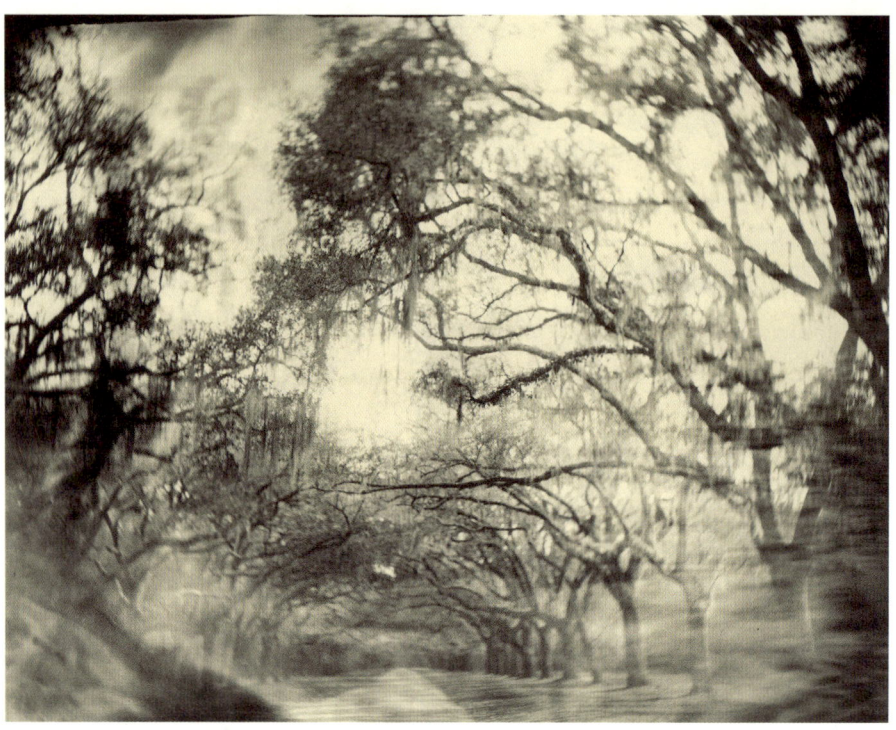

And nothing has changed—I mean, I'm *still* lucky. (I say this smugly, even as I toss to the ground the banana peel on which I doubtless will momentarily slip.) I've mentioned that I live way out in the boondocks, outside the small town of Lexington, whose phone book, when we used to have one, maxed out at the thickness of a Jehovah's Witness pamphlet—a quarter inch or so—and whose page of "Ts" from 1972 is something awfully close to small-town poetry. It reads: "Tutwiler, Tutwiler, Tweddle, Twiddy, Twiddy, Twombly." And although you can generally find Starbucks coffee in the grocery store, and probably get somebody to paint your nails, what you for sure can't find here in Li'l Chickenswitch is a forty-four-inch Epson color printer and a skilled technician to run it. This kind of solution to printing problems requires a trip of at least two hundred miles.

But I had gotten myself into a printing pinch and needed exactly those impossibilities, so I called the high school photo teacher to see what he could suggest. He allowed that the week before he had been to the local camera club meeting and there had been a guy there who said he had a big printer. I could perfectly picture the scene: a room full of dejected retirees, wearing droopy newsboy caps, their whisk-broom mustaches coffee-stained, digital cameras hung around their necks and resting on their paunches. But he gave me a number and I called it.

A bright-eyed voice answered, and I asked the hopeless question, and, well, yes, he did have a printer, yes, an Epson, and it was big. And, no, he wasn't up to much and would be happy to help if he could. My spirits rose a bit.

But then I asked the all-important spiky question on which those spirits were bound to be punctured: How well do you know computers?

There was a beat, two beats, and he said, "Um, pretty well."

Turns out that this man, right here, a few miles down the road, had created the animation system behind Pixar. Eben Ostby had been supervising technical director for almost all their films, until he had the good sense to move next door to me in the boonies. Knows his Photoshop, too, can code with his eyes closed. And as if that weren't enough computer luck for this poor rube who can barely plug in an external hard drive, he is also a fanatical—even more than me—alternative-process geek.

Fortune, not for the first nor, I hope, the last time, lowered her blindfold and directed a now-indispensable photo pal to my tiny little Appalachian dot on the map.

And while we're on the subject of exactly how small and how sleepy our Li'l Chickenswitch is, and lucky also, if a town can be called lucky, here's a story that illustrates all three: In late August of 2000, the evening before the official opening of Washington and Lee University for fall semester, Larry was helping Jessie move into her college residence. Just after 5:00 p.m. they heard an intense, high-pitched whining noise and looked up to see a small plane nose-diving into the middle of the town. A moment before it spiraled out of sight, a man dove off the wing clutching a black duffel bag, then they heard a sickening thwomp.

The single-engine Piper Comanche landed nose-first in the middle of Washington Street, bordered on both sides by residences and fraternity houses, their doors open to receive the hundreds of double-parked parents and arriving students, and exactly a block and a half from dead center Main Street. And dead center is right: The man on the wing landed in many places throughout the middle of the town; Larry and Jessie, in fact, drove past a significant part of his spinal apparatus.

As far as I know, only one person actually saw the plane drill into the pavement (at least five feet in, according to my friend Steve Crowder, the chief of police at the time), at what would be rush hour anywhere else but our little town. It happened to be the draftsman for the house I had been designing who had been working on his computer and looked out of the window just at the moment of impact. He stared for a minute, watched a tire bounce down the eerily quiet street, sighed, and went back to the CAD program, working another thirty minutes, then locking up and driving off in the other direction. I remarked at the time that maybe it took that kind of unflappable constitution to suggest "Cranberry Bog" from the Sherwin-Williams color chart for my exterior stucco tint.

Even more remarkable than my friend's blithe unflappability is that nobody in town got hurt, other than the man with the duffel—a boxer and the lead singer of the Johnny Angel band—and the pilot, Jack Gambino, who, at 1:45 that afternoon had assured his Daytona Beach mechanic that he was "on the way" to renew his plane's inspection. According to the

NTSB report, it had expired five weeks before, and Gambino's own flight review was eight months overdue.

Gambino had run out of luck.

———

In 1949 Branch Rickey, the beloved manager of the Brooklyn Dodgers and the first major league manager to hire a Black ballplayer, sat for an interview with a cub reporter after the team had won its fourth or fifth National League pennant. The earnest young man, his press credentials tucked into the band of his fedora, observed that Rickey must feel pretty lucky. To which Mr. Rickey replied, "Luck, sir, is the residue of design."

There is a time in most lives, and it varies in duration, when you expect the world will shower upon you the lucky blessings to which you have a perfect right. The sooner the day comes when you realize that this is not how it is going to go, the better off you'll be—the day you are shocked to discover the trooper really is going to issue that speeding ticket despite your casual mention of daddy's third-circuit judgeship. Or the hungover morning that you look in the mirror and the magnitude of your banality, your perfidious phoniness, and the vacuity of your ambitions are garishly revealed to you, and you realize the cost of what Emily Dickinson termed "fortune's expensive smile."

That is the moment you need design.

And design, in the wildly disparate worlds of both Branch Rickey and Emily Dickinson, is hours upon sweaty (at least in Rickey's case; surely Emily Dickinson didn't sweat) hours of—let's just call it what it is: work.

3

Rejection

Levin scowled. The humiliation of his rejection stung him to the heart, as though it were a fresh wound he had only just received. But he was at home, and at home the very walls are a support.
—Leo Tolstoy, Anna Karenina

That's right: work. It's hard work, all the damn time. And it's humiliation. It's rejection after rejection. It's bad reviews. It's painstaking, soul-crushing process. It's ruthlessly killing your darlings. It's—or it was in my case—living in the kind of poverty that when you bore your children with descriptions of it, they smartass you with, "Oh yeah, and you walked to school barefoot."

I told them I did. I believe artists should suffer.

Not just as an obligatory rite of passage, something that you can cut corners on or pay somebody to do in your stead, like the wealthy avoiding war service. You can't buy plenary indulgences for suffering remission or get some dust-bowl double credit by skipping the Starbucks and making your own coffee in a dented 1940s tin drip pot (as I still do). And I'm not talking about glamorizing suffering, or publicly displaying your personal pain in all the myriad, often self-destructive ways we devise to do so, nor do I see it as a cross-off-able Herculean labor. The point is not to get to the other side of performative suffering, to slide shut the dead bolt on the now-pristine Augean stable and stride out into the freedom of creativity— the point, as you have surely been told countless times, is to build character. Without character, you will have nothing to say.

But—and here's the nub of it—if you are an artist, or a writer, you will probably have plenty to say. It's not like you have to gin up the suffering to satisfy the character requirement: Suffering comes with the territory. Ted Orland tells the story of a filmmaker who hand-carried his first film to a teacher and theorist whom he very much admired. The teacher watched the entire film in silence. When the viewing ended, he rose and left the room without uttering a word. Ted's friend ran after him and asked, "But what did you think of my film?" And the teacher replied, "What film?"

Painfully familiar, right? Laying those character-building foundations.

Once I decided, at the age of seventeen, that I would try to make a career as an artist, it took me almost no time at all to realize how miserable it was going to be. I had just mastered the ironic tilt of my Left Bank beret and the requisite squint of the eyes—helped along by the smoke from the unfiltered cigarette depending in a Bogartian dangle from my sullen lip—when I wrote this in my journal:

> God-damned photography is so fucking tedius.
> And i don't have the patience — no, nor the talent.
> Discouraged. phooey.

Already!

Ready to quit at seventeen, before I'd even started. My first roll of film and I'm wondering if maybe I should look into something else . . . less "tedius," less demanding, more paint-slinging and pirouette-y and unrestrained. Not so many rules and formulas. And here is the word that you will never, not another time in this book, see again: talent—something I believed in back then. And, as I wrote, I for sure believed I didn't have it.

What I was wrong about was the patience part. Patience, it turns out, can be learned, and over a long period of time I have learned it. Patience, in conjunction with its sibling, tenacity, can take the place of . . . that other thing. So, not only can it, in its own deliberate way, shape-shift into the spark and vitality and intuition and physical form of Art, but where patience really saves your artistic bacon is in helping you overcome suffering.

There are a lot of ways you will suffer. Mostly you will experience rejection. This is just a quick screenshot of some of the rejection letters that I saved, but countless others were so humiliating and depressing that I balled them up and threw them away (you will note that the National Endowment for the Arts merits its own folder because there are so many rejection letters).

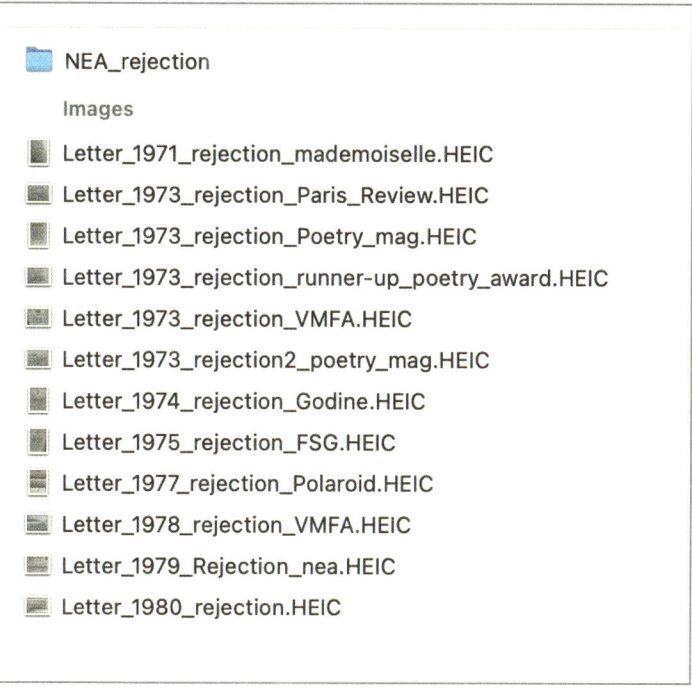

In fact, rejection letters became so commonplace that Ted sent me this all-too-true spoof:

```
Mrs. Sally Mann
223 McLaughlin
Lexington, VA
24450                                          November 6, 1980

Dear Mrs. Mann,

As you know, President Reagan has placed the highest priority upon naming
a woman recipient to an N.E.A. Fellowship in 1981. We are sorry to inform
you, however, that your name is not among those under final consideration
for this Girlship, which will be awarded on Mothers' Day, 1981.

Recipients of this year's awards, chosen by judges Harry Lunn, Victor
Schraeger, and non-voting representative author Curtis Casewit, are
Lewis Baltz, Stephen Shore, Nicholas Nixon, William Clift, and
several others whose awards will be announced by their respective NYC
galleries. Smaller "emerging photographer" awards went to Mrs. Stephen
Shore, Barbara Reagan, & Senator John Tower (R-Texas).

We hope you will not be discouraged that the work you submitted this year
was so inferior, and will feel free to submit more competent effort in 1981.
The necessary entry form and Loyalty Oath will be sent you upon receipt of
your $25.00 non-refundable entry fee.

                                         Yours Truly

                                         Senator Strom Thurmond (R-S.C.)
                                         Director
                                         Visual Arts Program
```

Rejection came in all forms. And why on earth am I writing that in the past tense? I am still getting rejections; my work has been turned down flat several times by curators in the last few years. Rejections still hurt, just like they always did. I felt like a piece of shit in 1977 when I wrote this to Ted:

```
There is just a certain pint beyond whivh I really hate to let myself
get talked into thinking I'm a piece of shit. That sentence doesn't make
sense but it makes ßßßgut sense. Every year just like cþookkwork I submit
grant applications and every year just like clockwork I get rejected
and every year I feel like a piece of shit. It makes me wonder at what
priçe fame and fortune, etc eç. Same old query. The people who like my
work are so few and far between and it's a temptation to turn toward
Emily Dickenson-dom. Well, you've heard all this before I know.
```

And in the end, that's just what I did. "Emily Dickenson-dom," or close to it, embracing the sentiment I once heard from my friend John Dickerson: "To be great, you have to disappear." Disappearing made me less vulnerable (if not great). I don't know if I'm unique in this—probably I am especially thin-skinned—but I can conjure up old slights with an elephantine recall, while being unable to even faintly discern the outlines of a compliment. But just in case some of the details escape me forty years later, like exactly what kind of sandwich a certain gallerist was eating as he fingered through my prints (Reuben), or what he was wearing (pink plastic belt and matching shoes), my contemporaneous letters from the time, written most often to Ted, bring them immaculately and vividly back to mind.

One from the spring of 1977 is excruciating in its details of my humiliation at the hands of a gallerist at what was then the most important photography gallery in New York. It's typed with such pounding despair and fury that certain letters of the alphabet actually tear through the paper (this was an old, manual typewriter). In case poor Ted did not know I was upset, on every third line, words like "ultimate degradation" and "utter speechlessness" and "brazen heel" appear in ALL CAPS.

The story isn't just a simple gallery rejection; I've had plenty of those, some more memorable than others. One of the more memorable was being shown out of a gallery clutching prints from my early Family Pictures (*Damaged Child*, *The Last Time Emmett Modeled Nude*, *Jessie at 5*, etc.) with the words "You'll never get anywhere with those; way too domestic" ringing in my ears.

No, this letter to Ted recounted a rejection with an extra twist of the knife, O. Henry territory. Funny, if you have a sense of humor bordering on the cruel.

It began with a box. A gorgeously undulating, custom-made portfolio, each wood in its striped pattern a different color: pale maple, warm walnut, ruddy cherry; wood cut and hewn from our own woods at the farm. It was lined with a dark green velvet. I had traded several of my rare—even then—platinum prints to have it made and I was convinced that the reverence-inspiring container would set the tone for viewing the work inside.

But the problem was, it was heavy. Really heavy. And pretty big. And it had no handle. But that did not stop me from deciding to carry my work up to New York on the train in this splendid vessel.

This was to be my second, confirmatory trip to the gallery. The first time I had gone, the director, nameless here but mud on my lips for decades after, viewed my work with much admiration, even without the awe-inspiring box, and proposed a show later in the year. But, just one thing: He wanted me to bring examples of new work back to him in exactly three months.

As unlikely as this sounds, I had an acquaintance who also had taken his work to that same gallery a week before me, and had an almost identical experience, right down to the "come back in exactly three months" directive. We were delighted and wondered if our shows would be at the same time, although the director was unaware that we knew each other.

As instructed, after three months, my friend made an appointment to show his new work, and I waited to hear from him the dates of his, or our, show. Instead, what I heard was a tale of dejection and confusion. When he had shown the new work, the director had leaned back in his chair, stroking his chin, and quizzically, haltingly, said, "You know, this is so odd; the things I liked about your work before are the very things I don't like about it now." My friend repeated that sentence to me three times, each time with more mystification and pain. He simply couldn't accept the unreasonableness of this reversal and the confusing, contradictory wording.

I did my best to console him, all the while having the, yes, I know, selfish thought that maybe without him I'd get the whole gallery now! I bought my train ticket for the next week, exactly three months, and set off at dawn with my box, so much heavier now that it was full of mounted prints. Almost as heavy as I was, or so the train conductor quipped as he hoisted it up the stairs for me. From Penn Station I somehow muscled the box and my little cardboard suitcase onto an uptown bus and went straight to my appointment at the gallery.

In the letter to Ted I describe my confidence, writing: "I breezed in feeling like a million dollars"—however unlikely it was that anyone was breezing anywhere with that box in their arms—and commenting on how good-looking the director was, how warm his smile. With great ceremony, I opened the box and he began flipping through the prints, pulling out every third one, stacking them unevenly to the side. I tried to disguise my concern at their treatment as casual indifference: Oh, ho hum. Just my life's work there that you're tossing around like scrap paper. But I consoled myself with the thought that obviously he didn't need to study each image with the reverential care I was expecting, since this was just a confirmation of his first impressions from three months ago and he was probably making a preliminary edit for the show.

When he was finished, there was a pause, and he sat down in his chair as I held my breath and mentally turned the pages of the calendar to showtime. He leaned back. He stroked his chin, his forehead creased with perplexity and distress, and he said:

Well, you know exactly what he said, don't you? It was the very words, the exact same fucking words.

My letter to Ted reports "a flush that went from head to toe and utter, UTTER speechlessness. A look of near-tearful agony on my face." It was not near-tearful for long. I have no way, even today, of cranking down the waterworks tap and I began to cry noisily, wiping my nose on my forearm, so blinded by the tears that I could hardly see to gather up the prints. Patting them into a roughly even stack, I turned them sideways to tap them like a sheaf of irregular term papers, but they were debossed platinum prints and would not conform. I was sobbing by then, and the office staff was peering around the doorway as I crammed the prints unevenly into the box and crushed the top down on them, their edges sticking out from three sides, some folded, one blocking the latch.

The director was pounding on the elevator down button when I finally scooped up the box with both arms, and the concerned-looking staff, one of whom was my (now) good friend Maude, pressed a Kleenex on me, and stuffed the rest of my belongings into the elevator with me. When I got to the ground floor, I sat on a bench and restacked my prints into the box. Almost all of them were damaged. I had spent every hour of the past three months printing those platinum prints under a blistering sunlamp, debossing the deckle-edged BFK paper that had to be special-ordered from Europe, soaking the sheets of precious paper, running them through the etching press at the university after hours, layering them in drying cloths, dry-mounting the delicate platinum prints onto the now-debossed paper, and then signing in light pencil. Like a real artist.

I went out on Fifth Avenue, where the buses went the right direction to take me down to my friend Robbie Goolrick's fifth-floor walk-up (the ground floor a Spanish restaurant, then two floors of Chinese brothels, he reminded me yesterday) on what had to be the noisiest street in New York, Thirty-Fifth. I waited at the curb until the right bus came and gathered together my purse, my sweater, my suitcase, and the box. No helpful conductor this time.

I rejiggered my belongings and hoisted the box up onto the stairs, followed by the rinky-dink suitcase. As I began to reach for the chrome bar to pull myself up, the doors wheezed shut. I jammed my fingers in the rubbery lips and tried to pry them apart, running beside the bus. No go. The bus picked up speed. I ran, losing my flip flops. Kept running, barefoot, as the bus picked up speed. As I frantically maintained contact with the side of the bus, I envisioned my ignominious death under the wheels, and the even more ignominious tossing of the box and its contents into the trash. And, fine, I thought. That's probably where the hell you belong.

When I got to the top of the stairs, Robbie let me into his stifling apartment, running his nicotined fingers through his thick, Pre-Raphaelite hair as he stared at my bare feet. This was not the first time I had collapsed there in tears of frustration, humiliation, and disappointment after a visit to a gallery. As he always did at these moments, he handed me a strong drink, then remarked: "Now is when you stuff the dog into the umbrella stand."

I stared at him, and he motioned for me to sit down and told me this story. Who knows if he had gotten it from somebody else, or if it was Robbie's own experience. The protagonist was a raw young man of straitened means who had seldom traveled and was in his first year at an East Coast college. A little like Robbie himself had been a mere decade before, so perhaps it indeed was him. This lad was making plans to take his first international flight, with a layover in Los Angeles. Mentioning his intentions to spend the night in a youth hostel before the flight to Asia, his wealthy suite mate insisted that he stay at his parents' house in Bel Air.

Arriving there by taxi from the airport, the astonished boy, let's call him Robbie, gawped at the enormity and tasteless opulence of the place. Terraces. Colonnades. A uniformed maid walking what appeared to be a cluster of leashed, yapping dandelion puffs. A water park. An observatory open to the heavens. Robbie shouldered his rucksack, climbed the stairs to the large front door, and pressed the bell, which released the sonorous chimes of Notre-Dame on the other side. Hardly had the last electronic clapper tolled when the door was opened by a liveried butler who, with barely concealed disdain, showed Robbie down a long hall and announced, "You'll be staying in the White Room."

And it was; the deep carpet, bed linens, rococo picture frames, ancien régime writing desk; all white. Even the pull cord to summon the butler (also white), who, with the pincerlike gesture of a man removing toilet tissue from the bottom of his shoe, had taken the backpack from Robbie's shoulder and placed it on a white chair, then withdrawn from the room. Overtaken by an urge to share a description of this place with his then-girlfriend, whom he called Sister Fang (don't ask), Robbie nervously sat on the spindly chair at the escritoire. He surveyed the white stationery, embossed with the name of the estate, the fountain pen, white, and the only incongruous element in the whole room, a jar of black India ink. Unscrewing the top of the pen, he reached for the jar and found that it had a crusty circlet of dried ink within the screw whorls and gave it an authoritative twist. It released suddenly and spewed ink across the room, on the carpet, the coverlet, the curtains, even pooling in the white ashtray.

Nothing in his background had prepared him for such a contingency as this. Panicked, he pushed back from the desk, grabbed his backpack, dashed down the corridor and within seven strides was down the stairs and fleeing along the shadowed drive.

Years later, after a successful career in advertising, Robbie was a wealthy and worldly business traveler disembarking again in Los Angeles. Reminded of the misadventure in his past, he thought to address the wince-inducing guilt of this sudden memory and apologize to his friend's parents.

Taking a taxi to the house, he was surprised to find it exactly as it had been a decade before. Standing before the great door, he pressed the bell: the Notre-Dame chimes; the same impassive butler sloping along, a tad worse for wear. This time, and with a little less butlerine condescension, he was shown to a room off the main entrance hall, which he noted with relief was decorated entirely in shades of brown. He sauntered easily to the comfortable-looking brown chair in the far corner, piled high with a beckoning disorder of fluffy brown pillows, and threw himself heavily into it.

The instant he heard the stomach-turning crunching sound, he knew. There are many breeds of small lapdogs, some so diminutive and delicate that they can be carried in a woman's evening purse . . . or mistaken for a pillow. He leapt up and confirmed the terrible suspicion, then snatched the lifeless dog from among the pillows and, in a frantic dash to the front door, stuffed it in the umbrella stand before taking those same seven strides down the stairs to the drive.

Robbie had nailed it. Stuffing the dog in the umbrella stand seemed the only possible response to those years of repeated rejections and failures, the bad reviews and unanswered letters, slights imagined and actual.

and it's just too hopeless to call, to write. It all passes and like that day in New York I'll get up the morning after and go thru it all again, starting as if the past had no life of its own, no lessons, no truth. I wonder where I will finally end, stopped like a heart gasping maybe, maybe just stopped.

as always, S

And, indeed, as I wrote in this letter to Ted, I got up the morning after every single one of them, as if the past held "no lessons, no truth," a gift of ignorance generously bestowed to Southerners, and I kept working. My heart did not stop. Perhaps there was some gasping as I sprinted from one bad experience to the next, but each time, the dog was dumped in the umbrella stand and I was moving ahead.

4

On Writing

Writing is easy: all you do is stare at a blank sheet of paper until drops of blood form on your forehead.

—Gene Fowler

The letter about that ill-fated gallery visit in New York is one of hundreds written to my friend Ted Orland, and since this is the umpteenth time I've mentioned him, you're surely wondering how he fits into this narrative. He could easily slot into the chapter about blind luck, but Ted's own chapter would best headline as "The Importance of Epistolary Friendships." He and I poured our frustrations, doubts, fears, sorrows, and, yes, joys into decades of letters from 1973, when we met in Yosemite at the Ansel Adams Workshops, until . . . well, until the present. Ours is a friendship based on writing—and I do not mean texts, I mean actual paper.

Paper is important: Toss your writing in a cardboard box and your life will still be there to hold in your age-spotted hands when you open it up again to re-create your past. You think you won't get there, I mean that age-spotted future, but I'm here to tell you: Blink your eyes and there you are, with Time's winged chariot shifting gears ominously behind you.

Or if you think that what you have to say doesn't merit the paper it's written on—and you may be right—then try harder, think more, write better. Or maybe you think you don't have time to put it in writing, so you'll just bang out a text, or push a button to dial a number for a quick chat. But it's not the same, and you are losing your past every time you do it the easy way.

For somebody as fundamentally insecure as I was, it seems odd to me that I saved so much of my inauspicious past: my writing, my letters, my cringe-inducing journals, my lists, and so much of the ephemera of my life. I have been asked if it was because I thought someday I might be famous, and I replied that it was just the opposite: I thought someday I would vanish into deserved insignificance and all that would be left to show I had lived, like the smear of adipocerous fat at the site of a body's decomposition, would be those pieces of paper.

I wanted so much to be good at *anything*. Fiercely, heartbreakingly, I strove for improvement at everything I did. Athletics were out, that became clear early on, not necessarily because I wasn't capable (I'm fit as a damn Olympian now) but mostly because there were few sports for girls when I was growing up. It's true! Ask your granny. We skipped rope and cantered around on stick horses. Also, given my personal and intellectual limitations, largely out were academics, especially the sciences and math, cooking, sewing (or "Home Economics" as it was called), and typing was definitely out, as well as a whole host of other avenues down which others effortlessly glided. Left to me were the exiguous footpaths of art and writing (although I was also good at flirting), and those I trod relentlessly, if unpromisingly at first.

The first year that I applied myself (a phrase my teachers frequently employed—in the negative—in reports to my parents) appears to be 1968. It was a year with a great deal of racial turmoil in America, which in turn caused a great deal of upset and tumult within my own Southern heart. As I passionately tried to express this, rolling the inks, gouging the wood, and abusing the canvas, it became clear to me, and especially to my dyspeptic art professor, Bill Hunt, that the traditional artistic forms might not be the right ones for me. (Sidebar: Hunt was right about that, but, when informed that I was marrying Larry Mann a year after my high school graduation, he sniffed, "That marriage won't last two years." This was fifty-five years ago.) Happily, it was at that moment of dispiriting realization that the chemical-stained curtain of the group darkroom at my school was pulled aside for me by a boy I wanted to make out with.

Writing, on the other hand, I didn't accidentally stumble into looking for a dark corner, like I did photography. Writing, in fact, was the thing I wanted to do well ever since I was a stripling, probably even before I could hold a pencil. To this day, it is the thing I want to get better at, the thing I want to be good at. And yes, I'm dangling my prepositions because I am hammering my spavined forefingers on the keys so rapidly that I can't be bothered with grammar right now, and why? Because I want to impress on anyone who is still reading this that being able to write, especially about your work and why you do it, is important.

> because the insecurity is there, regardless of the pride I have in my pictures, Sometimes I can just get awfully excited about shades of grey or curves or a clean print. I think I am not very good at writing about what I do.

As this journal entry from 1971 indicates, I knew that it was important from the beginning of my art practice (a wince-inducing phrase, probably more apt as "practice art" in my case). When you have a personality like mine, driven by an unattainable desire for perfection, admitting that you are not very good at something that you want with all your being is like the meaty whiff of an impala drifting across the lion's nostrils: Like the lion, I rose up with a primitive imperative, and from that moment I was going to run that damn impala to the ground.

Writing in journals (or "journaling" as another repellent neologism has it) is one way, and composing long, fevered poems late into the night is another, and of course I've employed them both, but more than either of those I recommend writing letters. It's a time-honored form of communication, it puts you in the best literary company you could ask for, and it keeps you fairly honest. The only problem with letters is, you have to fold them up and mail them off. They are still yours in a sense, the copyright remaining with the author, but they also physically reside with the recipient.

Years ago, a large box tied up with kitchen string arrived at my doorstep, scribbled with the familiar handwriting of my friend Davis Pratt, then the curator of photography at the Fogg Museum at Harvard. I had not heard from Davis in a while, despite having had a prolific and entertaining correspondence with him over the years. So, it was with some curiosity that I cut the bindings and discovered neatly dated piles of my own letters to Davis, tied up with the same yellow twine. Many had been written on the backs of failed prints, and all of them were dashed off in the moment, evidenced by my scrawling cursive, which started big and then got smaller as I realized I wasn't going to have enough space to say all that was on my mind.

There was no note, and it took a minute before I realized what this parcel might portend. My fear that I had somehow offended him was almost immediately replaced by the realization that this kind gentleman was returning my personal correspondence because he was not likely to be reading it again. Davis died several weeks later.

I have had equally intense correspondences with several other people, both personal and professional, in particular with a curator at the Metropolitan Museum of Art, where we were planning a show of the Family Pictures in the late 1980s. Of all the ways my heart has been broken, professionally—and good god it has—the cancellation of this show might have been the most painful. The still-twingey regret was re-twinged this year when I ran across the list of photographs we planned to exhibit, which had been pushpinned on my bulletin board for so long that the metal thumbtacks left rusted circles on the paper. When all hope for an exhibition of the Family Pictures at the Met was extinguished, I finally removed the list and protectively never looked at it again, until now.

The correspondence the curator and I shared during the course of the show planning, usually handwritten, would likely eclipse that of Davis Pratt's in volume, and also in fervor and candor. Which leads me to my cautionary note to any of you who are still writing letters, actual paper letters. Following Davis's lead, I have suggested to the curator that we each return the other's letters, but this has not yet happened, so be aware as you succumb to the old man's counsel to exaggerate, or to your own prolix sentimentality three glasses of Merlot into the night, that the words you put on paper are forever—they are not necessarily nuanced or accurate or how you would write them stone-cold sober or after years of maturation. But there they are, in your undeniable scrawl, written without the least thought that they would ever be seen by anyone else.

Which reminds me of a story I have told before, of the intemperate attack launched on my work, and more annoyingly on my children, by the writer Anne Bernays. After reading her four-line indictment in a letter to the *New York Times*, in a rage I grabbed a discarded 20 × 24–inch silver print from the offending series of pictures of my children and proceeded to scribble out a furious defense on the back. I then wrapped it up, the words still-smoldering, and marched it two blocks to the post office.

Boy, did I show her. I've been told that for years she delighted in displaying her poisonously personalized Sally Mann print, even once to a video crew who interviewed her about it. Doubtless, just a matter of time before it shows up on the auction floor to make somebody some money.

So, all that aside, I still say to write your friends, write what you truly feel, but bear in mind that your letters in all their searing honesty will stand for you for all time. And it's OK to look like an idiot, you are writing your friends, not a dissertation; don't try to be anything but who you are. Tell the truth as you see it in that exact moment, even if the next day it is some other truth (or an "alternative fact," a dubious concept recently forced upon us) and don't stint on the details; your letters should reflect the steep bell curve of sublimity and mundanity that is your life.

And they should be on paper. Of course they should. Everything you do should be on paper, paper you should keep; your letters, your lists, your accounting, and your journals (god help you). But the chances of that are pretty much zero these days, unless you've affected some nineteenth-century persona where you ostentatiously whip out your marbled fountain pen to sign the credit card bill.

Indeed, almost all my own correspondence, except for most thank-you notes, is now by email. Instead of the boxes and manila folders I have gone through for the material to write *Hold Still* and this book, I now scroll down through the folders on my computer. It pains me to realize how ephemeral and intangible all that I have thought, felt, and written in those folders now is. And how vulnerable: one massive solar flare or cyberattack away from extinction.

But I save them, nevertheless. The alphabetized email storage folders are routinely augmented from the main inbox and are grotesquely over-stuffed. My cheeks mantling with hypocritical shame, being a die-hard paper person, I tally up the contents of a few of the 199 folders stacked up on the screen:

"Hold Still" (mostly communications with my editor Michael Sand) logs in at 10,867.

"A Thousand Crossings" has more than 7,000.

The *"Creepy"* folder is broken down into subfolders: *Nutjob_Trumper_Russian, Whispery_Voice_Skitzo_Phone_Guy, Fashion_Shoot_Imposters, Fruit-bat_Letter_Writer,* and *Creepy_in_General.* Despite the main folder totting up 958 skin-crawling communications, the two bulging banker's boxes in the attic that hold the Creepy Letters written on real paper give off a way more ominous vibe.

"Photo_Related" is a not-surprising 21,168, just a smidge more than the *"Gagosian"* file, reflecting a panoramic 19,366 emails exchanged with the long-suffering and brilliant Putri Tan.

And then there's family, which is the saddest of all to see on a screen and not in packets tied with twine or even boxed up with the names Sharpied on the sides.

"Jessie": 7,505
"Virginia": 7,758

And, my heart breaks here, 3,964:

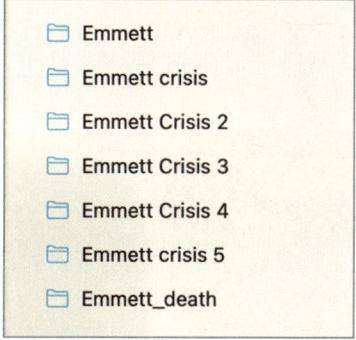

A few days before Emmett died, I was carrying a thermos of tea in a bag with my Day-Timer. I have maintained that three-by-six-inch yearly planner in a crudely repaired Filofax leather cover since the 1970s and (of course) saved almost all of them, neatly stacked, year after identical year. That day, the thermos top was incompletely sealed and tea soaked the 2016 calendar, smearing and wrinkling the pages for the second half of the year. Now, in the middle of the otherwise uniform stack of calendars, the planner for 2016, my *annus horribilis*, stands out, warped and stained.

Paper can tell stories in many ways, and although not even Bertha Rochester's attic would be capacious enough to hold all the letters in my computer, it still makes me sad to see so much compressed to ones and zeros. The solution, if I could offer some advice that I myself seldom follow, is to print out correspondence that is important to you. After you die, your children will doubtless take it all to the dumpster, as I predict mine will, but you at least will have it at hand, literally, until then. And, for god's sake back up your computer files.

As for me, in 1985 I donated my typewriter to the Stonewall Jackson Hospital Thrift Shop and plunged, cold turkey, into learning how to use a computer. It did not come naturally to me, to understate the case.

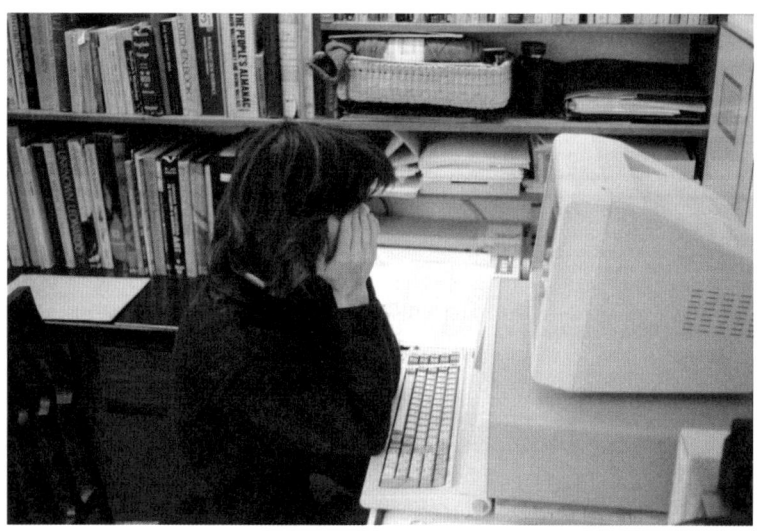

A small digression here. The first computer I got was an IBM PC, despite my smart brother's advice to get a Mac. That same brother had been buying Macs for years at that point, when they weren't even Macs, they were Apple computers. He bought the second-ever Apple computer and still has it, and his family has enjoyed the benefits of early Apple stock purchases. To gild the lily, he also bought our father's 1961 Aston Martin DB4, with forty-eight thousand miles on it, which he also still has. Between Apple and Aston, you'd have to agree that my brother is very smart indeed. Wish I had listened to him. End of digression.

I had been told by the computer salesperson to insert the various disks into the two six-inch slots, one at a time and in the right order, then I was to wait for the chug-chug noise and pretty soon a blinking speck would appear on the screen. Once that showed up, I began my frantic two-fingered rat-a-tat, as if the cursor might blink out at any moment, expiring like time at a pay phone. Once I'd mastered that, I learned how to save all my perfervid output, stuffing the floppy disks into hard-sided boxes and forgetting about them.

Until, twenty-five years later, I wanted all that writing, all those letters. By then I was well into my third Mac computer and the PC was far in my past. The letters were, I suspected, lost forever.

Larry and I have been married for an eternity, but at least a dozen times a year I think that we won't make it another week if he doesn't deal with all the SHIT (always at the top of my lungs) he saves for no reason. This 1982 letter to Ted details the magnitude of the pack-rat problem:

```
began sorting through the phenomenal amount of stuff
he had stored in there: every nook and cranny had
totally unsorted JUNK in them: for instance a horse'e
tail ( a real one), a pick-up truck load of ¼ inch
pieces of glass from a department store shelves, 5
100 pound boxes of nails, 5 window fans, 24 working
electric motors, 16 leaf bags full of aluminum cans,
a dishwasher, 3 gas heaters, several human skulls,
several glass jars full of dead birds, a mile of used
stove pipe, an acre of insulation scraps, plywood, 2x4's
and planking ( all from the construction), a mineature
Singer sewing machine, The last decade's receipts for the
Lexington-Rockbridge Fire Department, 1956-66, the
blueprint for the proposed sewage plant in Fairfax County, Va,
(46 pages_) 3 empty typewriter cases, a year's subscriptiion
to air-gun news, a file in the filing cabinet entitled
" sculpture" which consisted of tear sheets from his
father's collection of Playboy magazines ( and worse).(he
says he needed them to help him model the breasts he
was going to use in his sculptures) a complete blacksmith
shop of tools bought by Larry in 1974 and never really
sorted through, merely/ deposited in the shop in
cardboard boxes and wooden cases labelled: "We loned no tools" sic,
and "kep yore mitteys out" sic also, a thousand universal
joints and bearings and bolts and nuts and"useful" things
like bottels designed to suck ladybugs off plants without
damaging them, 3 cases each of gallon jugs of hydrocloric
and Nitric acid, 3 toaster ovens, a carton of calling
cards that his mother had printed for him when he was 14,
his pewter mug engraved Fireman of the Year, 1976,
an army cot and a suitcase of bedding, 2 gas masks,
dozens of books ranging from Chinese acupuncture to
How to stay alive in the woods, a dozen broken intercoms,
a broken waffle iron, broken regular iron, broken tensor
light, broken stereo, broken refrigerator, broken water
heater, etc etc and to top it off a moving crate for
a couch filled with styrofoam peanuts. Never can tell
when you might need that he said as each and every one
of the abovemeantioned things was ignominbously thown
into the trash heap/ which was monumental in scale.
```

He still won't throw any damn thing away because we might need it sometime, and, OK, in fact, he is often right. What I needed in 2010 was my original 1985 computer that could read those old disks with all my letters on them, because otherwise they were lost for good. And there, stuffed between a collection of stereo vacuum tubes and a disassembled 1946 toaster, was that very computer, saved by Larry. By god, we fired that sucker up and after an interminable wait came the chug-chug, the cursor, and, inserting the disks, there were all my letters, written in the passion of the cursor-blinking moment, for me to cringe my way through.

The pack rat gets a pass.

———

This year Ted sweetly sent me back every letter I wrote him from 1972 to the present, doubtless freeing up a capacious new storage space in his bungalow, no longer awash in reams of my puerile and passionate ramblings. I, of course, have saved all his letters to me (more on saving shit later), and have mated his and mine together chronologically. The resulting stack rulers in at nearly thirteen inches. There are hundreds of letters; single-spaced, double-sided, smudged, crossed-out, wine-stained, barely readable—almost like those eighteenth-century letters written at right angles to save paper—sometimes several sent in a week.

Most of this letter writing was, of course, before computers, but thank god it wasn't before *typewriters*. I'd pack up my little portable Olivetti in its traveling case, unfold the beach chair and a table, plop the baby (there was always a baby, it seemed) in the Swing-o-matic, giving it enough cranks to allow me fifteen minutes of metronomic, clicking baby-peace, and pound those keys. I'd write furiously, two fingered, hunting, pecking, cursing, exactly as I am writing still, the abused joints of my two forefingers now arthritic and painful. My mother tried when I was a teen to get me to take a typing class, but I utterly disdained the idea. Among my many regrets.

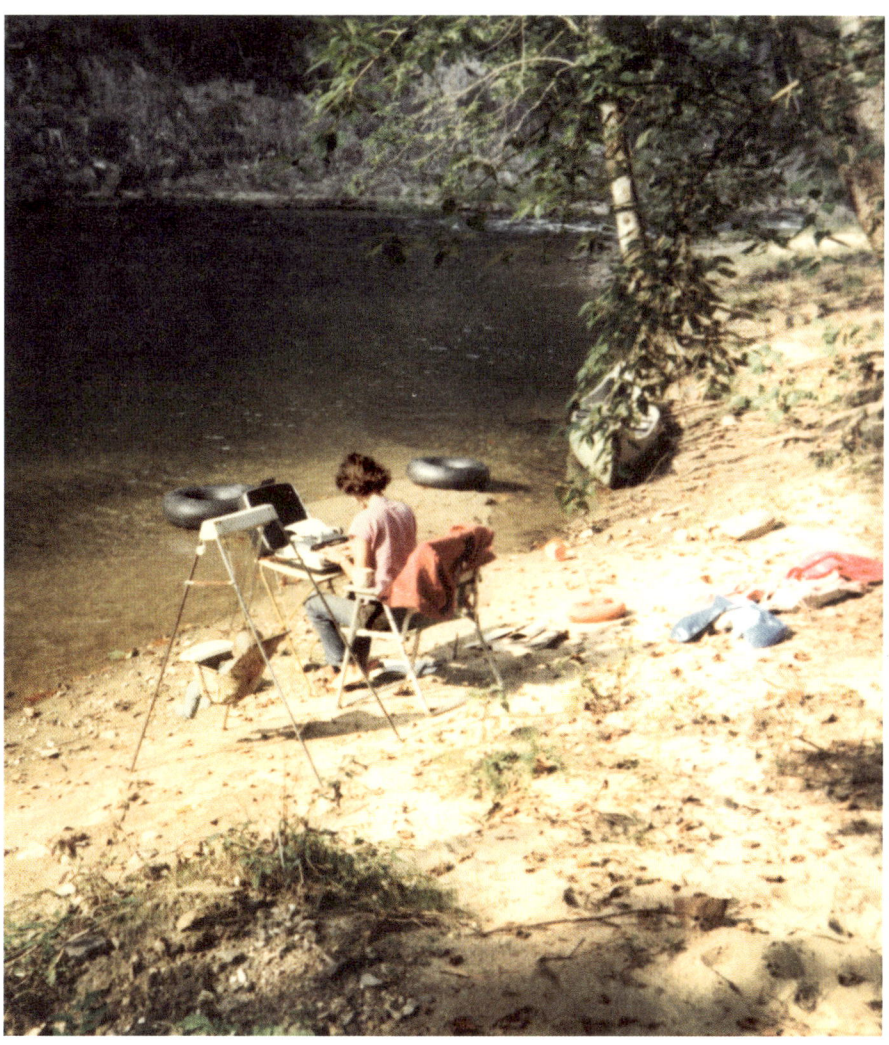

When they invented the erasure paper stuff, that helped, and then Wite-Out, which doubled as an intoxicant, and finally the miraculous rotating-ball IBM Selectric that literally lifted the mistaken character off the page. But, boy, once computers came on the scene, it was Katie, bar the epistolary door. The below is one day's letter to Ted:

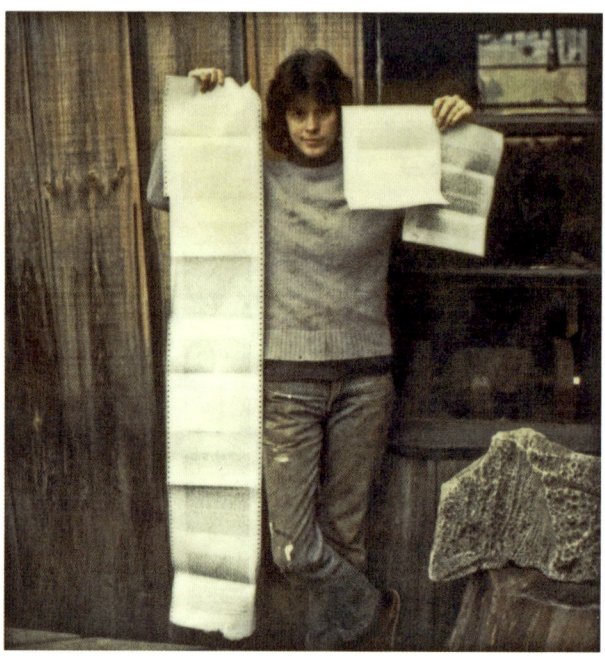

I wrote to Ted about everything: shutter speeds and apertures, sex and poverty, food and booze, family squabbles, shoulder pads, hair styles, successes, and—more often than not—resounding failures. The sanitized version of many of these letters could be produced by typing out the line of symbols residing above the numerals on your keyboard, concluding with a heavy finger on the ! above numeral one. (And can you believe this? There's a word for the use of symbols to replace profanity, and it showed up this very week on my Word-a-Day calendar: "grawlix." That's one to remember.) As I reread these letters now, they set off depth charges of long-forgotten emotions, and I recognize in that young writer the same snoot-cocking fakery of confidence I display today, fifty years later, and so often the same indecision, regret, and doubts. Hair styles might be better now, however. And no shoulder pads.

But while I was bleating, whinging, and exalting my hyperbolic way through the decades, recounting problems that would make Pontius Pilate quail, Ted more often than not applied droll humor and a positive philosophical spin to every setback and dead end we each encountered.

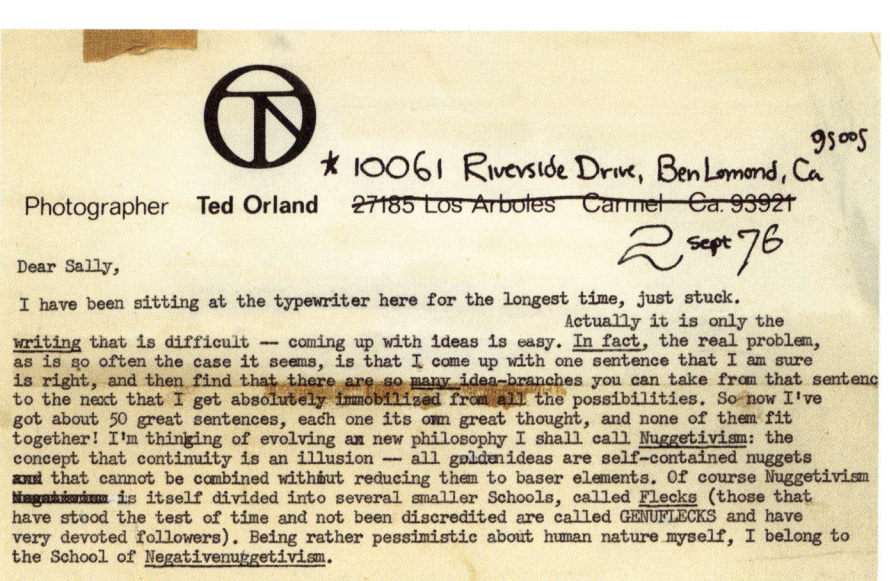

Photographer **Ted Orland** ~~27185 Los Arboles Carmel Ca. 93921~~ * 10061 Riverside Drive, Ben Lomond, Ca 95005

2 sept 76

Dear Sally,

I have been sitting at the typewriter here for the longest time, just stuck. Actually it is only the writing that is difficult — coming up with ideas is easy. In fact, the real problem, as is so often the case it seems, is that I come up with one sentence that I am sure is right, and then find that there are so many idea-branches you can take from that sentenc to the next that I get absolutely immobilized from all the possibilities. So now I've got about 50 great sentences, each one its own great thought, and none of them fit together! I'm thinking of evolving an new philosophy I shall call Nuggetivism: the concept that continuity is an illusion — all golden ideas are self-contained nuggets and that cannot be combined without reducing them to baser elements. Of course Nuggetivism is itself divided into several smaller Schools, called Flecks (those that have stood the test of time and not been discredited are called GENUFLECKS and have very devoted followers). Being rather pessimistic about human nature myself, I belong to the School of Negativenuggetivism.

(Along with his coauthor David Bayles, Ted actually made something out of his half of those thirteen inches of stacked-up letters, brilliantly weaving them into the bestselling book *Art and Fear*—a GENUFLECK of the highest order with countless devoted followers—from which I copiously borrow each time I write about the process of being an artist. Or trying to.)

If misery loves company as much as they say, then no Gore Vidal, Christopher Hitchens, gravelly voiced Dorothy Parker, no swashbuckling Southern yarn-spinner, no raunchy raconteur plopped down on the neighboring barstool with a swizzle stick and a cigarette could have been better company than Ted was. He endured my detailed descriptions of transporting a puking python while trying to navigate interstate traffic (the rhythmic heaving began at the tail and continued along six feet until he noisily disgorged a putrid vomitus of nearly digested rat on the floorboards), how to skin a groundhog (mindful of the scent glands under the forearms), my friend Splinter's twenty-seven consecutive orgasms, my episiotomy stitches, the dying plants in my garden, and my many humiliating rejections, one of which I transcribe here because the original is handwritten in an illegibly furious scrawl, underlinings tearing through the thin paper:

> . . . [the curator at the museum] with heavy-lidded eyes flipping through my work & being pompous about my matting or my framing—the humiliation and anger that arose in me.
>
> I resolved one thing for <u>sure</u>: other than my friends and people who <u>ask</u> to see my work, I am never going to take it to someone for <u>criticism</u>—<u>never</u> . . . I find that I impose my own criterion [*sic*] & opinions over anyone's and I don't give a flying fuck anyway.

Ted, of course, being the kind friend, forbore comment on the obvious hypocrisy of all the flying fucks I supposedly did not give.

For years I wrote Ted about whether I should have children. This is a question I am sure many young artists are confronting as you find yourselves, suddenly, not quite as young as you used to be. There is no minimizing the difficulty of being responsible every hour for both your children's lives and your creative life as well. Each one is, to paraphrase Wendell Berry, a vexed privilege and a blessed trial, both of them necessary and neither altogether possible. In fact, sometimes destroyingly impossible. Head-in-the-oven impossible.

But women have done it forever. When asked the question "How did you make your art and raise three kids," the artist Betye Saar responded: "What's the difference?" And while Mr. Harriet Beecher Stowe got a room of his own in which to study Biblical literature (and drink), his wife was at the kitchen table writing a novel so morally compelling that it has been suggested it effectively ended slavery, all the while caring for and feeding seven children.

So, I say do it, if you want children and are feeling especially heroic, but take heed of what Ted wrote me when I asked him about it:

> You are hopelessly optimistic if you think that somehow you can have the child at the beginning of summer vacation and then send it off to childcare in September and go back to work. Housewives don't make their small children a full-time occupation simply for lack of a more meaningful profession to engage in—they are a full-time occupation because they ARE a full-time occupation.

And, boy, was he right about that. Those of you hoping to make art and be a parent, even of one child, had better be prepared for years of frustration, distraction, exhaustion, competing priorities, and, at least in my case, occasional despair.

```
I have hardly taken a good picture--let's get it right-- I have
takeen hundreds of pictures and none of them are any good. Well,
maybe one or two. One lovely picture of naked Larry.
And a portrait or two. I don't really know what's wrong except
that sometimes I think it may be just that I have two children
who wear me down to a little nub.

In any case, I simply don't have enough time to do anything
right. Every thought, every sentence is inevitably interrupted.
Every long-term project faces certain defeat and interruption
and finally I am left with the only alternative: to do little,
mindless, unessential jobs all day: alphebetizing the herbs and
spices, dousing the mealy bugs individually with alcohol, one
by one with a q-tip, taking the children for walks.
                              inevitably
Whateverproject I choose is ßßßßßßßßßßß punctualted  with a
temper tantrum, with Jessie being pushed backwards
down the stairs_____ over
```

Again to his great credit, Ted also denied himself the pleasure of the dozens of rightful "I told you so's" as I struggled, painfully and sometimes comically, with the balancing act of child-rearing and making pictures.

No word on the book yet but I've been on the phone to Time Life about every day. You wouldn't believe what ■■■■■■■ (critic for the NY Times) wrote about me. The headline for the article was:
HOUSEWIFE AND MOTHER MAKES PHOTOS IN SPARE TIME

I SWERR that's what he wrote. Then he went on to say how "secure" my life is, my husband a lawyer who's supported me for 11 years(!) and how after the birth of my first child I started using a lot of "pale pinks and blues" in my pictures....it was NAUSEATING. It was like a parody.
you couldn't have done any better if you had spent the night drinkin good napa wine and chuckling over it. The editors at Time Life are women and they're horrified. Nobody exactly knows what to do to shake the idea out of his head: He seems DETERMINED to make me into a mousy little house frau with raw knuckles from diaper washing on the washboard. Argggggggh. I get too angry to type.

I don't really know why I was so angry; I was, bottom line, a housewife and mother, a mousy little hausfrau, and I did wash my baby's diapers, but just not on a washboard (Ted took this picture of Emmett and me, diapers hung in my sunny kitchen in the absence of a dryer).

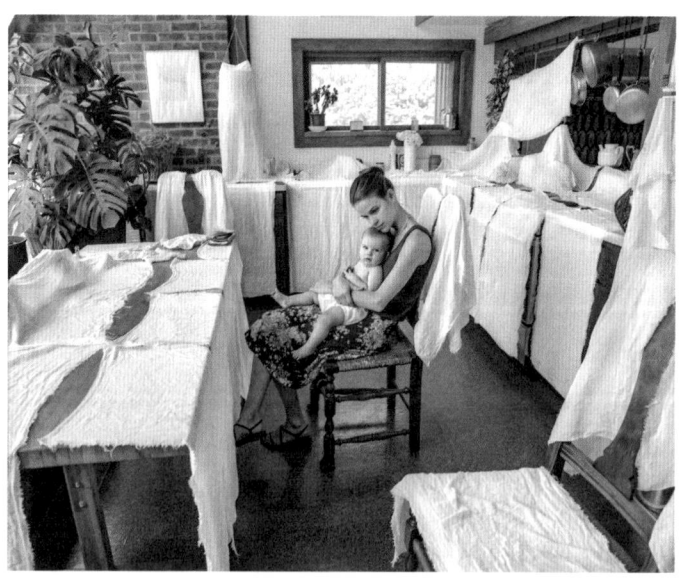

But the household income with which this critic assumed Larry was supporting us was, in fact, earned by me. That got my hackles up; I had for years worked full-time as a commercial photographer while Larry was trying to build a career as a blacksmith, only quitting my job when Emmett reached toddlerhood and Jessie was on the way. While I had miraculously received a small grant from the Virginia Museum of Fine Arts to tide us over, there was nothing "secure" about our lives, and our pantry supplies always hovered on the Scroogeian end of the Dickensian curve.

There was, however, one calcified reality within that precariousness: the needs of two babies, coming less than two years apart, and then Virginia three years later. For almost a decade, I had one baby or another strapped in the Snugli (I had contrived a hole in it so they could get access to the boob without my having to stop work) or in the backpack, their head lolling over the back while I made and developed pictures. I had a playpen and bassinet set up in the darkroom and don't give me grief about my inadequate air-handling system. Desperation is the mother of those adorable triplets—compromise, creativity, and final reconciliation—and, in my case, the trio managed to triumph over the psyche-ravaging alternative.

I won't say the pictures I made during that time are groundbreaking, but I was determined. Here is a scrap of a letter from February 1984:

```
over 8 pounds and got me up every hour and a half at night. Oh god
was I miserable. 2 babies in diapers, Poor sweet Emmett uncomprehending
and at that fragile age of 2. Jesus I thought I was going to die.
I don't remember much of what I was doing at that point, artistically,
but I do remember that I worked along on some project or another
with some constancy. That's one thing for sure: having children
hasn't hampered my art any and, in fact, to the contrary it has
really helped it. I have become maniacal in my pursuit of good
pictures, mostly because I refuse to let my art go by the wayside
because of children. But, I'll admit, times like now I wonder.
```

Of course, there's only so much you can do with an 8 × 10 camera set up in the living room and a friend you have bribed with cheap gin to model for you, especially with a baby upstairs just starting to ramp up a hunger yowl. That crying baby will kick the sunshine out of ambition, no matter how maniacal, how determined.

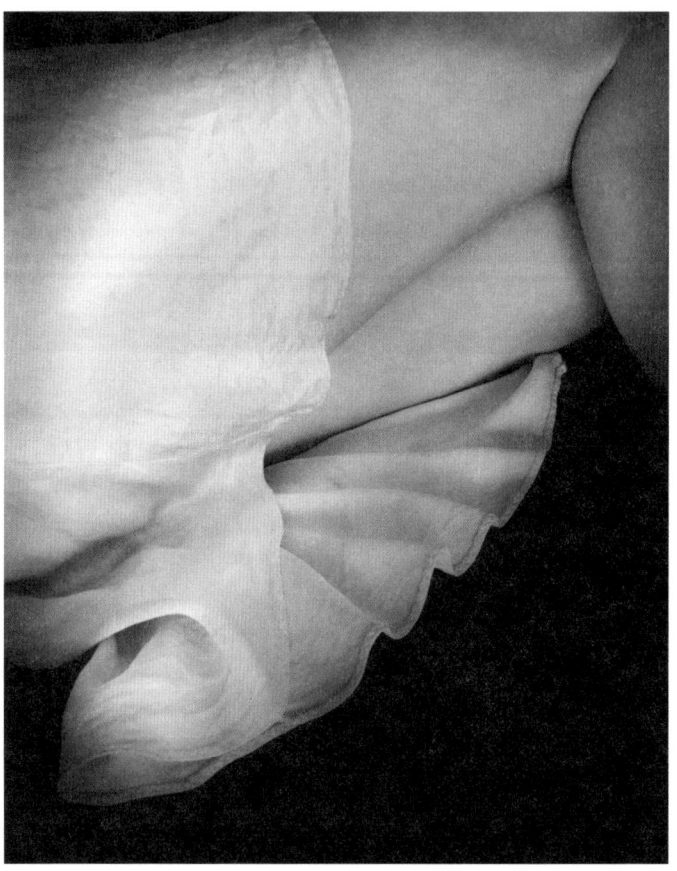

(It should be noted that when there was no model, or cheap gin to pay her with, I would occasionally use a child as my model on the living room floor, which for some reason puts me in mind of Fagin, in *Oliver Twist*, yelling at the kids: "Shut up and drink your gin!" No gin for the under-age working models, but my friend Splinters, a fairly reliable model, got plenty. In an unconscious but felicitous segue, those early pictures of the babies on the floor, filling in for a "real" model, evolved over time into the Family Pictures series.)

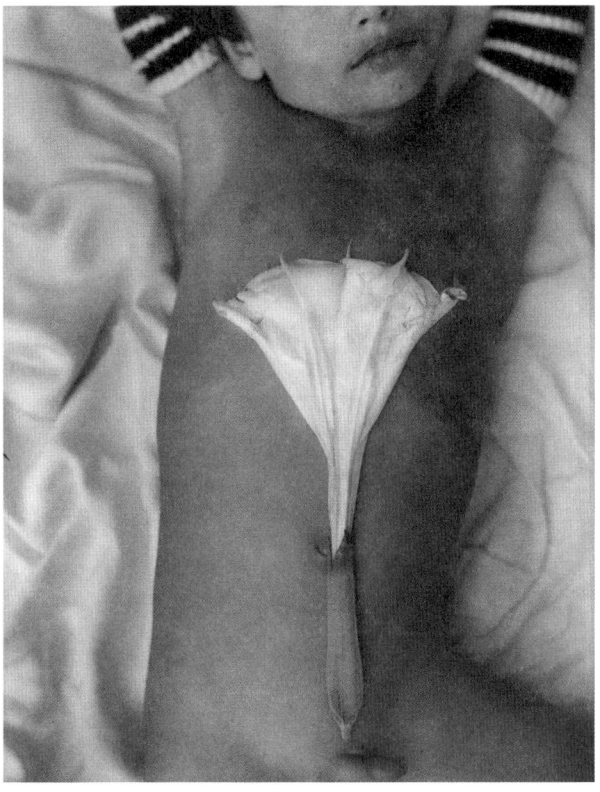

Despite repeatedly staggering beneath what I was convinced was the last, backbreaking straw—Jessie's forty-one ear infections and seven pneumonias in one year, for example—I kept taking pictures. Through all those years, all of those letters, neither Ted nor I ever lost faith that photography was our lifeline. Ted patiently listened to my despair and my disappointments and in turn shared his own—but this is the important thing for anyone trying to work through a complicated, impoverished, and fraught life as an artist: An artistic friend—a true friend, not just someone who might give you a leg up when they make it to associate director at a gallery—can identify when that despair reaches the point where it is not merely an excuse for an entertaining anecdote, but real despair. A true friend will write something like this:

> Your Christmas letter is still right here on my desk, bringing me happiness, and sadness, each time I re-read it. Your Christmas Day sounds warm and wonderful, and the fact that you are continuing to pursue your poetry assures me that there is a lot of inner strength in you yet. But from there on, I worry. Underneath your mock anger and mock despair, I sense real anger, real despair. From this vantage point, I feel that all those things you ruefully and hilariously describe as destroying you _are_ destroying you. I don't think that's what you want me to say, so I won't go further, not just now.

Or this, from 1977:

> That is all that I worry about for you Sally: that you spread your passions too indescriminately between the things that sustain you and the things that destroy you.

And, the most germane to the decades that followed, this one from August 1976:

-3-   *for your happiness*

> to me, and I pass no judgement. I envy you for many things, for your cabin and your darkroom and your beauty and your Dubbonet, but never have I envied you, nor even for the briefest moment suspected you _were_, happy. Most all of us lead lives of quiet desperation, as someone wrote. I tend to be a little less quiet than you, that's all.
>
> But it is not a thing to be ignored; it must not be ignored. You are at a crossroads, Sally. You (not everyone, but _you_) exist to serve Truth through Art. Nothing Less. And all the other things, the cabin and the darkroom and your youth and the Dubbonet, are just fleeting niceties along the way. Enjoy them, but don't take them seriously.
>
> In the beginners mind there are many possibilities, in the advanced there are few. You are an artist, and it's too late to back out. You have no choice, now or in a year or two, but to take aim upon your life and discard all the debris that holds you back from doing what you know you have to do.

• All My Love •

The "debris that holds me back" has taken many forms, as I am sure it has in every artist's life. It can be our day jobs, our poverty, our wastrel siblings, our shithole apartment, the rotgut wine we drink too much of, our broke-down, half-assed car, our lying son-of-a-bitch former best friend, or the *two* speeding tickets in one day, both issued by the same cop, a tall drink of bucktoothed biliousness with the too-apt name of T. J. Eager. And that's just for starters; there are a thousand things like that. But in the same way that our definition of an alcoholic is someone who drinks just as much as we do but whom we don't like, we ourselves would never admit that what actually holds us back is that we just plain waste half of our life not making art but instead doing dumb things too embarrassing to repeat. All the while telling our partner that he's the one wasting time and how come the chicken house never got cleaned out.

5

Distraction

Hitherto I have hoarded up mementoes and monuments of the past;
been a worshipper of all heirlooms; a fond filer-away of letters,
locks of hair, bits of ribbon, flowers, and the thousand-and-one
minutenesses which love and memory think they sanctify: —but it is
forever over now!

Herman Melville, *Pierre*

It's hard for me to imagine Tolstoy cleaning out the chicken coop, and yet I know even he must have had those kinds of quotidian obligations and distractions. I'd be willing to bet his writing days were disrupted by just as many insistent demands on his time as my days are. He walked the dogs. He gambled. Like Levin, he scythed the wheat. He rode his dock-tailed horses through the birch forests of Yasnaya Polyana, his management-intensive four-thousand-acre property. I assume he had some interaction with his ten surviving children, and, given the evidence, also with his wife.

Luckily for him, he didn't have to repeatedly refresh the *New York Times* app to be given the gruesome geopolitical news, or obsessively maintain his social media presence, like just about everybody does now. Except me, who refuses. But I manage to find plenty of other ways to waste time without being on Facebook or Instagram or whatever Twitter is now called. When I look back at earlier years in my Day-Timer, pages heavily leaded with penciled irrelevancies mistaken at the time for urgencies, I wonder what the hell actual creative work I got done in those crowded days and weeks.

Is it possible that these myriad, time-gobbling intrusions—the crossed-out chores, the appointments, the forgotten fertilizer, the remembered wormer—might actually enrich or refresh the creative mind in some inexplicable and necessary way? It would be nice to think so, since there are so damn many of them. But then, if they don't, we have to figure out a mechanism to shake free of their tenacious fuckupery and limp back to work.

I know in my case, I'm conspicuously open to time-sucking distraction, maybe even a little on the obsessive side, what with the organizing and all, but conversely, I also hate wasting time. Anybody who knows me, even a little, knows that I like to keep busy. I'm a fidgeter, a cuticle-picker, a harrier, a martinet multitasker from before that word was even invented. If I were a dog, I'd be a border collie, a hyperactive breed that even I won't own. I bring darning to dinner parties, listen to audiobooks and podcasts while doing almost everything, including riding my horse, and back when I still used the telephone, cricked my neck painfully to free up my hands so I could slice off the tips of my fingers trying to mince garlic while having a phone conversation.

But, even spinning the platter at 78 RPM, double speed, with all the stuff that consumes our time, and assuming not many of us have a Mrs. Tolstoy, how do we get our work done?

As far back as 1973, Ted addressed the issue, riffing on Pogo's offhand remark (anybody remember Pogo from the funny papers—or, in fact, remember the funny papers?) that we are faced with Insurmountable Opportunities:

```
How do you work it to your xxx schedule, I mean work in the important things,
to keep the trivia from overrunning you like a creeping vine that slowly
strangles you and saps all your energy in the process?
Unimportant things are obvious, that get done quickly (giving at least some
transitory feeling of Accomplishment) but reappear again at the next mealtime
or the next house-cleaning etc.

We Are Faced With Inopportune Surmountables..
```

As Always

Ted

I know how true Ted's simile is, having grown up with vines of such exuberant, indiscriminate growth that you can actually hear them inching up the stucco of your house toward the open window as you lie awake at night. At moments when the distractions of my life pull me from my creative work, when I am sapped and strangled by what I think of as trivia, I imagine myself becoming just one more unidentifiable mound of kudzu, triumphantly smothered with the rest of the landscape.

The general perception of how creative people live is different, I think, from the reality. While I am convinced that I am uniquely beleaguered with the humdrum mundanity that seems to fill my days, I suspect that's not true. I remember as a child being taken out to visit Pierre Daura, the Spanish artist who taught Cy Twombly to paint and who lived just a few miles up the road from our farm. He was sitting by the warm mineral springs that bubbled up into a slimy pool by his house, repairing a strap on his sandals with an awl and waxed thread, a sweating glass of iced tea beside him. No easel. No paint-smeared smock. No production deadlines, no guilt, no artistic angst anywhere.

It has taken me six decades since that summer morning to finally figure out that Daura was doing what artists actually *do*: They live their lives. Their everyday, boring, mundane, tedium-filled, sandal-repairing lives. Just like yours. Just like mine.

When I was little and told to find something to do in my room, I would pull out *The Family of Man*. Stretching out on the cool concrete of my bedroom floor, I would turn unfailingly to the well-known Wynn Bullock image *Child in Forest, 1951*, of the naked girl on the ferny forest floor. Holding the book in my grubby hands, I envied and craved her perfect marmoreal serenity. I visited her so often that the page was dog-eared and smudged, but only a little less so than my second favorite image, W. Eugene Smith's *Walk to Paradise Garden*. Rather than sensing abandonment and vulnerability in those images, I saw the children as safe and protected by the overarching and encircling arms of needle and leaf, the gestural protection of nature.

I spent a lot of my childhood alone, but occasionally my father, a country doctor, would take me with him on house calls. One Sunday when I was quite young, four or five, we went to see a pair of aged sisters who, as I remember it, had been told by their father that if they ever married, he would disinherit them and force them to move out of the family's grand eighteenth-century stone home. So, of course they remained spinsters and bitterly rattled around in the echoing rooms of the deteriorating house, set deep within a grove of trees. Reclusive and frail, they were almost identical, each of them with pencil-thin gray braids bobby-pinned at the top of her head.

When Daddy pulled into their long drive, our eyes adjusted from the windshield-spangling sun to the shade of the trees. As he turned off the car and reached for his medical bag from the back floorboards, he told me to stay put, he wouldn't be long. I knew he wouldn't, since he was just checking to make sure the sisters were still alive and getting enough to eat. But as soon as he went in the house, I got out anyway. That's the kind of obnoxious kid I was. Peering around in the shade of the understory I saw we were parked beside a gentle bowl, probably an old sinkhole, carpeted in a uniform green ground cover. Pulling off my underpants, which was all the clothing my mother could get me to wear, I sprinted for the Wynn Bullockian scene. Wading into the not-quite-ferny setting, I sensed a prickling on my legs, but nevertheless threw my naked body into the thickest, greenest part, setting up the tableau of the immaculate child on her stomach and began the wait for my father to return.

By the time he did I was in anaphylactic shock, gasping for breath, my bluing body splotched with angrily burning hives. He high-stepped into the mass of stinging nettles, snatched me out by one arm, pulled open the frog-mouth edges of his medical bag, and overturned the contents on the ground, frantically searching for the hypodermic.

Decades later, when I came upon an aging house trailer, set in a similar green bowl within its own bower of protective trees, I did not sense there could ever be a stinging, spiny, poisonous underside to the scene. Until a few years ago, I hadn't even known it was there, across the river from our farm. It sits well above the water at the dead end of a long dirt road that winds down through old-growth forest until it emerges into the sanctuary-like ring of exceptionally large poplar trees, often pierced by a shaft of light, as if from a cathedral window.

Encircling the trailer with unnatural, Euclidean precision, the trees were all about the same age and their trunks remained uniformly smooth until seventy feet up, when they finally arbored their arching limbs. Their mythological size diminished the trailer almost to the point of miniaturization, as if in fact it was a Hobbit home within a fairy circle. And until an unfortunate sale of unclaimed shit-brown paint at our local Sherwin-Williams, the trailer had been painted a Hobbit-y tealish green, a color especially popular during the 1950s, when it was often used on the lower half of two-toned cars, but apparently it was still popular in the seventies, the trailer's vintage.

Sometimes when the river was low enough, I would swim my mare across and thread up a fern-sided road dug into the hillside and pass through the almost perfect circle of trees to reach the trailer. I never saw the occupant and there was not even a twitch of a curtain as I rode by, but the lawn was always mowed to fairway specs and the glass of the crank-out louvered windows shone. Neatly edged flower beds surrounding the trailer sprouted spindly, sun-starved perennials, manicured boxwoods, and triumphantly adaptable ferns, their pale green tips queen-waving gently in the breeze.

As a child, I remember seeing the hand-drawn advertisements for these mobile homes in *Life* magazine, shown as regally setting sail down the virtually empty highways of the time. In the pictures, they were towed behind a four-door automobile driven by a resolute man, his blonde (Clairol: "Winter Wheat") wife languidly supporting her cigarette arm in the palm of her left hand, and their two children hanging out the back windows. The kids, a boy and a girl, were waving and, one imagines, yelping with the pleasure of hauling their own yacht-like home behind the sharky fins of their powerful sedan.

This trailer, manufactured in Bean Station, Tennessee, couldn't exactly have sailed into its dry dock among the poplars. Indeed, because of the remote location and the twisty road, the stately flotilla required an overland passage cut through an adjoining pasture. Neighbors, curious and skeptical, would have stood along the dirt road to watch the lead car with flashing lights and pennants flapping, followed by the tow truck and the majestic long mobile home, haughty with unconcern. As precipitous as that dirt road is going down to the bowl there must surely have been a few onlookers placing bets as to the braking power of the tow truck.

———

By the time we bought the trailer and a few acres around it, it retained little of that hauteur and self-possession, but instead had the serene dignity of a treasured but valueless object too long burnished and beloved to be discarded. The inside remained just as its advertisements had touted: the "glowing veneer" of the built-in cabinetry still polished, the unblemished white of the shag rugs suggesting a childless occupant, and "Arctic White" curtains by the windows, although maybe a part of the Arctic near a particle-emitting power plant.

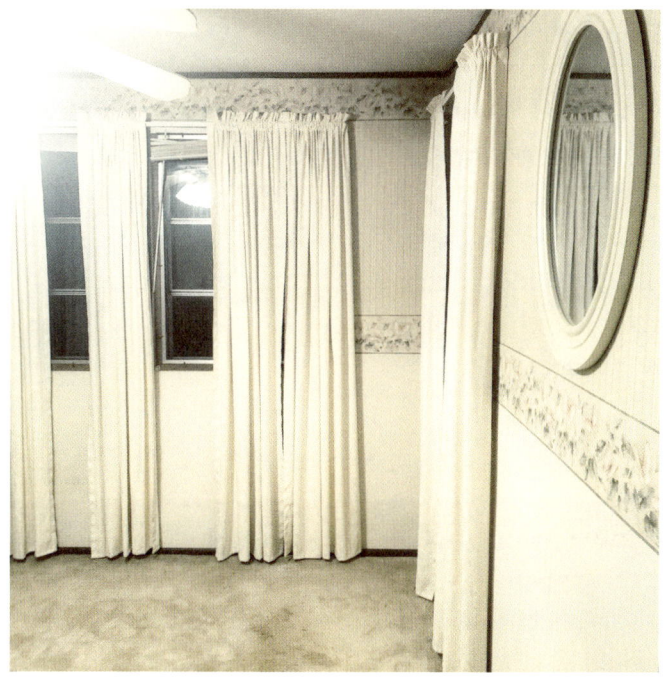

The color scheme, besides slightly sooty snow, tended toward pink, with a rose-petal wallpaper scroll, perhaps reminiscent of a chair rail, unnecessarily breaking up the white wall below the alarmingly low ceiling. Plastic floribunda roses in delicate vases sat in the windows and on the lace tablecloth covering the oval dining table. The drawer pulls in the kitchen had been replaced by handmade papier-mâché flowers, and the burners on the white enamel stove were disguised, as if too utilitarian to be exposed, by flower-painted tin covers. On the refrigerator door, held there by magnetized (yes, you guessed it) flowers, was Vergie's recipe (*"very good recipe"*) for homemade starch.

I'm guessing that Vergie was one of the church folk who came every week to help the trailer's owner, Peggy L., mow the lawn, divide the iris, and, unfortunately, paint the exterior shit-brown. Apparently, Peggy was fairly self-sufficient right up into her late eighties, when she became too frail to live by herself and had to be taken to an old folks' home. She left behind on the walls evidence of her pride in her humble trailer home: flowery plaques advising that we "Cherish the Little Things" and reminding us that "Simple Pleasures Are Life's Treasures."

Standing in the old-woman-smelling trailer after she was gone, I tried to imagine what it felt like for her to leave this Simple Life Treasure that she had so tenderly loved for so long. Being myself not so far from that eventuality, I found the poignance of her care reflected in those pink-and-white plastic roses, which I otherwise would have tossed in the trash without a second thought.

Not wanting to open myself up to a deluge of desperate tenants in the beginning of the pandemic, I was selective when I placed ads for the trailer, limiting them to a nature center website and a local university. I figured it would be a perfect, if funky, getaway for a writer or an artist or a naturalist—the remoteness and quiet, plus the access to the peaceful half mile of deep river, overhung with sycamores.

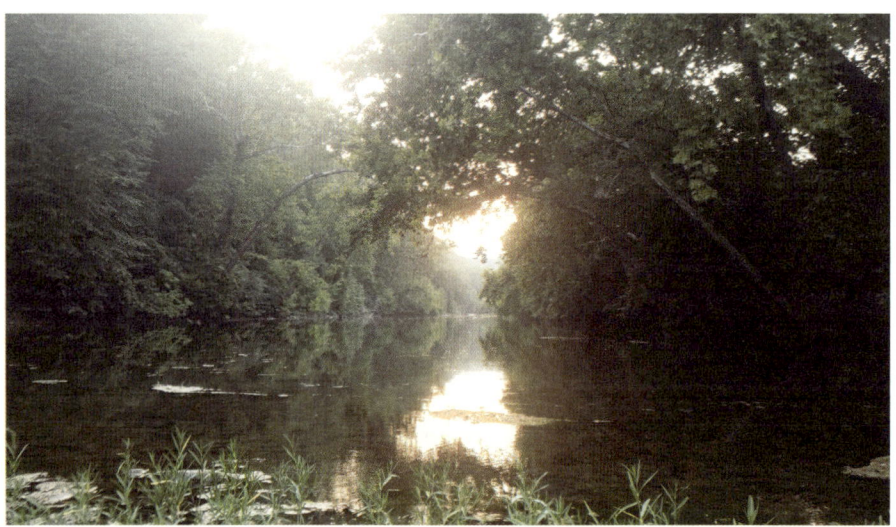

And it came semi-furnished: immaculate, if dated, appliances, all with their warranty cards filled out and mailed—something I never seem to manage—their instruction manuals tucked into folders; a spartan but not inelegant set of plates; cutlery; a knife set; the necessary cookware; and clean dish towels in the lined drawers. As if it were a motel, the folded pink towels and washcloths formed a pyramid on the bathroom counter, and the toilet paper was a fresh roll, its dangling starter piece V'd. And all through the house were objects of china and yellowing plastic, Peggy's Cherished Little Things, the last pleasures as she became increasingly housebound.

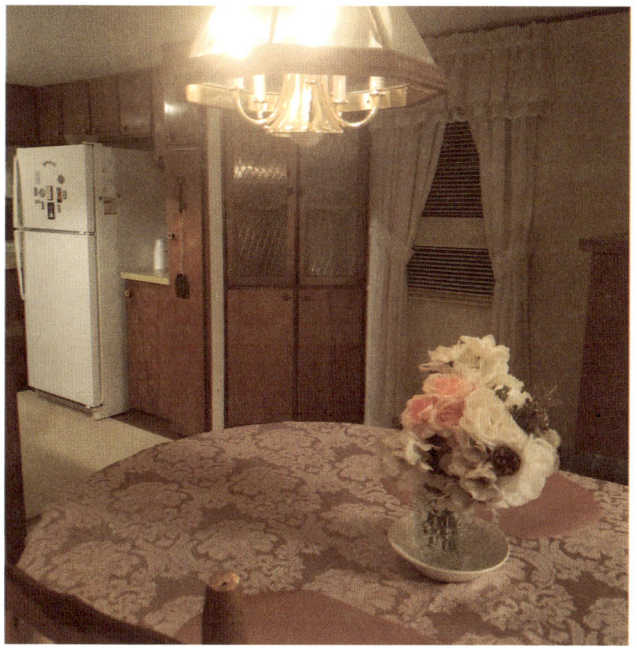

Of course, I knew that those and the plastic roses and the Tara-like curtains would be the first things to go when a tenant moved in, but I felt that even if the trailer were reduced to its essential retro-ness, the sanctity of her simple joys would not be violated. And for some reason it mattered to me that her 1950s ethos of wholesomeness—her churchgoing-ness, the friends who took care of her without recompense or opportunism, the sense of stopped time within which she lived—be preserved.

No artists or writers or naturalists responded to my ads. The monthly rent I was asking, eight hundred dollars, carried with it the whiff of suspicion, of a cover-up: Who charges just eight hundred dollars in rent for a furnished home along a beautiful river, even in small-town Virginia? Must be a piece of shit. Which, I suppose, objectively, it was, but all the same I was disappointed.

I heard from a man with fifteen house dogs, from another who asked how many people the bedrooms could hold, and from a woman who had been living in a tent for three years. Finally, there was an excited response to the ad, breathless almost: This was exactly her dream house. She could tell from the pictures. She loved it all. Her own little place in the country. No, no, she didn't really need to see it, she knew it was, finally after all the crappy apartments, her perfect home.

Of her many subsequently discovered surnames, she introduced herself to me with the least Yoknapatawpha County–sounding one, in fact it had an Englishman-on-the-moors ring to it. Her actual, present name is so Snopesian that had I invented it for this story, any self-respecting editor would have urged me to use something less redolent with unsubtle mockery. So, let's just call her Cindy Snead.

I left a set of keys so she could take a look at the trailer, and afterward we met at an intersection close to our house. She emerged from a tricked-out hatchback, her forehead flocked with still-vivid acne scars, kinky red hair in a scrunchy, and eraser-colored lips that looked like they belonged on a goldfish. She spoke softly with a slight lisp, which gave her that subtle sense of being on the verge of baby talk, and as I strained to hear her, I was surprised to learn that she had children (what children? And twins??) and that she liked to be far out in the country where nobody could find her (red flags should have gone up here). And, oh yes, come out, honey, and from the back door of the car emerged a wraithlike, stringy-haired man with a chin cleft so deep you could niche a toy soldier in it. His whole affect was dark; I felt like I was looking at a late Rembrandt come to half-lidded life. Her fiancé. Yes, yes, would be living with her. Like the unknown number of children, hitherto unmentioned.

———

Larry and I are still bickering about whose fault it is that we rented the trailer to these two. I say Larry's because he was the one who called the references, relatives and friends, and never thought that maybe he wasn't getting the objective truth. He says it's mine because I was the one who actually met them, and I should have been more discerning. He's probably right.

But I was charmed by their excitement at finding their own place, and their eagerness to move in that very afternoon to get started with the "cleanup," immaculate though it was. Rather than ask questions as we stood by the side of the road that afternoon, I put words into their mouths: "With children around, of course, you don't do drugs . . ." and, "You wouldn't be smokers, no, of course you wouldn't want to stink up your nice home." And after the fiancé had spun a long, sad tale about being injured in a hunting accident, being unable to work and failing to get disability but, oh no, no way would he take those pain drugs they offered, I was nodding in vehement agreement with his righteous attempt at self-care. We drafted a rental contract that evening.

A few months later, I rode my mare across the river and heard an odd chiming noise as I began the climb up the ferny road leading to the trailer. Farther up, still in the woods, I heard it again. A little fairy twinkle of a sound. Emerging into the enclosure of trees, I smelled acrid smoke and discovered a multilevel circle of cinder blocks off to the side of the once-perfect lawn enclosing a still-smoldering trash heap. Approaching this, I realized it wasn't just paper trash—iron-clad cookware, plates, mugs, and cutlery were in the ashes, topped with a colorful melt of plastics. With retch-provoking dread, I urged my mare forward but even she wanted no part of what we discovered: All the perennials and carefully tended shrubs, even a mature dogwood had been hacked down to stumps or dug up, as if by a truffle hog.

Looking past the smoldering trash and the piles of dead plants, I realized that the yard was now a blighted panorama of tarps, with mountains, valleys, and lakes swarmed by greenbottle flies. This new landscape perplexed me for just a moment, but not my mare, whose irrefutable sense of smell told her to flee from this scene of destruction and putrefaction. Where the coverings had been chewed through by animals, the geologic underpinnings of the tarpy landscape were revealed to us: black plastic bags of garbage. As far as the eye could see.

Allowing my mare to follow her natural instincts, we spun around from the landfill that was once lawn, and as we moved off, I thought to glance down at the three wooden sheds lined up below the trailer, trig and tidy. Walker Evans already had done a memorable job on their ilk, but nevertheless they had cried out to be photographed; weathered, modest, and, on one, a flowering vine wending fetchingly along the doorframe. Or, it had. Before it had been ripped out of the ground. Inside, Evans would have surely set up the tripod for a few images of the contents, many of which I remembered as being what you might find now in a pricey antique mall—worn tools and pinioned tables, a splitting maul with a handmade handle still nearly twanging in a chunk of sycamore.

But the doors now hung open and what appeared to be the blackness of the interiors was in fact the mountainous blackness of trash bags. And one with a snowcap of the lacy tablecloth, now stained and torn. Nothing left there to tempt Walker Evans, or me, for that matter, to crank out the bellows of a camera.

I tied my mare out of the range of olfactory threat and picked my way back through the reeking landscape to the trailer. As far as I could tell, it was locked up tight, although, as I drew closer, maybe just a little bit too tight—it was positively barricaded. Several new locks had been crudely screwed into the thin pasteboard of the trailer, and the lower windows were painted black. Those were no longer curtains in the windows, I realized, but blankets and towels jammed into the louvers and cranked shut.

Passing around the perimeter of the trailer, kicking aside the drifts of trash, I kept hearing that little fairy chime, so incongruously sweet. And, increasingly, so ominous. I looked up. Cameras were in every third tree, facing all directions. There was a steady line of them in the trees bordering the gravel road going up the hill, and at the top of the remaining dogwood there was a camera jerry-rigged with glue, tape, and a barbeque fork. Several cameras, blinking softly, were nailed to the trees facing down toward the river where I had ridden up. Each time I moved, a chime.

Glancing again across the yard to the telephone pole, I realized the glass housing of the electric meter was wrapped in tinfoil, a surefire way to keep government and paranormal beings from surveilling it. My own tinfoil-hat instincts suddenly all atingle, I sprinted back to my uneasy mare and we took off, the accompanying twinkle of sound landing on us like unwelcome fairy dust.

For legal reasons, I have had to add up the number of hours I have spent dealing with the trailer since the day I discovered its . . . well, its *violation*. A big number. In fact, I spent most of four months on it, time I could have been taking, say, some pictures! Or making some prints. Or writing a book. Or walking my dogs. Or doing almost anything but calling the sheriff, banging on doors, hiring a lawyer, researching the toothless eviction laws, setting up my own motion-detecting cameras, meeting with the deputies who offered some cover while we ineffectually begged the Scarecrow, as I now called the emaciated man with the chin cleft, to open the door of the trailer for which he had paid not one penny in rent for five months, and finally, once he was removed, and when I wasn't waiting on hard courtroom benches, shoveling up the crap outside the trailer, and I'm not about to make this sentence any longer by getting into what we found inside.

But, having taken a deep breath and given my furious hunt-'n'-peckers a rest, I will. It upsets me, even now. Resembling nothing so much as a rock band's postconcert hotel suite, where let's say the lead singer's kleptomaniac sister had stashed her stolen clothing for the last several months, there was very little left of Peggy's Life Treasures to Cherish, if those plaques and refrigerator magnets could even be found anymore.

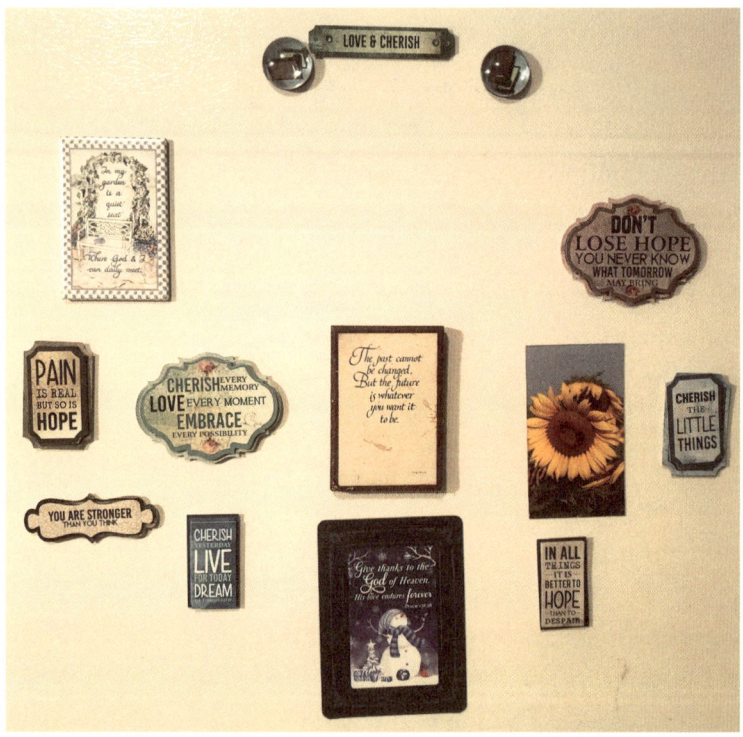

Just getting through the doors, nailed shut from the inside, required pushing back a mountain of stuff on the floor, which left a fan-shaped clearing resembling the wingspread of a one-armed snow angel. Given the now near-Himalayan landscape of garbage bags outside, my first surprise, once inside, was the amount of food left everywhere; cooked, uncooked, half-eaten, uneaten, and regurgitated. And there was plenty to wash it down with; open, half-drunk sodas, beer, sweet teas, and unnaturally colored fruit drinks spilled across the white carpet. I discovered something about beer that I didn't know, even though I have lived in some very cold houses: When there is no heat in the middle of January and you leave a beer can tipped over, the contents turn into something most closely resembling a semisoft foam. Not frozen, exactly, just weirdly chemicalized.

The dining room table, now swarming with cockroaches so big they could have enrolled in kindergarten, had been used for crafty projects of various kinds, and was paint-smeared and gouged, covered with scraps of lumber and broken tools. There was no food on the table, but it was everywhere else; chicken bones, pizza crusts, near-empty peanut butter jars with spoons still jammed into the jelly-swirled remains, half-eaten plates of SpaghettiOs, Halloween candy, and take-out cartons with contents so mold-covered they were unrecognizable. Even the rats and mice didn't eat those, but they had been hard at work on most everything else. Except the vomit. They drew the line at that, apparently, although there was plenty of it, especially atop the waist-high piles of clothing, much of it with price tags still attached.

It wasn't hard to figure out how the rodents had gotten in—there were several holes in the walls, some apparently from fists or feet, but others seemed to be part of a Rube Goldbergian system of homespun security devices. Whether the balls of copper wire stripped from appliances were intended to be part of this protective effort or for sale is an open question, but for sure one very interesting bit of handiwork had been created with the wire, using an overworked glue gun, a button switch, and a small blue light.

I was with my indefatigable Mountain Boys, Sam and Royce, who had helped me kick my way into the back bedroom, when we spotted this peculiar object. Royce picked it up, and Sam said, "Whoa! Drop that shit!" then immediately, "Don't drop it!!!" For a click, Royce stood holding the device by the dangling blue light as if it were a dead mouse and then gently lowered it to the bureau, and we all backed up a step.

The state police bomb squad has an impressive mobile unit, but that afternoon they were miles away when the picture of the homemade device I had sent to the sheriff was forwarded on to them. Nevertheless, almost immediately two extremely personable local deputies in black shirts, cargo pants, and wraparound sunglasses showed up to secure what everybody seemed to think could be a small plastic explosive. Eventually, the bomb squad vehicle, I'm guessing a military hand-me-down, showed up, and we all moved back while the technician gingerly removed the device that mere hours ago the Mountain Boys were handing back and forth, turning over, and speculating about the degree of resistance on the kaboom! button.

As the specialist placed it several yards away in a heavily protected scanning device, he noted that it was consistent with the components and design of a mini IED. A half hour later, after he received the all clear, he took it from the scanner and handed the absurdly glued, meth-mad device to one of the deputies and told him to push the button.

The dangling blue light came on.

We went into the house and had a drink.

―――――――

That afternoon was a giant waste for everybody concerned, not least of all the taxpayers. But for me it was not a total loss, waiting for hours with the deputies in the milky winter sunshine. As we chatted, I learned a lot about the kinds of behaviors that local law enforcement has come to expect from the child-diddlers, methheads, girlfriend-beaters, schoolyard masturbators, pit bull killers, and house-wreckers living in, OK, more often than not, trailers at the ends of dirt roads.

Bomb-making, thankfully, was not usually one of them, although in terms of house-wrecking the Scarecrow was right up there with the best of them. "Bad, very bad," remarked the sheriff looking around the trailer, "but I've seen worse." Strains the imagination, that.

He also seemed unsurprised, but possibly not unconcerned, when I told him that we had found the bank records for what appeared to be a cashed stimulus check that had been immediately converted into a 9 mm pistol. The receipts, the empty box, and ammunition had been among the flotsam pressing against the door as we pushed our way in. Ordinarily I would have just taken the approach that, hell, everybody has a pistol around here, we even have one, somewhere. But a friend had shown me Cindy's most recent Facebook picture and there she was cradling an AK-47. So, on those occasions when I went to the trailer alone, I always took my Belgian Malinois, Cartouche, who whenever he had seen the Scarecrow in the past had commenced such a barking frenzy that mouth lather flew all over his filthy Crocs. Those dogs, as everyone knows, are smart as hell.

Larry and I had Cartouche with us one mid-December evening when we decided we should just run by and make sure that the poor trailer was not now just a pile of embers. We pulled up among the trash mountains in the middle of the circle of poplars. Stark, bare, and creaking in the wind, they no longer seemed sheltering and magical but threatening instead. When exactly, I wondered, had the moment come when nature became no longer protective? When had the tall trees that sheltered me for most of my childhood and watched over the sleeping child in the ferny glen become summer branch-drop hazards, insurance liabilities, collaborators in surveillance, cell-tower imposters, wildfire fodder, and camera supports? When had my role changed from the serene nude in the landscape to the shrieking, gasping child with a needle in her ass?

It was fully dark when we arrived at the trailer, but we turned off the car and got out, Cartouche running in protective circles around us. For a while, we leaned against the hood together, two old people who have seen it all, sad and once again disappointed in humans, ourselves, the world.

The creepy chimes had been disconnected but we were both still a little freaked out by the bomb scare, the pistol, the AK-47, and the dark, now minatory, landscape, so we got back into the car and quickly hit the ignition button. No go. Again. Not even lights on the dashboard. Shit. This was the third time this virtually new Subaru had run its battery down for no reason. There we were, at the end of a long, dark road, no phone connectivity, far from anyone, my imagination running wild with scenarios of the imminent arrival of the vengeful, armed-to-the-teeth Scarecrow.

Larry has muscular dystrophy and can barely walk. There was no way he was going to be able to get away from the car, nor was there any way he could defend himself if, as I feared, the Scarecrow showed up to torch the place. There was no leaving Cartouche with him for protection because he won't leave me, so I told Larry to get in the car, lock the doors, take a nap, and I'd be back with another car. I gave him my useless cellphone, and Cartouche and I took off down the road toward the river, using the bright bits of plastic trash on the edges to guide us along. It was pitch-black now and getting colder. When we got to the river Cartouche hesitated only an instant then followed me into the rushing black water.

Soaking and shaking with cold when we emerged, I grabbed the roots of the sycamores and pulled myself up the sides of the riverbank making for a barely cleared electric line that I knew went straight up toward our house. As I ran, and then scrabbled up the almost vertical power line, through the vines, multiflora rose, and thorny Elaeagnus that love those clear-cuts, I had a good laugh at the—wildly incorrect—image most people must have of a relatively successful artist rusticating in bucolic Virginia.

Just the afternoon before, I had been informed that I had won the prestigious Prix Pictet award for photographs I had made in the Great Dismal Swamp. When it was announced that night in London, champagne flutes had been raised to toast an artist the assembled crowd could not possibly imagine was now man-hauling her muddy, scratched, terrified self up an escarpment to protect her husband from the possible wrath of a nutter with an arsenal, after having wasted two perfectly good months not making an iota of anything resembling art.

———

Reading this, you are perfectly within your rights to complain that this isn't what you thought the creative life was like, that you wanted to read a book about what real artists do, not about what goes on in the boonies where you hardly know anyone who makes art. But people make art everywhere; they have made it in caves and on the sides of subway cars and hunched over a prison cot writing on toilet paper. They do it when they are exhausted, discouraged; they make their work in spite of not having the time or resources, never mind a computer or a studio. And they make it in the moments cobbled together from a day just as jam-packed as your day is, as you plug yourself into your soul-destroying day job or juggle a baby on your hip while packing the school lunches or while you recover from yet another catastrophic family holiday, because they always are. Catastrophic. Like this one described to Ted in 1987:

```
Instead, of  course, the  tree falls  over first thing and breaks
all the ornaments, the children are begging to be taken  to Roses
to buy  a new  toy (!!!), and the house is filthy with the little
scraps of wrapping paper and tinsel  and  the  dirt  of  weeks of
neglect suddenly emerging from thair larval state into full-flung
dustballs. I remember my mother on  Christmas eve  with two bowls
of soup  in her  hands closing  the refrigerator  door by leaning
back against it and sinking, slowly,  down the  refrigerator door
into a  pile on  the floor  and sobbing. And this woman had full-
time, 7 day a week help! (That was an aside) Well, I  fell apart
just like that only the rage came out, it didn't stay in. There I
was shrieking and wailing in rage,  the baby  cowering behind the
amaryllis, Jessie  under her  covers and Emmett standing agape in
astonishment. Poor, poor Larry. He spent  the afternoon vacuuming
noisily while  I  sat  down  to  write  thank  you notes sighing
conspicuously.
So, it  was sweet  and simple: I gave Larry a new work vest and a
squeegee for washing his windows and he gave me a pair of kitchen
sissors and  a book  of photographs about a woman dying of breast
cancer. Christmas night my brother Bob called from  Bermuda where
he and  his girlfriend and their collective families were lolling
in the sun and I admit a little pang did go through me and  a few
moments  later  my  friend  Robbie  stopped  by on his way to the
airport to go to the Virgin Islands, and Larry allowed as how his
secretary and  her family  were off  to the  Virgin Islands and I
started in astonishment at  this as  we waved  beaming Robbie off
and then my friend Joan called. She asked me what I'd gotten from
Larry for Christmas. I said a kitchen sissors and a  book about a
woman dying of breast  cancer. I  asked her  what she  had gotten
from  Malcomb for  Christmas. There  was  a  pause.  She  said,
haltingly, that  she had  gotten a  lovely pair  of binoculars to
complement the season's tickets  to  the  Kennedy  Center  ( with
hotel and meals for the weekend with Malcomb included..) and then
there was another pause and she said, Oh, yes, and I got  10 days
in Cancun  next  week.  That  was  when  the day after Christmas
started falling  apart.  I  began  to  imagine myself  tied down
forever to  great balls  of dust,  to wailing children and shitty
diapers and falling Christmas trees and finances that  never EVER
seem  to  stretch  the  necessary  amount,  and  I  sank down the
metaphorical refrigerator.
```

Somehow, despite all the distractions and the despair, art gets made; words form on the page like blood on the forehead. Because it has to. And because, in fact, it's you who has to make it.

———

Sam and Royce are both large, strong young men who grew up on the side of a local mountain, hunting bear and racoons and caring for their eleven hounds. They are hardworking and tough, but cleaning out the trailer wore all of us out. That hourly account of my time spent on the trailer I mentioned a while back? The cleanup alone was at least twenty-three hours over several days with three people and barely a break for a Mountain Dew. A lot of that time was spent shoveling up trash, clothes, towels, curtains, shattered furniture, moldy shag carpet, broken appliances, a Gordian tangle of what turned out to be thongs, a few "Tight Pussy" jerk-off aids that I wondered for a minute (only a minute!) if Cartouche might like to have as chew toys, and, of course, food. All of this went into black plastic bags, and these weren't your regular kitchen bags, either; these were giant "contractor bags," their packaging showing a hard-hatted construction worker confidently tossing cinder blocks and steel beams into the unfazed and capacious sack.

In 1995 I had bought a green Suburban, initially to drive our son, Emmett, to and from boarding school in Massachusetts, but later to haul my mobile collodion darkroom all over the South. You can't kill that damn thing, and we have it still to pull the sixteen-foot utility trailer that has infinite uses on a farm but is the devil itself to maneuver. Only my Mountain Boys could back that rig up next to the trailer so that we could load all those bags and return them to Cindy and the Scarecrow.

Return them? Yes, we returned it all; packed it all up and hauled it to them. They wanted "their stuff" and this seemed the perfect moment to employ my father's time-honored "take one, take 'em all" policy. In a reversal of the clever trick of burying a bitter pill in the hamburger for your dog to swallow, my father would bury some very desirable treasure in a pile of junk he wanted removed. If you wanted, say, the lovely Chinese fu dog sculpture, then you had to haul away the broken push mower and the cracked birdbath and all the other junk that surrounded it.

So, operating on that principle, the Mountain Boys and I bagged up and jammed into the Suburban or piled on the trailer every scrap they had left within the now-ruined fairy circle, except the mattresses, which were so stained and repulsive that even an incontinent dog would refuse to use them. Everything else though; rotting, leaking, reeking; we loaded every bag to be returned.

The utility trailer is designed to hold 3,500 pounds, and by the end of the day, we had far exceeded that capacity. The Suburban was bulging with bags as well, and by the time we pulled out, we had only the front seat in which to cram two very large men, one tiny, gray-haired woman struggling to see over the wheel, and seventy-pound Cartouche. And all seat-belted, even the dog.

I worried that our rusted-out Suburban with Farm Use plates and no inspection sticker pulling a grotesquely overloaded trailer with a desperate dog gasping for breath at the window might attract a bit of law-enforcement attention, but by creeping along the back roads we made it safely to the motel where Cindy and the Scarecrow were living. Sam and Royce knew I was afraid, but they assured me that they weren't worried about a titty-baby like the Scarecrow, adding that his butt had been ingloriously kicked by their cousins just a few weeks ago and he wasn't likely to mess with them again. Looking at these young giants in their lumberjack boots with Vibram soles so platformed they almost looked fashionable, their large, reddened hands hanging out of too-short coat sleeves, I reckoned they were right: I probably had nothing to worry about.

While Cartouche protectively circled the operation, the Mountain Boys and I unloaded over two tons of bulging black contractor bags, a real-world advertisement for the brand. Cindy, a pistol strapped conspicuously at her hip, filmed us with her iPhone as the pile in the parking lot grew so high we were soon hidden behind it.

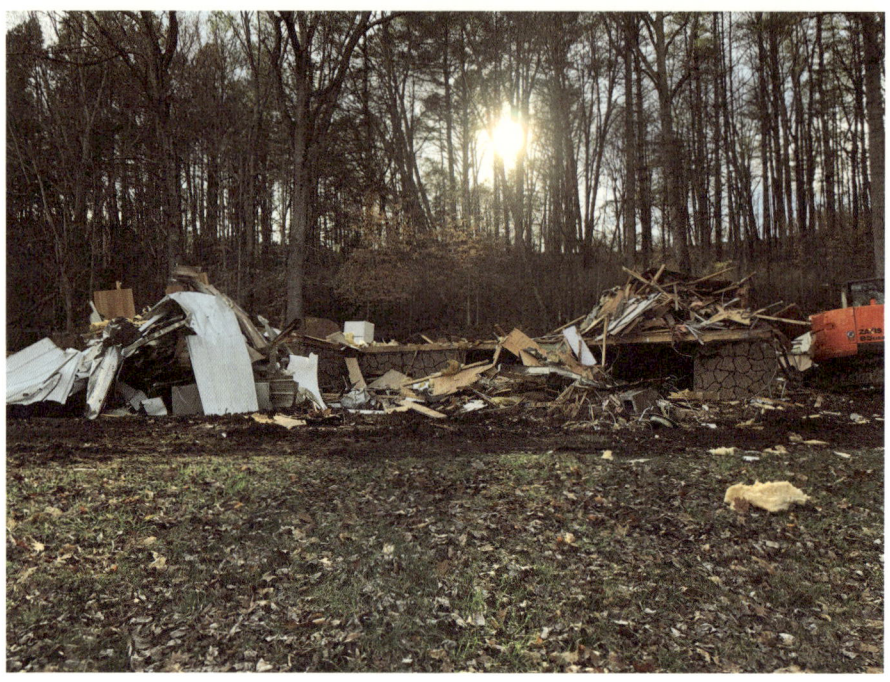

It rained on the March morning they demolished the trailer. Not cats and dogs, but enough so I was soaked after one last farewell tour around the bowl. I arrived at the same time as the prehistoric-looking track loader and experienced a little heart lurch when I saw that two frilly yellow daffodils had survived the flower bed massacre and were bobbing, earnest and oblivious, to either side of the steps. I walked through the empty trailer one last time, opening the kitchen cabinets to make sure I didn't need the brittle plastic cake carrier with Peggy's name written in block letters on it (so that it would be returned from the church potlucks), or the doilies, or the laminated "11 Easy Substitutions" still taped to the inside of the last cabinet. The door to the electric panel was hanging open, and I could see the switches carefully notated with strips of floral paper behind yellowing tape.

I left the plastic roses that I had rescued from the debris leaning on the windowsill, where they would be the first thing to go when the giant excavator claw smashed into the flimsy structure. It was no flimsier, really, than the tissue of fantasies, fabrications, and memory in which I had lovingly wrapped the place and no less thoroughly gone by the end of that day. All that remained to be seen by anybody who happened to get to the end of that road—the lost Google Maps truster, the dead-end turn-arounder, the lovers' lane parker, the napping VDOT workers— were some gouges in the bark of several of the big trees, some scraps of plastic, a shard of floral crockery, and the two miraculous daffodils protected by god knows what.

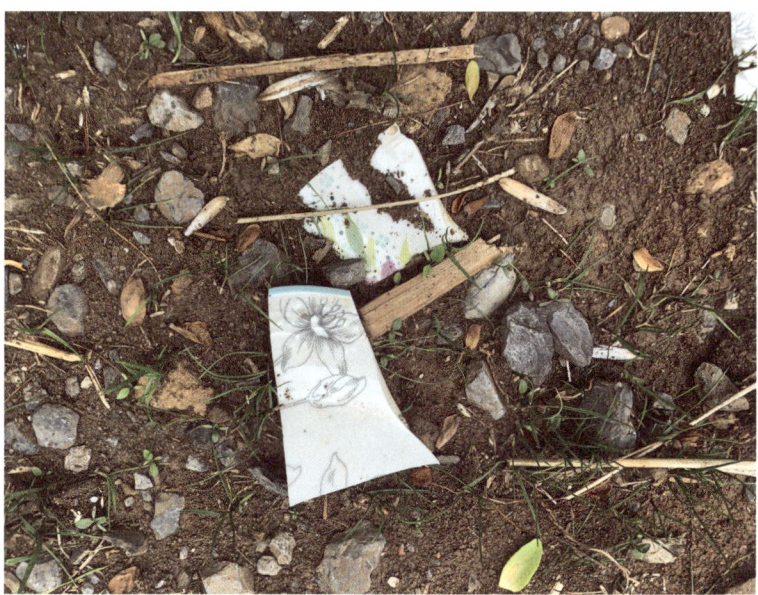

Except for evidentiary iPhone snaps, I didn't take a single meaningful photograph through this whole ordeal. I am a *photographer*! In interviews since forever I have banged on about how we should "photograph what's important to us," the things that matter, the things that are close to us. Make the local universal, and all that. Yet here was something so close to me that it was truly under my skin; I had fiberglass insulation embedded in the back of my neck from elbowing along the snakeskin-y crawl space under the trailer to check the ruined plumbing. For days I itched and burned like the nettle-stung child, a physical reminder of yet another mistaken expectation within a different budding grove.

This whole trailer debacle joined the unhappy ranks of dead ends, lost causes, failures, disappointments, betrayals, and all-around time-wasters in my life. Viewed through the lens of the collective fantasy to which we seem unswervingly dedicated, the fabled "artist's life" is Olympian in its lofty disdain for the ordinary and the tedious. As susceptible to this fantasy as anyone else, my subversive brain says: Real artists don't spend their time the way I just spent mine. Real artists make art and when they're not making art, they are drinking absinthe with friends and vacationing on St. Barts and even then they are probably provisioning their art larders.

Of course, I'm all about making art even in the unlikeliest situations (see: bathroom, airplane, page 192), but is there any art, or any benefit at all, that could possibly emerge out of this trailer fiasco? At the time, I would have said hell no. What woman in her eighth decade needs to be swimming a fast river in December? But I see it differently now. There was value in those wasted four months. Not the least of it being that I now have an especially entertaining story for my next visit to the part of the world my friend describes as having "knob heat"—that is, the non-Appalachian world with thermostats instead of woodstoves. I love bringing good redneck stories to my often-amazed urban friends. But there is also an ineffable and complex accretion of human experience—and I am hardly the first to liken this to the calluses on a plowman's hands—which is said to redound to the equally ineffable and slippery virtue of "character." My children will happily recount to you the repellent tasks they performed with the assurance of character-building.

If it's to be built by the hardships, by life's slings and arrows, then by god I've got a ton of it, and my kids do, too. Beyond entertainment, there's value in that. It gives you something to say in your art. It gives you the *right* to be saying it.

———

When I went over one final time to rake up all that was left of the trailer into the last of the contractor bags, my arms and back were still aching, but I identified another pain that was just as insistent. It was the pain of not working; of not making art, of not writing. Artists really get down to the business of making their art when it is more painful to *not* make it than to make it. And that's saying something. Because sometimes making art can be excruciating. But the desire to create is a real thing, if elusive and unquantifiable, and as elemental as any other hunger. It is fueled by the life we are living, and, paradoxically, discomfort and impediments can up the octane. Not entirely unlike an addict, you crave the almost illicit high, the skydiving exhilaration of art-making. The degree to which you will go to satisfy your passion to create establishes the level of risk you face at not doing so.

We work soul-sucking jobs to buy us the relief of a few hours of creativity, and it's not just us—it was Philip Glass, who worked as a plumber and once showed up to install a dishwasher for an astonished art critic, Robert Hughes; or the filmmaker Werner Herzog, who worked night shifts in a steel factory to fund his films; or William Carlos Williams, a physician who wrote poems on his prescription pads in between seeing patients. In his autobiography, Williams ventured that his disparate vocations were paired parts of a whole: "One rests the man when the other fatigues him." My vision of every artist but me spending the winters on a tropical island with a paintbrush in one hand and a fruity cocktail in the other is absurd, and when I am not feeling sorry for myself, I know that. Artists have regular lives doing regular, tedious things that take us away from our art, but those things also serve as reminders of how very much we want, and need, our creative life.

So, despite time's sands rushing the waist of my particular hourglass, I don't feel like the four months away from my art practice were without value. And I'll even posit that there is value in the time you just spent dicking around at whatever *you* just did, too (maybe even in reading this), despite it appearing to have no redeeming artistic benefit. I'd go so far as to say that even when you stop working altogether, for long stretches, there is ultimate good in it for your creative work, whatever it is. Inactivity isn't failure; like an athlete, your artistic muscles need time for recovery; repose is restorative. Paradoxically, not making art can teach you as much as making it, and if nothing else, it fills the reservoir of desire.

***

As I have said, during those years when the kids were toddlers and I seemed to always have a baby at the boob, I barely made any pictures. I was exhausted and broke and positive the well had run dry, after scarcely moistening the creative soil I had so sedulously tended. That overused dry well trope has been my lifelong refrain, and every time I sing it, I believe it with all my heart.

Well, there are good days and there are bad days and there are days that I dn't even remember but there are no lazy, easy-going days anymore. The times I used to have/for sitting down with a tall drink and witing a long letter to you are gone: in their place are afternoons spent with ▒▒▒▒▒▒▒▒▒▒▒▒ one baby on the hip and the other underfoot, pots bubbling over on the stove, phone calls interrupted by shreiking that ends the minute I hang up, laundry moldering forgotten in the machine, and always that nagging feeling thatthe well must have run dry and in its place I have taken to wife and motherhood. But the tall drink remains. One constant.

So, I'm thinking instead, of taking local, REAL local pictures. Even, believe it or not, BABY pictures. What could be more local. What could be more difficult?

1982

Take a look at that last paragraph. Even as my life was overwhelmed with distractions and mundanities, when the only constant was a tall gin and tonic at the end of the day (and thank god for that), I was beginning to feel the unignorable pull of the nascent Family Pictures, or, as I put it, of the "REAL local." Out of the mess of shitty diapers and an unemployed husband, out of myriad crises, many rising to red-alert levels, I had begun to formulate an irresistible creative way forward; photographs that could embody anew the Wynn Bullock image of the serene, naked child in the ferny woods, an image abiding and still vivid from my childhood, yet complicated now by my awareness of her vulnerability and evanescence: I had decided to photograph my children.

So, sure, go ahead and ask yourself the famous Rilkean question: "Must I?" "Will I die if I don't make work?" But I'm guessing that unless you're a Romantic poet with too much ether at your disposal, the answer is probably no. You won't. If you're anything like me, you probably don't have all that much to say anyway, so give it a break. Knowing when to stop can be just as important as knowing when to keep going. So, sit back and observe. Go to the benches on the southeast side of Walmart and watch the American parade. Observation and experience, including trashed trailers, are the cornerstones of good art. Regroup. Remember. Dream a little. Feel. Volunteer. Cement down a few more cinder blocks in the character edifice. Write a letter. Organize. Make lists. Clean out the chicken coop. Practice your craft; do your scales, memorize a sonnet, copy a Rembrandt. Over and over. Do all this so you will be prepared to come roaring back when you have something unignorable and irrepressible to say. And you will.

6

Organize

"The horror of that moment," the King went on, "I shall never, never forget."

"You will, though," the Queen said, "if you don't make a memorandum of it."

—Lewis Carroll, *Through the Looking-Glass*

Making art is your job; you go to it every day. Even if there is no set place to go. Even if you are sitting on the hard seats at the General District Court waiting for the judge to call your case, or hauling out contractor bags of trailer trash. You can be doing your job—making art—even in liminal moments like these.

Art, if it were a verb, would be intransitive, requiring no direct object, unlike, say, the verb "need"; it would "need" no nouns to complete its action. Art is often more question than answer, the first word of an argument that you have not yet formed an opinion about. Art can be illusory, invisible. Art is, above all, ordinary (and the only reason it's been capitalized here is that it's the first letter of those four sentences). Plus, it can be boring. Sure, there are ecstatic moments when whatever you're doing turns out, by some miracle, to be pretty damn good, but most of the time it is just a routine job, not that different from the everyday *jobs, jobs, jobs* that politicians are always promising to deliver. An artist is like every other working schmuck.

And, like any other job, it helps if you have your shit together. I never weary of repeating, like the tiresome old scold I am, this line I once thought so clever: Until you can paint like Vermeer, don't start flinging like Pollock. And I'm sticking with it. *Learn your craft.* You learn it like you learned typing (or we should have) or baking a soufflé or driving a backhoe. It's not everything, of course; the poet Charles Wright summed it up this way: "Pure technique is the spider's web without the spider—it glitters and catches but doesn't kill." Your technique will be invisible if your art is good enough, if it kills. If it doesn't, if it's all glitter, technique is all you'll see.

It's worth noting that art's etymological family is of Greek extraction, some distant progenitor being *techne*: technique, craft, skill. Then, by some ancient linguistic sleight of hand, *techne* embraced *ars*, another of those frolicsome linguistic alliances, and over time there came to be no distinction made between the artisan and the artist. The latter was no more highly prized or revered in their practice of the fine arts, the *vulgares* as they were tellingly known, than any other laborer. Their job was, in the words of the Oxford English Dictionary, "the *skillful* production of the beautiful in visible forms" (emphasis mine). What a terrific definition, right?

It was not until the seventeenth century in Europe that the artist was perceptually decoupled from the common laborer as part of the nascent but increasingly dominant narrative of individualism. (And frankly, given where the extremes of that individualism have brought us as a culture, I have some doubts about that particular trait but never mind.) Those of us who work at art know that we need a hybrid, nuanced narrative; we know that we are lucky, yes, and we have certain freedoms, but we also know that to be successful at our job there are rules, concessions, and unyielding strictures within which we labor.

For starters: You need to organize your time. Like craft and technique, the humble structural underpinnings of your meteoric artistic career, should you have one, will likely be invisible, but they will be essential. Anne Truitt wrote in *Daybook: The Journal of an Artist* that there is an appalling amount of mechanical work in an artist's life, and to manage it, yep, right at the top of her list is *lists*—an artist needs the time-management skills of a small-business owner. One trick to save time, which was revealed to me by a very successful Hollywood actor, is to decide on a day's menu that is toothsome and healthy and eat it every day. Think of the time you waste standing with the refrigerator door open, that annoying door-open dinger getting louder as the minutes pass while you try to figure out what to eat. The other thing she suggests is to find an outfit you like and buy a bunch of them, varying the colors day to day. She could tell I knew the clothes part already, wearing the same Levi's jeans every day (bought first when I was sixteen at the Putney School store—and still in 28 × 30, can you believe?), the same Blundstones from before every Brooklyn hipster was wearing them, the same cotton shirts from Goodwill. I have so few clothes, you couldn't adequately pad a crutch with them. If you can pare your daily decisions down, food and clothes are no longer things you have to waste time thinking about. Yes, maybe you appear to live a boring, undeviating life, but that is one thing you should not be afraid of. Your work will not be boring.

Ideally in your day "at work" you did indeed make some art, but you also checked off the list "change oil" and "stool sample to vet." The measure of artistic success is not money; it is time. And you must regulate it like the metronymic steps of the most unflappable Beefeater on parade. Let people make fun of my Day-Timer, clutched to my breast like a rosary. But knowing what I have to do, every hour of every day and every week of every month, is what allows me to schedule, yes, schedule, creativity. It doesn't drift down and lightly settle upon us like a gauzy visitation from the muse. You have to clear a well-lit and GPS-coordinated landing strip for it.

I was just out of my teens when I began to realize that I had a touch of what we used to call an obsessive-compulsive tendency. I'm sure there's some more correct way of saying what I've got, but here's a hilarious (if you call the weeping I'm doing hilarity) and sadly accurate account of one time, among many, that I have been derailed by my compulsive behavior. I wrote this to Ted in 1981:

```
now remember, spalling isn't  my long suit...

what is, however, seems to be about to consume me: compussive prganizing.
I talkled my darkroom/ studio area one day: actually, to be strictly
correct, I walked in to wash out a graduate to give the kitty some water
and I started to rinse out a few more graduates and then I began to
wash out the trays and then I scrubbed down the sink and then I
decided the walls needed a little brightening up and so I pinted
the whole entire room and ø moved into the studio and painted it and
with that, of course the shelves began to look a little dingy and
so I painted them and then the counters which had to be done in oil
base enamel so while I was painting in oil base paint I figured whu not
paint the stairs and once I got the stairs done I decided to shampoo
the carpet and strip the linoleum and re wax it and when that was
done I completely revamped my filing systems and my cabinets.

Bet you're wondering what happened to the kitty's water, aren't you?
```

I'm no better now. How many times have I bled the well dry by leaving the hose running in the horse troughs after I wandered off to do something else that took all day? There's always the chance that it was genetic, since on the day of my birth my organized mother began stockpiling money for me, beginning with a whopping five-dollar deposit; savings for a dire eventuality:

. . . which she couldn't have known would be an Ansel Adams Workshop in photography, as well as a precursor to a lifetime of exhausted savings accounts,

and also, of desperate frugality.

For years I kept a financial ledger in which I noted every day's expenditures (and, once in a while, meager income) in fastidious detail. Now, many decades later, I flip through it in wonderment. It has twenty columns spread across two pages, listing normal living expenses like "Housing," "Light, Fuel, Telephone," "Food, Dry Goods, Clothing," "Churches and Charities," "Amusements and Vacations." Needless to say, the latter two columns never saw a pen stroke, as all my notations were limited to a primitive, cheerless attempt to keep body and soul together. Rent was $72.97 each month, food and utilities each averaged about $30.00 a month, with the highest numbers often registered under "Automotive," the cost of keeping my ancient shitbox—a two-stroke Saab (yes, like your chain saw: add oil to the gas)—putt-putting along. There was nothing in the "Insurance" column.

And that included medical and home insurance, of course, so in 1971 I made a poor-person's list of home remedies for everything from warts to sticking griddles:

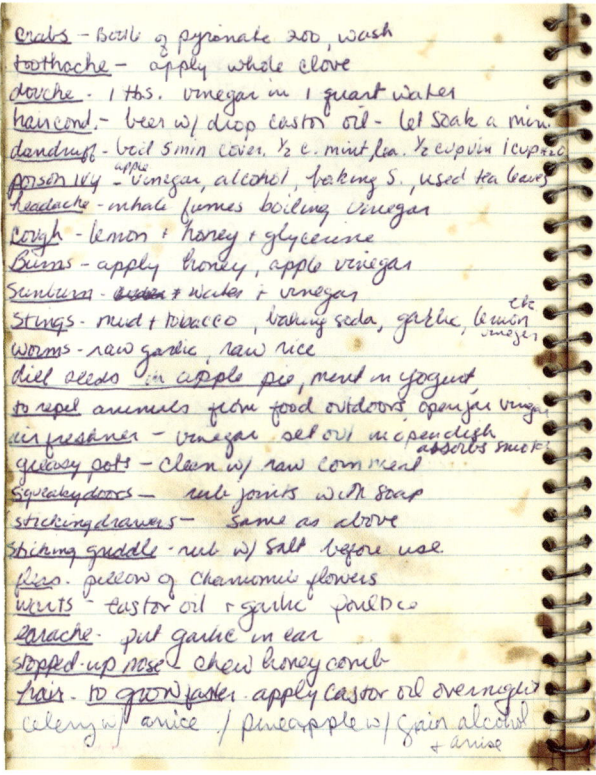

You will note about halfway down that intestinal worms are to be treated with raw garlic and rice, but of course you clever young people know I was wrong about that: the best treatment for worms—pinworms anyway—is diatomaceous earth. Mix a spoonful of that with some honey, gag it down, and the little spiny diatoms will cut even the tiniest worm to bits. This is way easier than the two-person job (one person has to hold the flashlight) of snagging the pinworms with the rounded end of a bobby pin as they crawl from the butt at night. I have a picture I could show you of this operation, but my squeamish editor has nixed it. Anyway, after you are done with the seven teaspoons you'll need for your worms (I recommend a full week of the honey and diatom treatment), you can use the rest of the bag of diatomaceous earth to make a beautiful, velvety varnish for your prints, as I did for my Battlefield series. And to kill slugs, of course. Same principle; cuts them up. Versatile stuff.

Anyway, besides pinworms within that painfully detailed financial ledger, there are some promising moments: one atypically prosperous month in 1975 we came out $13.01 in the black, our month's earnings being $237.50 and our outgo $224.49. But in earlier years, we struggled to stay even $13 in the black. Right after our marriage in 1970, when Larry was working at the local blacksmith shop, I simply wrote down those days where I actually had made any money to spend.

And, yes, that is the month's menu in the lower right corner, which in the summer depended heavily on garden vegetables and sour milk (almost free at the A&P). For the jot-and-tittlers among you, yes, I, too, have noticed the several errors in addition—nine plus seven, by my computing apparently equaling eighteen, and the final tally being off by one digit. You now need no further explanation for my becoming an artist. My math SAT was so appallingly low that if it hadn't been for my Latin and English scores, no college would have taken me. I don't remember ever being tested, but I wonder if my IQ would have exceeded room-temperature range. As it was, I squeaked into Bennington, the artsy-fartsiest school in America, which thank goodness didn't really care about test scores.

Because I was convinced that I wasn't all that naturally smart—and the test scores on those despised standardized tests only reinforced that belief—I have spent my life in a deliberate and relentless program of intellectual self-improvement. And, believe it or not, I use lists for this, too. Since there was no point in hoping for math improvement, I concentrated on language. I began to write down words and their definitions in my late teens, including their phonetic spellings and sometimes their Latin roots. I loved Latin and inexplicably excelled at it, under the riding crop of my Latin teacher, the Germanically punctilious Felix Lederer, who to this day I remember as being at the head of the class in thigh-blooming herringbone jodhpurs and tall, polished boots (this outfit as imaginary as the crop). I found that just writing down the words helped me remember them, having what I believe is a reasonably good eidetic memory, but every day I would try to memorize a new batch, like these from the late 1970s, and Larry would call them out to me. Looking at them now, I think I need a refresher: "rachitic"? When have I ever used that word? And how on earth are we ever going to be able to distinguish between "tumid" and "turgid"?

So, now for the really embarrassing part. I still do this. I keep lists of words I want to learn and use and I am seventy-three years old. My car has a shoebox full of Word-a-Day calendar pages for Larry to call out to me on road trips, and—this is killing me to admit—they are broken down into rubber-banded categories: words I need to learn, words I already know but need to be reminded of, words I'd never use but should know anyway, etc.

Can you begin to see why I say patience and tenacity are more important than that word I swore I wasn't going to use in this book? If I can be said to have had a small, innate spark of brilliance, it has been as tirelessly nurtured as any flickering campfire of damp sticks by Scouts desperate for warmth.

103

The path to being an artist or writer can surely be less tortuous than mine has been. For one thing, you should try to embark on it with some money, as you would any other journey. I won't further belabor the poverty of our first fifteen years of marriage, but there's no question that it has affected every aspect of my life, even until now. And I also won't pretend that I am not a very fortunate person to have been born where, when, and to whom I was. I unquestionably had a safety net; if I had experienced anything of an urgent medical nature, for example, I am pretty sure my parents would have stepped in. But in general, except for educational expenses, they were done supporting me after I announced my engagement to Larry at age eighteen, and they didn't revisit that decision.

I don't think they cut me loose financially in a punitive way, but maybe to make a point about consequences. I was obnoxiously independent and strong willed, and those tendencies had often made my parents' life miserable, so their basic attitude was: *Sister, have at it; here's your damn independence!* Everyone recognizes that moment of actually getting what you say you want and finding yourself suddenly not so sure you really meant it—that moment when the door you've been pushing against for years is unexpectedly opened and you sprawl into your future. The parental door I'd been pushing against opened just enough to let me out, and I'm pretty sure I detected a sigh of relief as the bolt was shot from the inside. Who could blame them? But then, I dusted myself off, married Larry Mann, and soldiered on.

In this cocky letter to my parents from February 1972, not quite two years after our wedding, I seem confident that I can manage without a college degree, that "piece of paper," banking on my (still nascent) "skill," and the potential of my photographs to "move people."

```
          Other than my skill, there is only
the question of the piece of paper and that is the most
 insignificent t̶h̶i̶n̶k̶ thing in the world when I can take
 the photographs that I do and when I see them move people
as they do. That will give me work whereever I gon..
 tho the thought of being really poor and refused a job
  by some goddamn stuffy basterd because I don't got that
 pretty BA is really infuriating.
```

Whether they could be so moved that they would reach for their check-books was another matter, as was my impotent rage against the system. But, despite all obstacles, I was going to make my art the way I wanted to make it, putting a point on it with the solecism "I don't got that pretty BA." And I was going to make it in the place where I wanted to make it, Lexington, Virginia, and the world by god was going to bend around that ambition.

Here are a few of the painful ingredients I collected for my character-building: overconfidence, arrogance, fantasy, and ultimatums. Perversely, the ingredients are subtractive. The character edifice is formed by extraction and replacement, suffering being the more durable structural component, glued tight with passion and belief. Like a form of art boot camp, just one thing must survive the breaking down and rebuilding process: that *I'd-rather-eat-crabgrass* passion.

I once read a trenchant quote by William Wharton in the *Washington Post*—and yes, I keep a list of quotes, too, presently 257 pages long, from which I now produce this one:

> I say to a lot of people, the secret to the good life is: find something you really like to do. Find out if you're good at it. If you are, work hard to become very good at it. Then hope you can find someone to pay you to do it. But almost everybody does it the other way. They look for a job, and then they hope to get good at it, and then they hope to learn to like it.

The salient thing about that overconfident 1972 letter to my parents is that even by age twenty I knew what I really liked to do and it was to take pictures. I didn't feel I had a choice; it was the thing I loved and I was going to pursue it despite the parental concern that I had no safety net, no teaching sinecure, no fallback skills. We make our art because we have to—if you're not sure whether you are an artist, then you probably aren't and you should look elsewhere. There are far easier ways to earn a living.

Which we all find out, usually the hard way. In my case, as Wharton says, I knew that in order to get somebody to pay me for doing what I loved, I had to get good at it. Very good. I started by, of course, making a list: a list of what it was going to cost me to learn how to take pictures. The obstacle was the cost, always the cost, never the desire or the unwavering belief that this was my destined path.

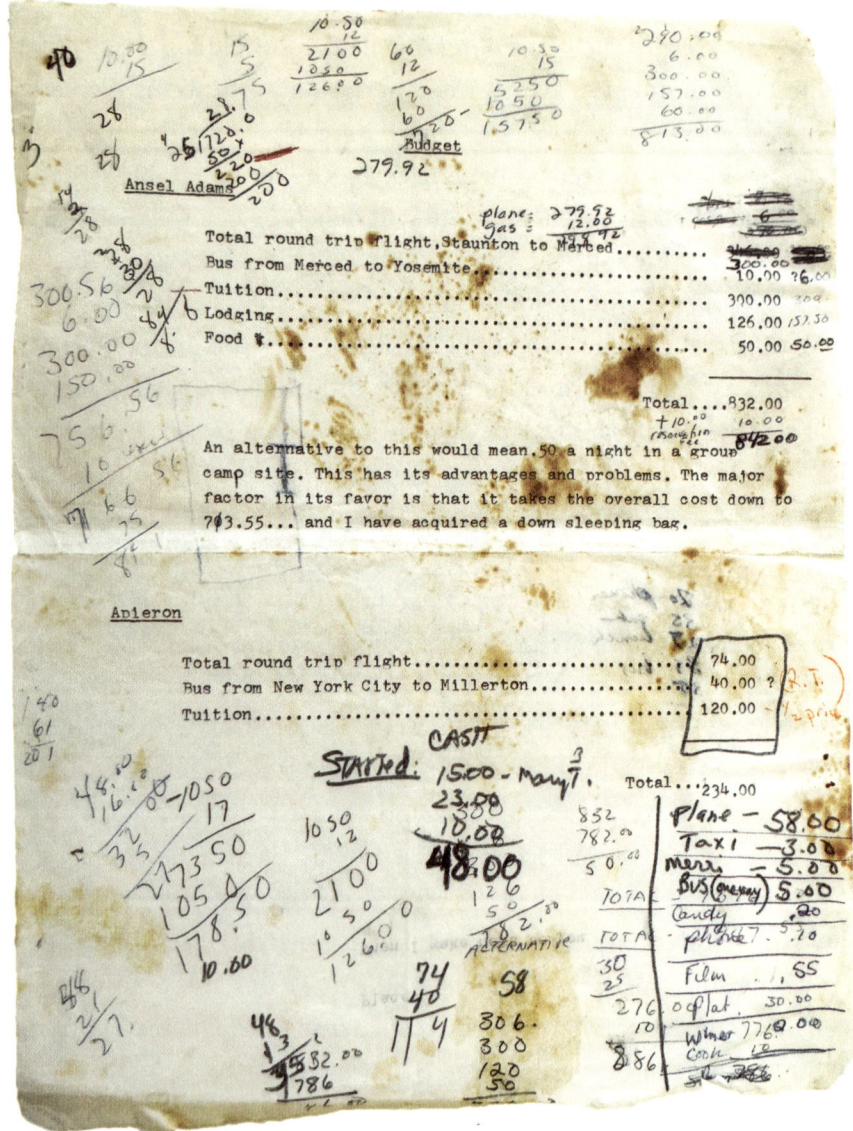

When you look at the bottom-line number of $842.00 for the Ansel Adams Workshop, you know exactly what happened to every penny of that money ($887.73) from the savings account my mother opened at my birth, and you know also how, for all intents and purposes, this particular photographic journey to technical competence (lists, formulas, budgets) and revelation (my long epistolary friendship with Ted Orland) began. If you were to envision an inspirational figure similar to the embodiment of Lady Justice but for artists (she would have defiantly torn off the blindfold, of course), Lady Art's set of scales would contain competence on the one side and revelation on the other. Like those of Lady Justice, they have to find some kind of stasis, but they also can shift up and down as they are unevenly weighted over time.

In those early years, I loaded her up, first one side, then the other, but, torturing this metaphor even further, Lady Art remained resolute, striding forward, skirts tucked in at her waist, arm raised in defiance. And so I strode, off to the only technical photographic education I ever got, those two workshops eked out of my lifelong savings account, the first one a week in Yosemite at the Ansel Adams Workshops, the other a weekend at Apieron [sic] with the master printer George Tice.

There's a scene—I may be misremembering—from *Light in August* in which a poorly dressed, thin girl steps down from a bus at the end of a long driveway, strands of hair plastered to her sweating neck and forehead, clutching a cheap suitcase. She has come to find her man. In 1973, when I arrived in just such a state in Yosemite, I was looking for my man, too.

He was Ansel Adams, the most technically skilled photographer perhaps ever, and I found him there, but I also found Ansel's assistant and printer, Ted Orland. As it turned out, Ted was the man I was really looking for.

The suitcase I was carrying was a white Samsonite overnight case with red sateen lining I'd gotten for my twelfth birthday. I had been inordinately proud of it then, but now I was embarrassed by its childish appearance, although it did a great job of protecting the rickety, wooden 5 × 7–inch view camera I had brought with me to the workshop.

Ted was one of the workshop assistants that year, and he surely must have noticed that I stood out from the other students, most of whom knew what they were doing and had the equipment to prove it. The first evening, while sitting on a wall miserably eating Triscuits from the box, I watched a boy in aviator sunglasses unloading Pelican cases and tripods from his Benz. Superciliously glancing over at me as I washed a big mouthful of crackers down with a bottle of Coke, he asked, unforgettably, "Were you raised in a barn?" I looked down at my filthy fingernails and the dirt seeping up on either side of my flip-flop thong, and knew I was in over my head, on all levels.

Ted immediately caught on to the fact that I was alone and overwhelmed and, even more importantly, so broke that the Triscuits and Coke were in fact my meal plan. One of the first nights there, he invited me to join the assembled assistants at the Ahwahnee Hotel for dinner and bought me a square meal and a big glass of red wine.

He also began to teach me what photography was really about: pushing the limits, having fun. Doing stuff that the Kodak guidebook said not to do. That first night after dinner, we all went out into the grasslands and Ted set up a camera with Polaroid 4 × 5 film to take a picture *by moonlight!* It had never occurred to me to try. I mean, there's no light to even meter. (Of course, Ted owes much of his crepuscular photo knowledge to Ansel. See: *Moonrise, Hernandez, New Mexico.*) He showed me things about the view camera and about printing that I use to this day. He introduced me to Ansel, who appeared wearing a large apron, his chemical-stained fingers holding a bulbous goblet of red wine. I adored him on sight. Soon we were both drinking wine and looking at my pictures, 5 × 7–inch contact prints mounted on cheap brown board, about which he was scrupulously kind. Ansel was welcoming, he was encouraging, he gave me information and hired me to be an assistant for the next year, but it was Ted who really gave me my way forward.

And I took it. Like so many of his workshop students over the decades, I am grateful for that moment in the moonlight when I watched my future come into focus. Or, close to focus. It was, after all, a fifteen-minute exposure, the grasses unsharp, gently moving, as if underwater. But I didn't miss a class, making sure I got my money's worth, learning everything I could, filling notebooks with formulas and shutter speeds and film characteristics, the technical information I needed to be competent,

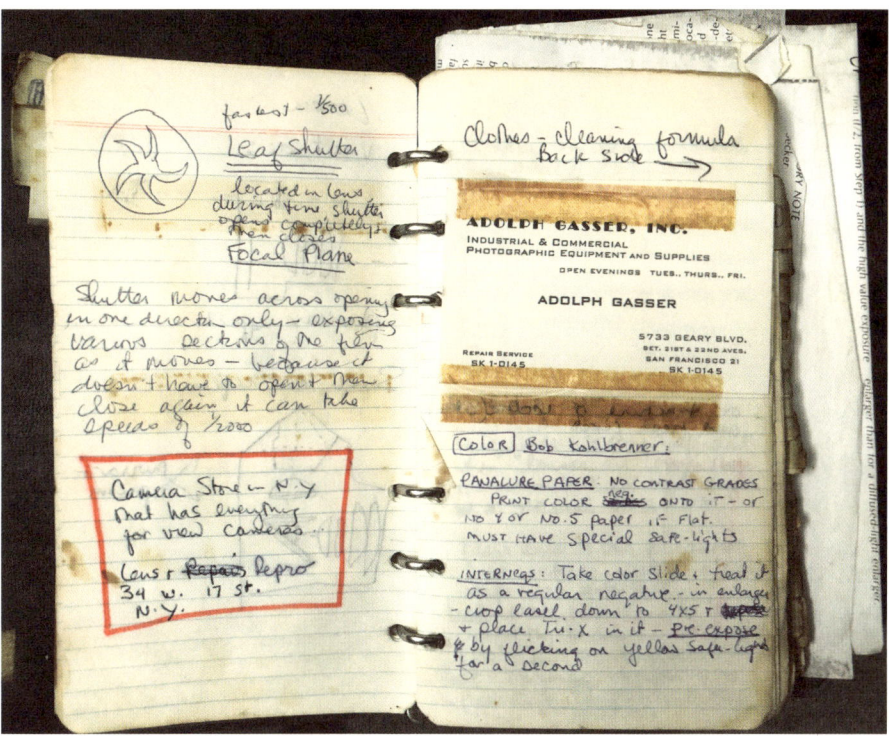

but also with revelation: sketched-out ideas for pictures yet to be taken, my own particular evolving aesthetic. And they were pictures that I soon took . . . and took . . . and kept taking. Over and over again. I am still taking them.

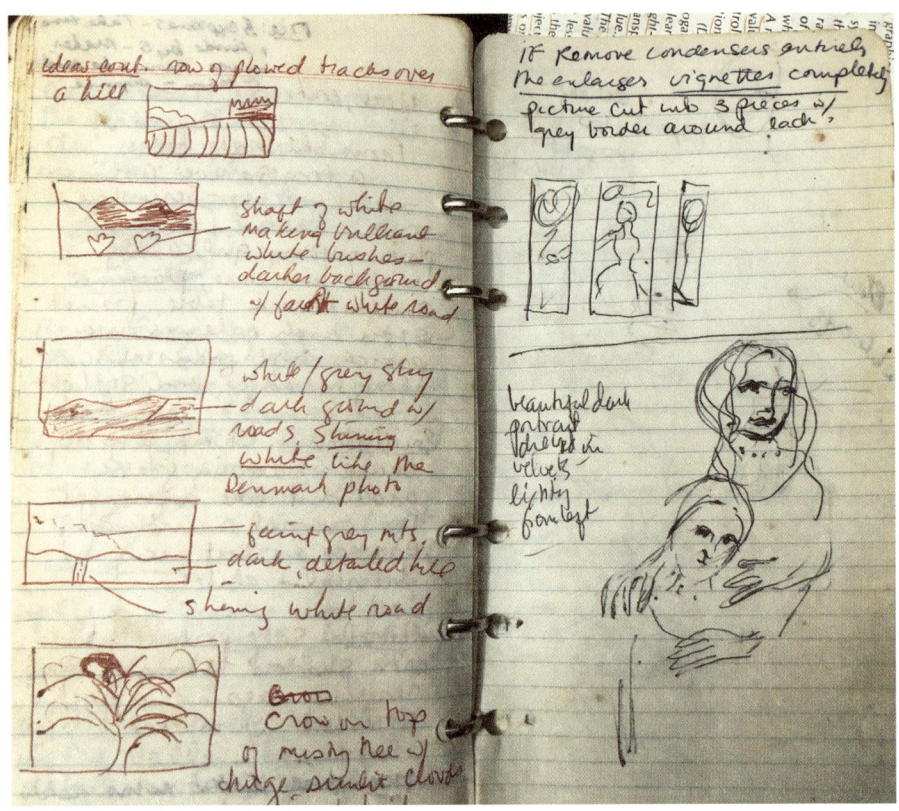

The images on the left side of the page drawn in red ink are ideas for photographs from my 1973 imagination—pictures that, in fact, I have taken several dozen times over the subsequent fifty years.

Here is a picture from a few years ago that is a mirror image of the third one down:

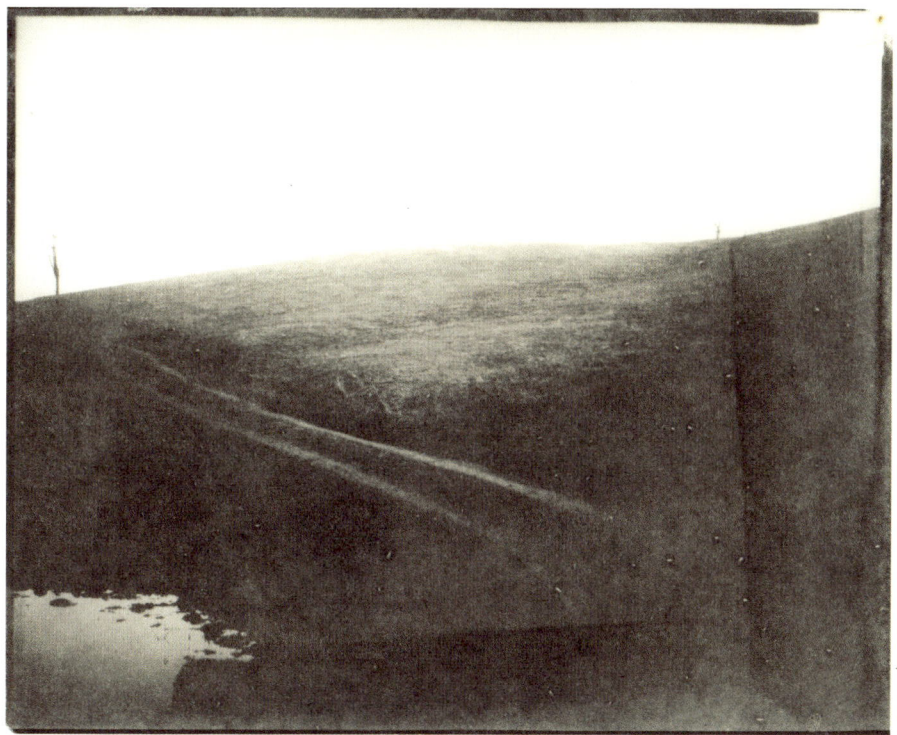

(Incidentally, this is the picture I was taking with the camera setup opposite the title page to this book.)

And this sketch of the idea of presenting one body part in perfect detail, like a Da Vinci drawing?

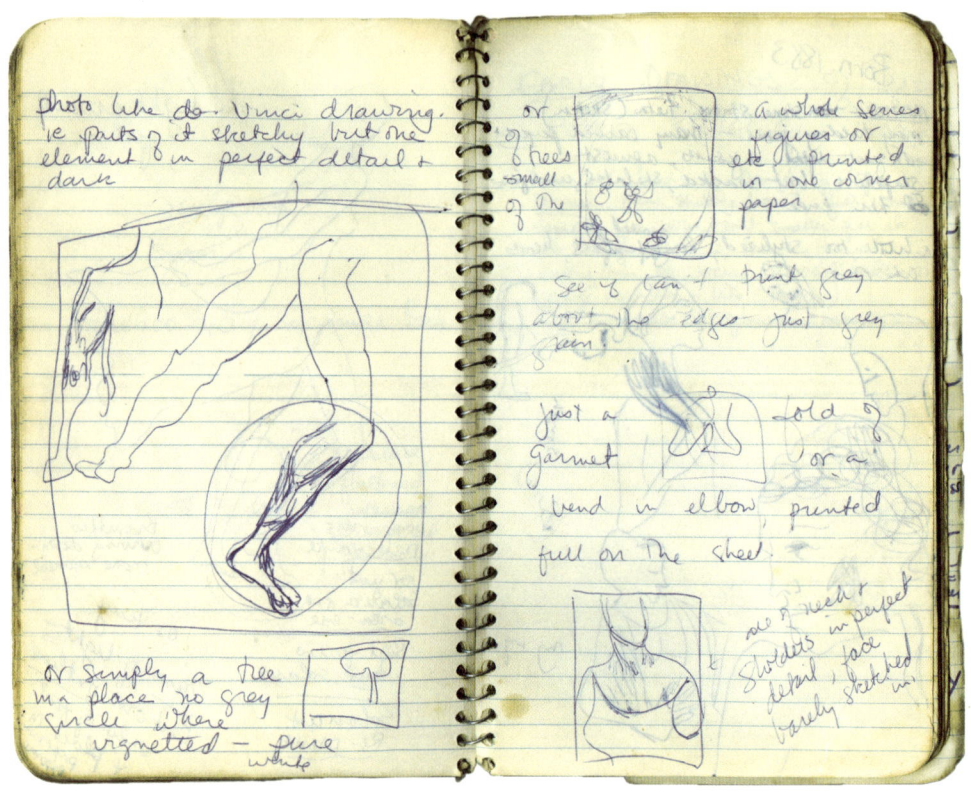

It percolated through the decades, appearing off and on in my work but reaching its ideal manifestation in 2006:

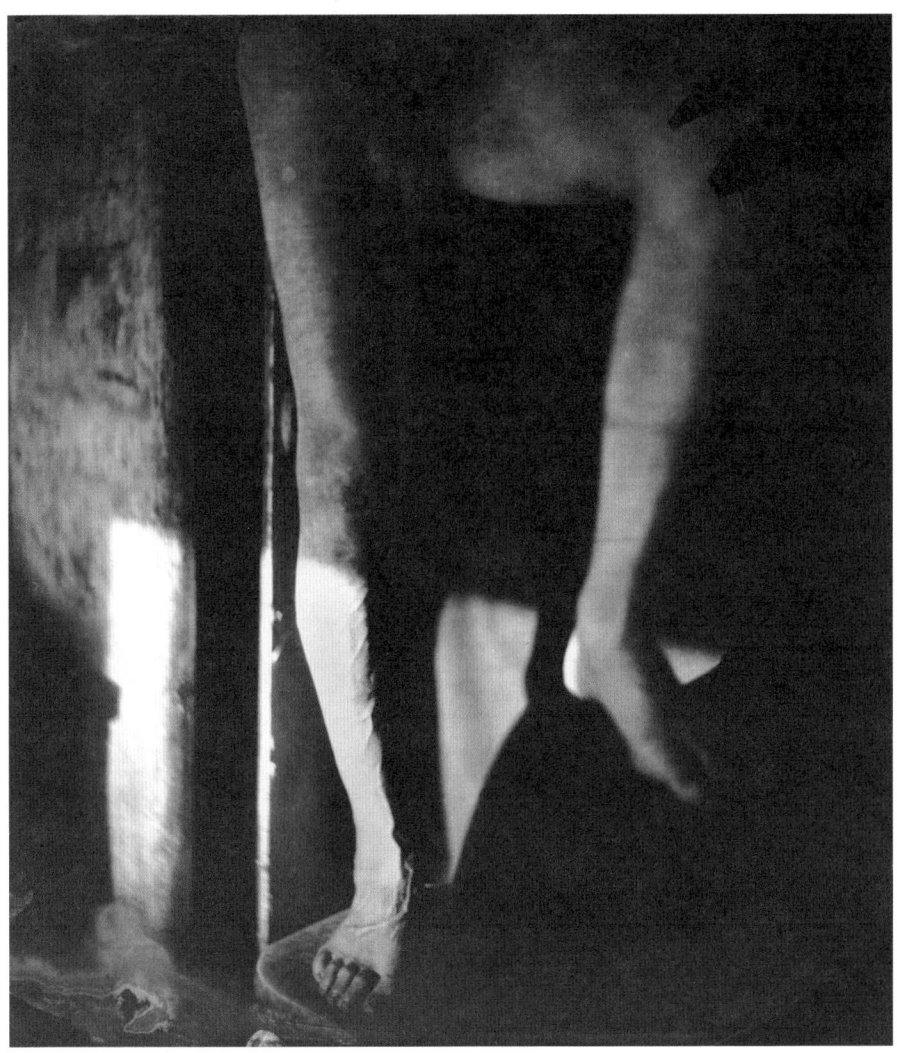

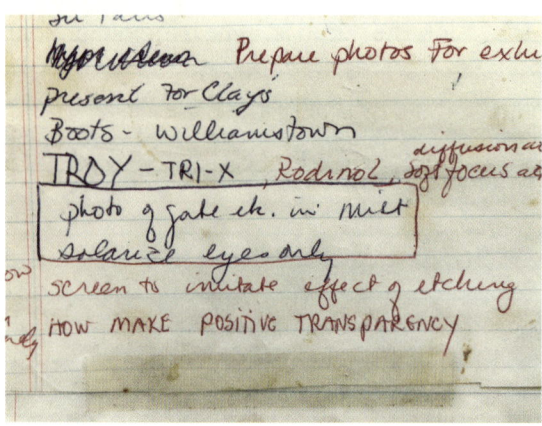

"Solarize eyes only," an idea jotted down in 1972? Right off the bat I can think of two of them, both taken decades later:

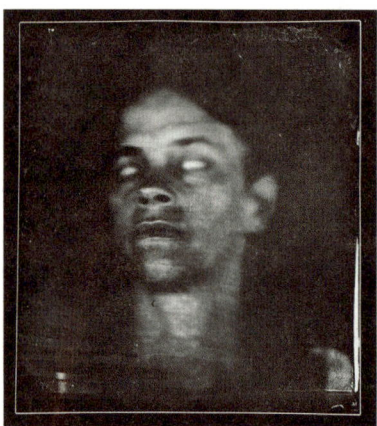
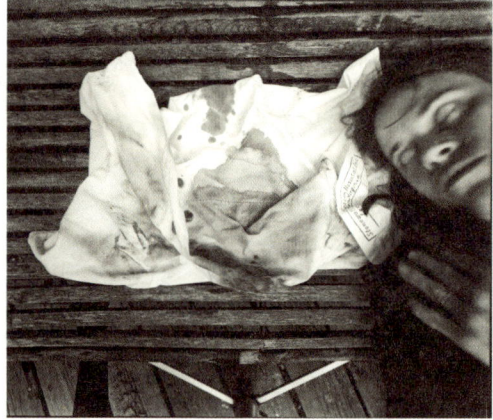

And, above the note about the solarized eyes, "photo of gate etc. in mist?" Good Christ, how many times have I taken *that* picture!? Over and over again, dozens of times, right up to just a few months ago:

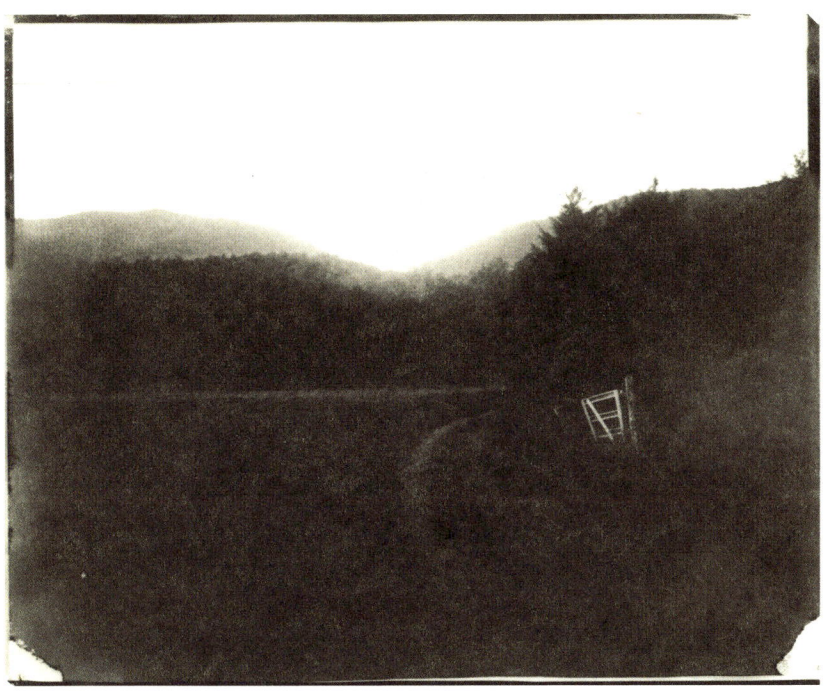

A decade or so later, I made multiple lists of ideas for the Family Pictures:

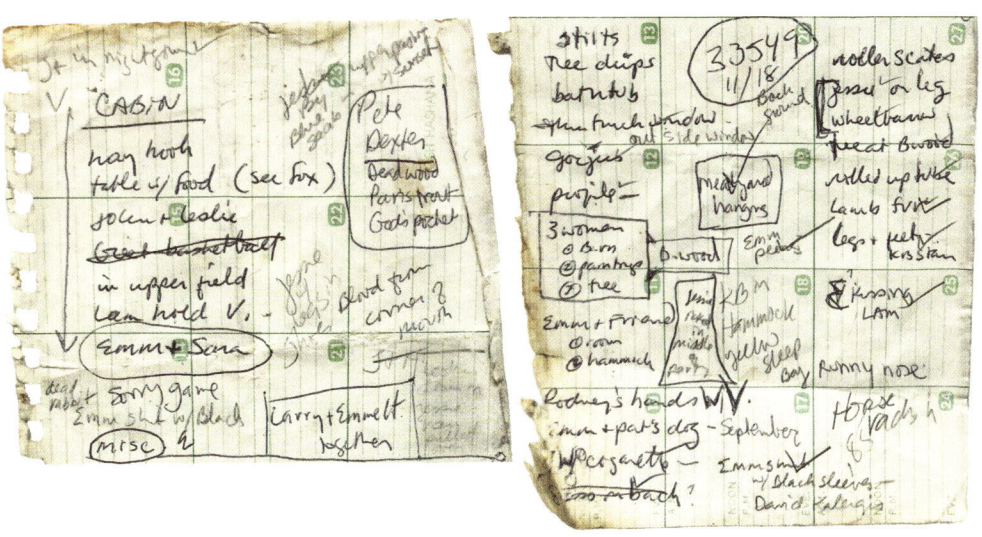

. . . and many of them got realized. Obviously "hay hook" is *Hayhook*, "Sorry Game" (farther down the list) similarly obvious,

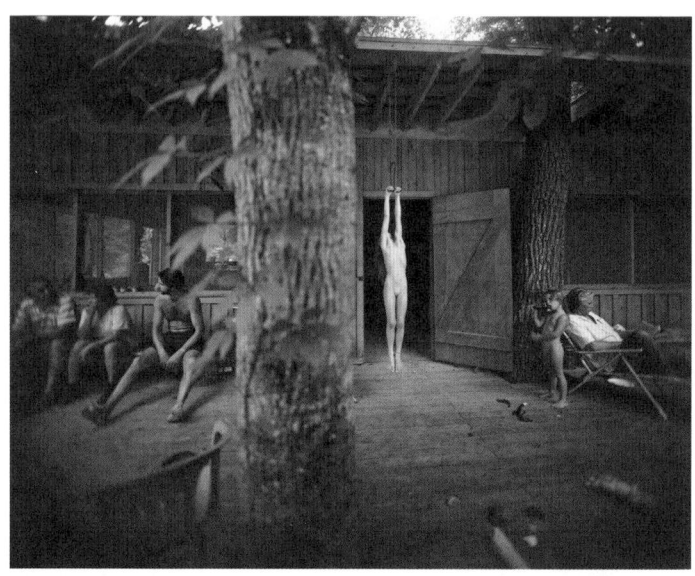

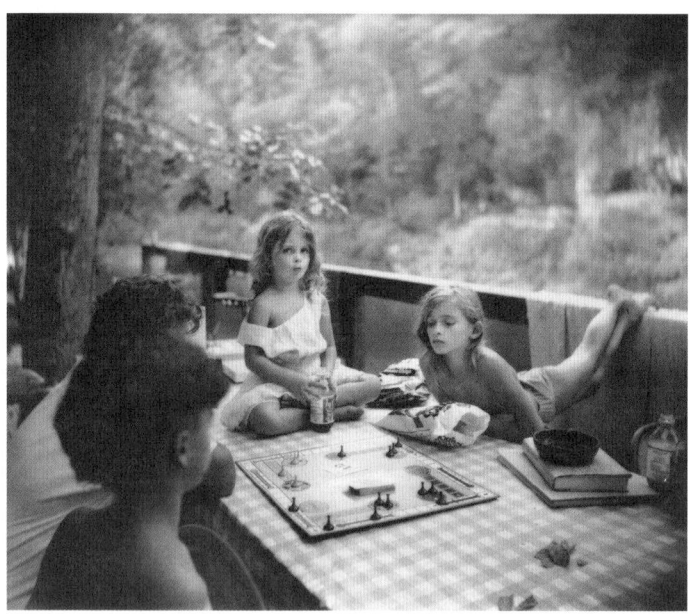

. . . and below it, "Emmett shirt with black sleeves" has an emphatic checkmark on it because in fact it was perfectly realized as *At Charlie's Farm*, one of my favorite pictures,

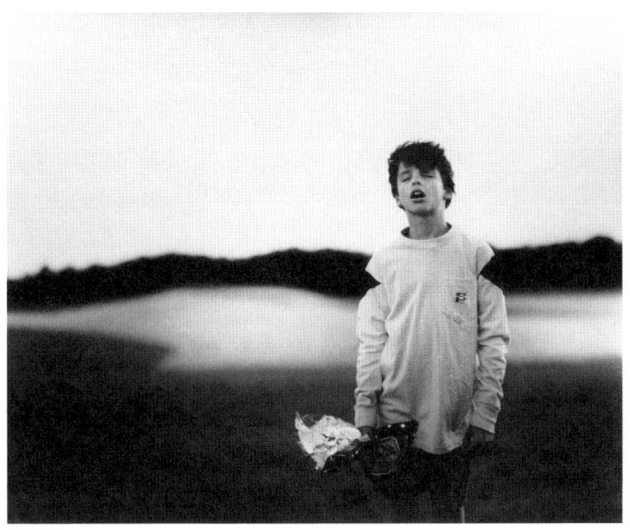

along with "LAM hold V," which became *Last Light* . . .

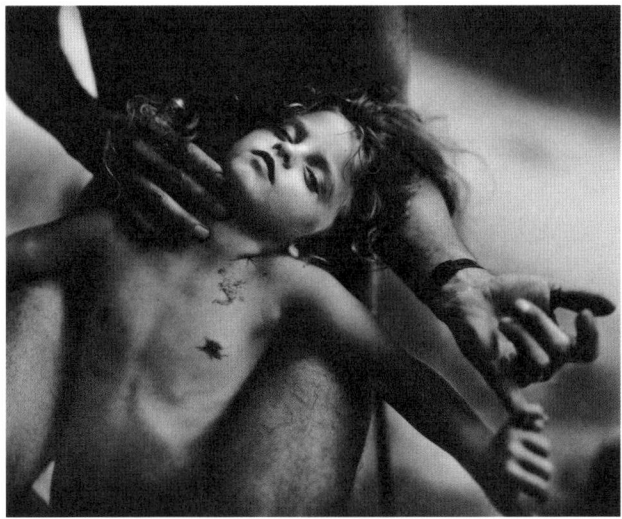

and "Larry and Emmett together" had dozens of tests and permutations.

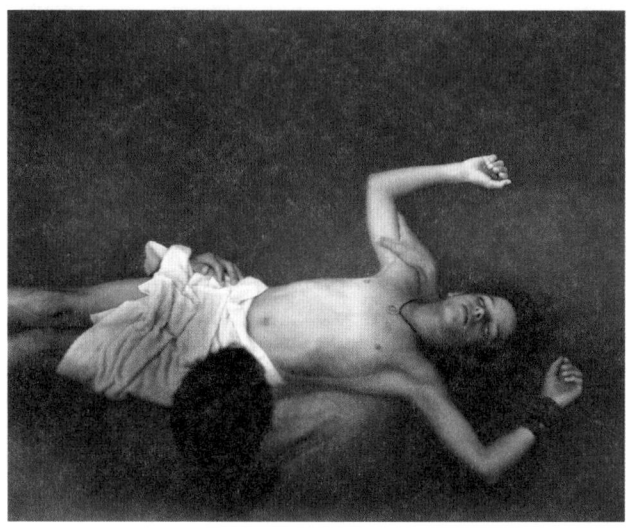

. . . While, of course, "gorjus" became *Gorjus.*

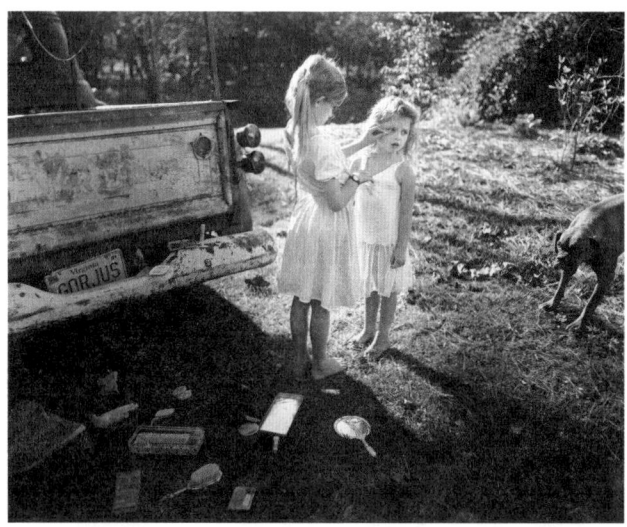

All of these pictures were ideas before they became words on a Day-Timer page, and then, when I could schedule in some time for creativity—because, yes, "be creative" has to go in a timeslot in the Day-Timer when you have three kids—they became imagery. That's just how my mind works; if I write it down on my list of things to do, by god, it gets done.

"Make Art."

Check.

And then, there's a different kind of list. This is an unwritten list of remembered images, magpied up and stored in what I think of as my visual memory. Which, I insist with probably no scientific evidence, is different from, and likely dangerous to, what I think of as my regular memory. What's left of it. My visual memory is composed of images—photographs, paintings—I have stored away as references with the hope that they will appear when I need them, like when I am composing a picture under the dark cloth. But my ineffectual system of retrieval from the mind's musty archives has forced me to employ the simplest form of mnemonic device—images on paper.

A close look at my bulletin board from the late 1980s reveals the unabashed evidence.

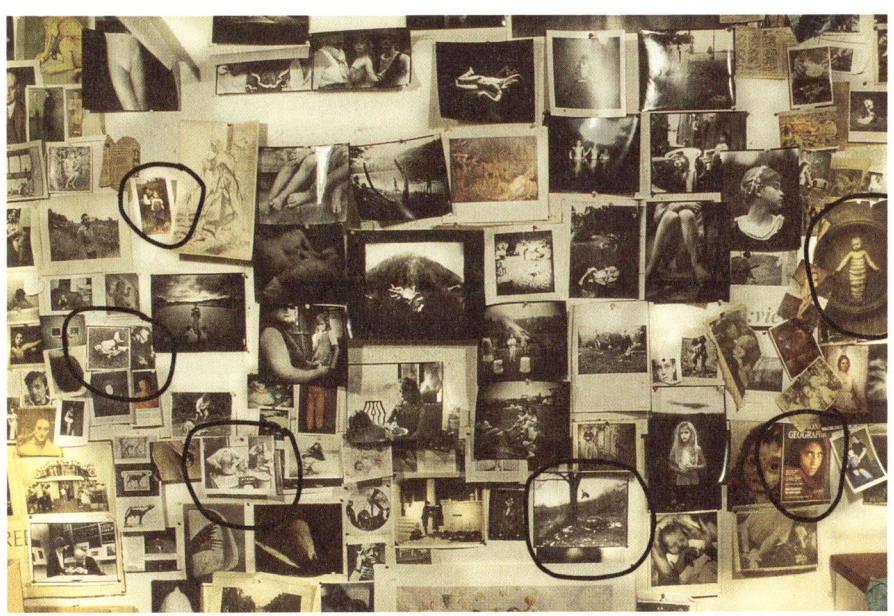

Let's start with the image circled on the far right. I must have felt safe so closely borrowing from Donatello, assuming that he wasn't going to reach through the ages and slap a copyright suit against me, an issue to which I am acutely sensitive. Relevant here is the frequently invoked Wildean bon mot that almost never includes the second half of the actual quote, italicized here: "Imitation is the sincerest form of flattery *that mediocrity can pay to greatness.*" Those of us who practice such flattery would do well to keep that second clause in the back of our minds as we "imitate," inadvertently or deliberately, but probably invariably, the works of others.

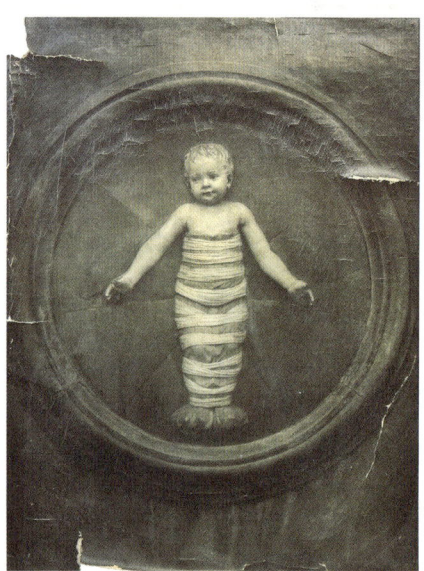 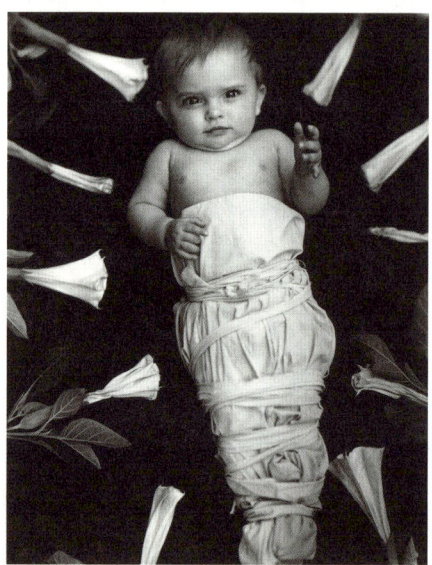

Just outside the crop of this snapshot of the bulletin board is the well-known Lewis Carroll picture of Alice Liddell—the inspiration for *that* Alice—costumed as a beggar girl that was pushpinned there for half a decade at least:

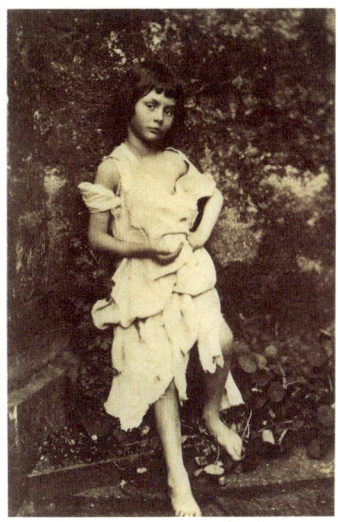

. . . and which was replicated by my own beggar girl, Virginia:

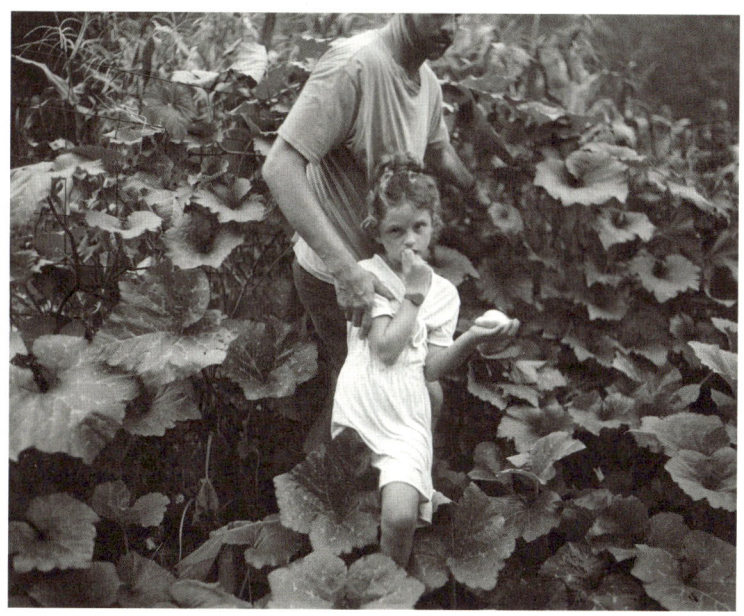

Moving clockwise, the next one is Steve McCurry's stunning *National Geographic* cover of Sharbat Gula, an Afghan refugee girl with heart-piercing green eyes. Who could open their mail to that face and not experience what Robert Frost called the "immortal wound" of great art, from which, he asserts, you never recover? I'm betting half the extant issues of the June 1985 magazine are coverless, as ours became almost the minute I saw it: That torn-off cover went straight onto the bulletin board, and moved with me over the years, from darkroom to darkroom—at least two dozen tack holes in it.

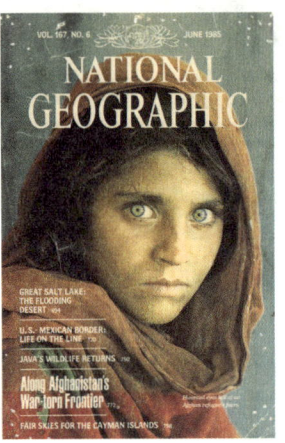

Steve McCurry, I hope, will forgive my attempt, as part of my mid-eighties series At Twelve, to render a portrait with as much piercing eyeball power as his portrait of Sharbat—at least as much as was possible in black and white:

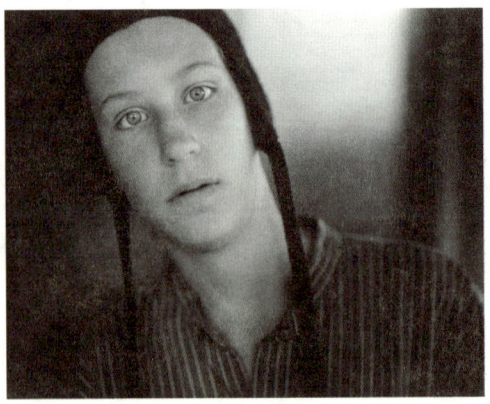

Over to the left of Steve's picture is an image by my pal Andrea Modica:

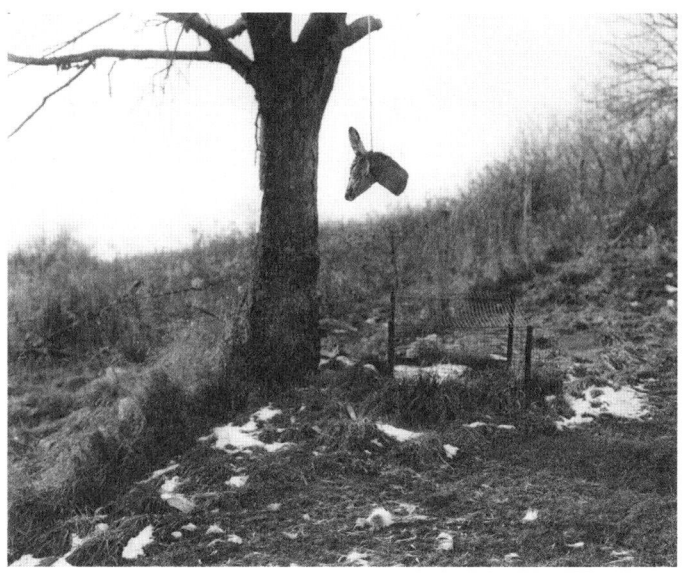

. . . and here's my version:

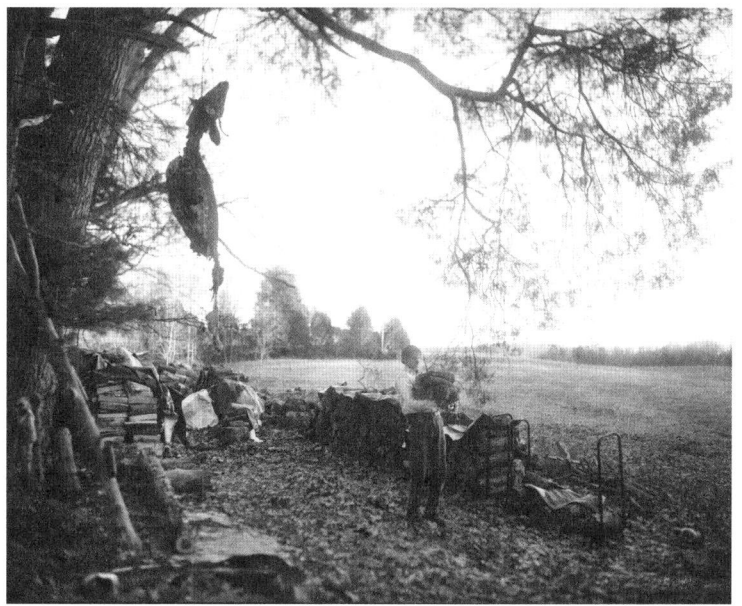

Next up, a personal hygiene photograph by another friend, David Spear.

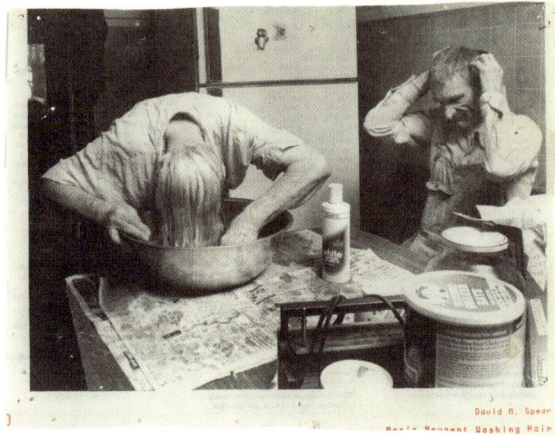

. . . which got me to thinking about how we bathed all those years at the cabin with no running water:

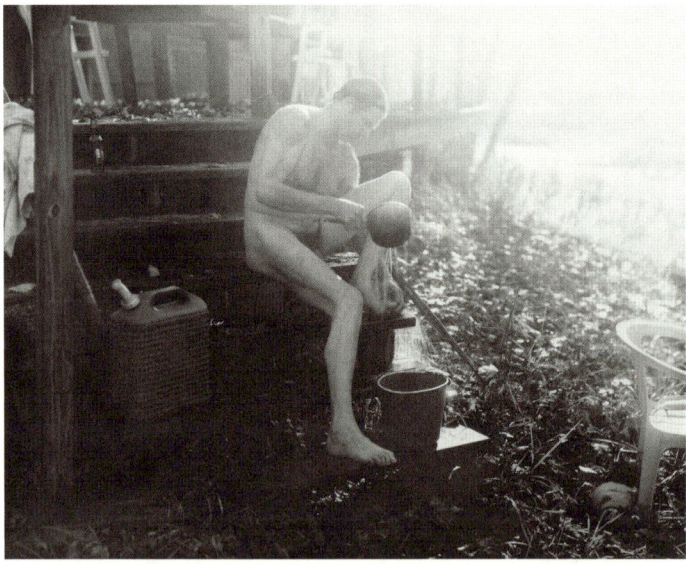

. . . and this, clockwise above the Spear print on the bulletin board, is another example of image borrowing—or shall we say "conceptual evolution" as a palatable euphemism? This is a prime example of mediocrity paying homage to greatness, the greatness of Emmet Gowin. Emmet very sweetly gave me a print of the image of the two children wrestling in the newly mown grass, perhaps motivated by the principle attributed to Dashiell Hammett, which goes something like, "Things belong to those who want them the most." It is a treasured print, among my very favorite images ever, a vivid, synesthesia-provoking evocation of rural childhood.

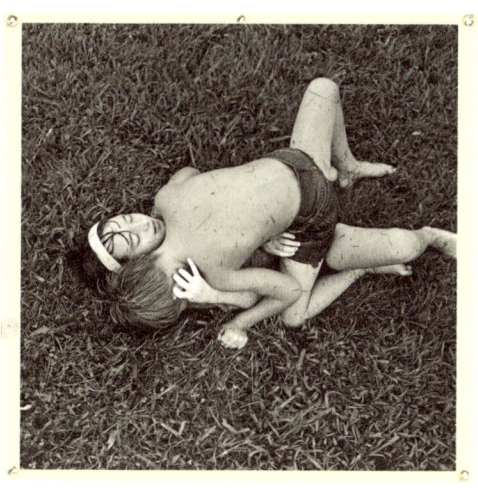

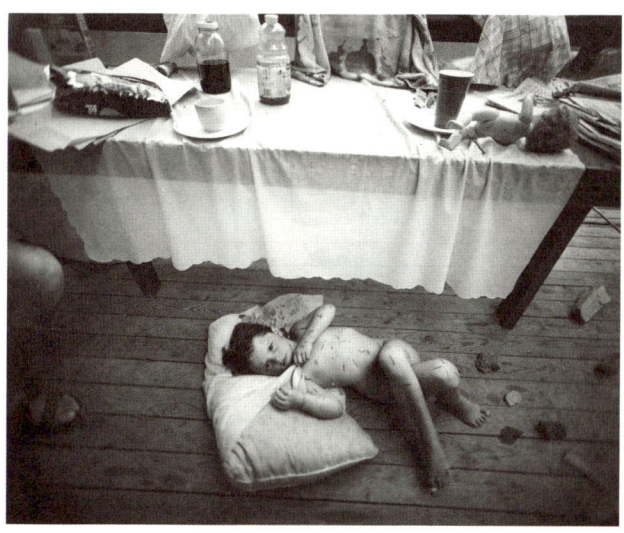

And finally, rounding out the grab bag of inspirations from my 1980s bulletin board, I tried a dozen ways to replicate the feel of the nineteenth-century flower child painting, but one day when the girls were Magic Marker–ing themselves, we made this picture and I realized I could, at last, pull out the pushpins and retire it from the memory board.

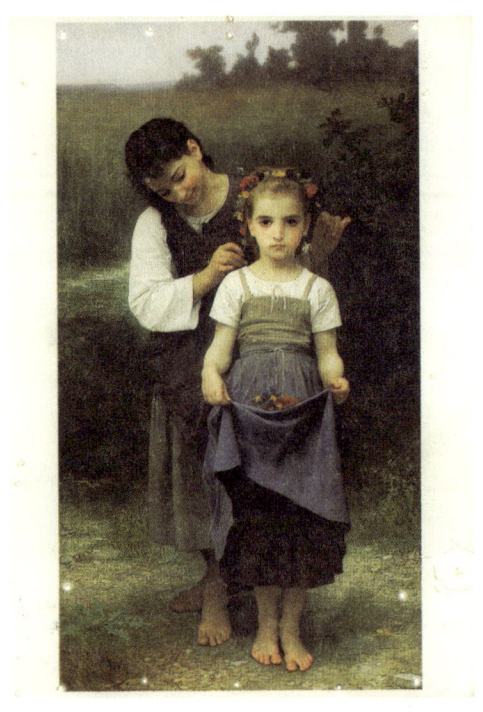

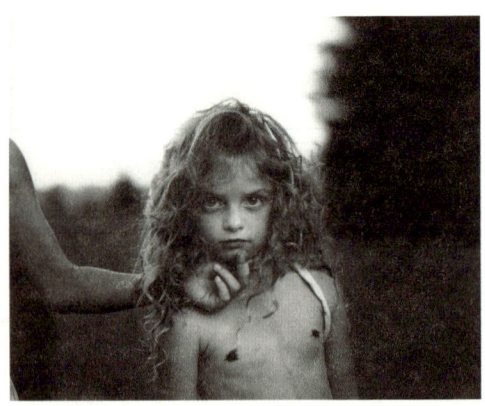

Of course, this interplay cuts both ways—a five-minute Google search produced innumerable versions of my photograph *Candy Cigarette*; photographs, of course, paintings (several marked "sold"), T-shirts, collages, refrigerator magnets, even a tattoo.

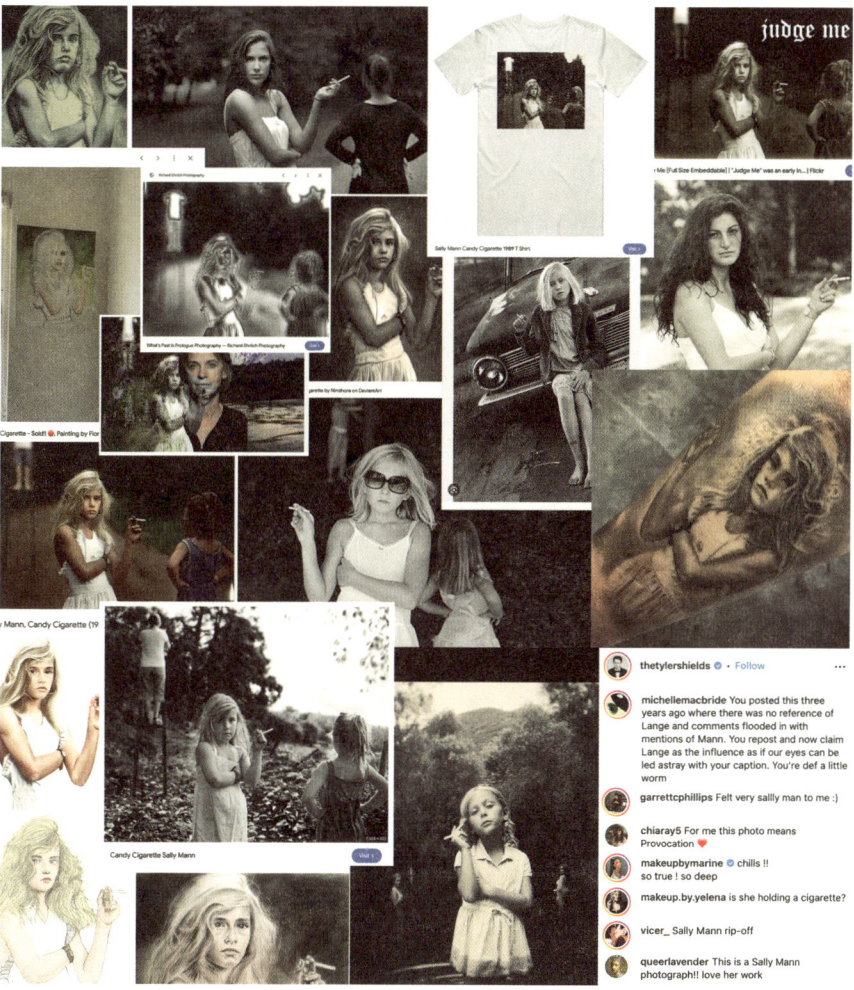

Some people are cashing in from their versions of the image and some are just reinterpreting it—to my mind, there's a difference between an homage and a vampiric rip-off. In the lower-right screenshot, the commenters are fiercely critical of the man selling this picture, whom they feel (correctly, I believe) has ripped me off.

I, too, bristle when my work is appropriated, and in some cases have taken legal action when I feel a line has been crossed. But we have to accept the porosity of art, the democracy of it, the infinite and multifarious ways it enriches not just its audience, but other artists as well. When we are just starting out, we usually begin by emulating the work that moved us, that spoke to our nascent sensibilities. This is derivation, but not necessarily plagiarism or forgery, any more than Beethoven's early work was stolen from his instructor, Franz Joseph Haydn. I am not ashamed to show how I, either by unconscious osmosis or deliberate stimulus (i.e., with a thumb-tacked image on the board), have borrowed certain visual elements from my predecessors for my own work, in this case Mary Ellen Mark on the left, Joseph Szabo on the right.

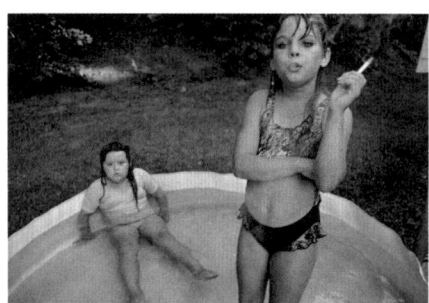 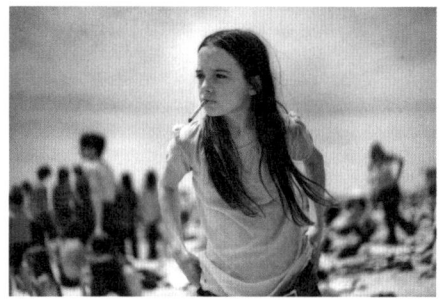

It may be that all art is a creative concatenation, a free-for-all, in which infinite parts ping and constellate, each generation resonating with the next and bringing its own contribution to the evolution of an idea. Because each time we look at pictures—and most of us look at thousands of them these days—we are building and reinforcing a memorial aggregation, a subliminal mimetic impulse, which informs, consciously or not, our artistic output. The goal is to organize (yes, there it is again) the cacophony of images—this cross-pollinating description would make sense to Nabokov, my favorite synesthesiac—in such a way that you can access them as near-involuntary memories to be subsequently braided into your artwork. (See: Proust/madeleine.)

Another literary lion, T. S. Eliot, joins Oscar Wilde in nodding his approval to creative appropriation, but here again, his most famous leading clause ("Immature poets imitate; mature poets steal") is qualified with a lesser-known secondary imperative: ". . . good poets make it into something better, or at least something different. The good poet welds his theft into a whole of feeling which is unique, *utterly different from that from which it was torn* [italics mine]."

In other words, if you're going to imitate, or steal, you'd damn well better do an irreproachable and transcendent version that is entirely your vision or voice. As somebody once said, you can be a great gardener, bringing in piles of produce, but it does no good if you're a lousy chef. But, then, I guess that's the crux of my argument throughout this book: Make the best work you can make. Make it uniquely yours. Make a lot of it, and you will know what yours is supposed to look like.

7

A Thousand Ways

"You will have only one story," she had said.
"You'll write your one story many ways."
—Elizabeth Strout

I hope your nose isn't out of joint because couple of chapters back I wrote that you didn't have all that much to say. I didn't mean you, personally; I meant that none of us do. We each have our unique narrative, and its power derives not from what is sieved in from the surrounding culture, but from what you wrench out of the dense nucleus of chance and circumstance that is your life. The art we make is inevitably autobiographical; the accretion of interpretation and embellishment that has at its core our own personal experience.

As Ted once wrote, no matter who you are, or how musically gifted, you are highly unlikely to be able to convincingly complete the closing movements to Schubert's *Unfinished Symphony*. It is not yours. And, if you are unable to tell a coyote from a Malinois at a hundred feet, you cannot meaningfully incorporate the Native American trickster myth into your work. That story is not your story, its power is not fungible; it cannot transfer to you. In summary, there's a difference between meaning that is embodied and meaning that is referenced; that Greek fisherman's cap you are so fond of wearing doesn't make you a Greek fisherman.

However, never mind that you are not a Greek fisherman, or how pedestrian your life may seem, or how white-bread suburban your upbringing; you still have a story to tell. Over the years, I have watched, say, in an airport, all the lucky people walking past, most appearing to be happy, unblemished, carefree. By all appearances their lives are not afflicted with the self-doubt that scours at me or scarred by the kinds of events that have sent gashes of devastation through my life. But at this point, I have come to know several thousand strangers, not unlike those surging by in the airport corridors. And I have repeatedly been surprised to find that the bubbly sorority sister has an adored father dying of ALS at home, or that the successful CEO battles debilitating depression. Once, long ago, in a wealthy enclave of Southern California, I was teaching a workshop in which the most engaging and striking participant was a woman in her late fifties. She had the perfect life, as far as we could tell; a large house, manicured lawn, expensive car, well-maintained body. We all tried to resist feeling jealous, but with her in the group, it was hard. Until she raised her shirt and revealed the crudely stitched, two-inch-wide scar that rose from her butt all the way up her back and into her scalp and, excepting her perfect face, all the way down the front. Dr. Mengele had wondered: Can a baby survive flaying?

So many of our fellow humans, unbeknownst to us, are quietly bearing a load of pain that would make Atlas groan with the weight of it. Despite outward appearances, most of us have an interior edifice of complex emotions, whose dimensions are unexposed, unexpected, and profound. And some of us are lucky enough to have ways to express that dark geometry, to tell our own unique stories.

Of the images on those lists I showed you, like "gate etc. in mist," a significant number are simply hardwired in; they are my aesthetic default and it's not like I need to write them down. It might make more sense to write down "try not to take *Gate in Mist* for the zillionth time."

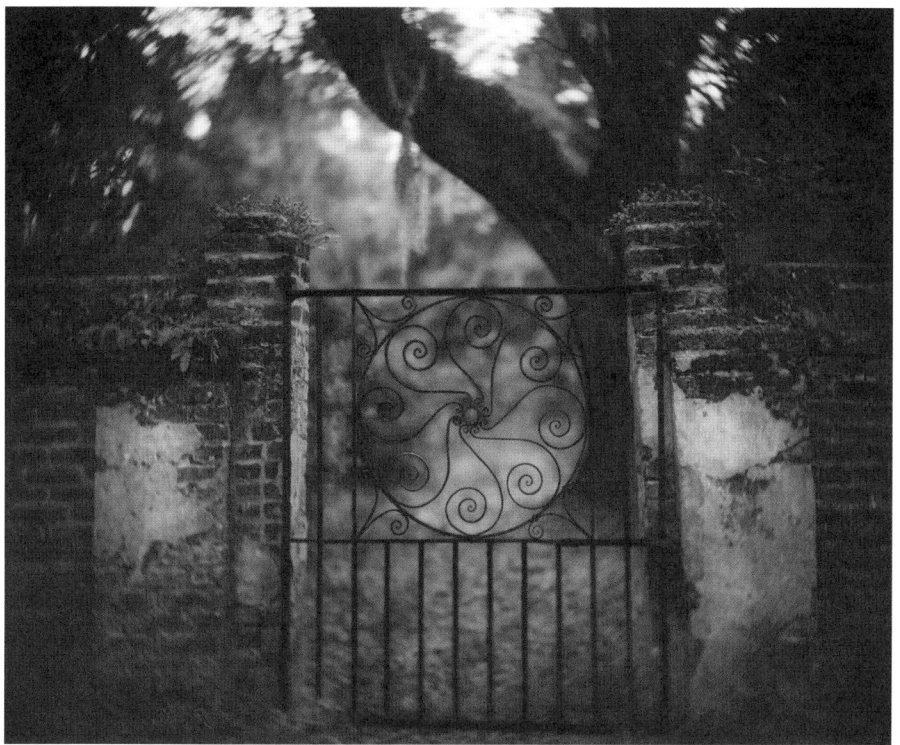

I know exactly when the wiring happened, and it goes back to that Wynn Bullock image of the pale girl on the forest floor and my unkempt wild-child self, studying it on the cool concrete floor of my bedroom. All of my creative work is based on a few sensations, experiences, visions, and ideas that were imprinted as durably as those of a gosling peeking out of her shell. In all of us, the unique events and emotions in our past will have carved a trace in our soul. And no matter how distant or tenuous that trace, it will ultimately reemerge, enlarged to easy legibility and unignorable; the tyranny of *memoria*.

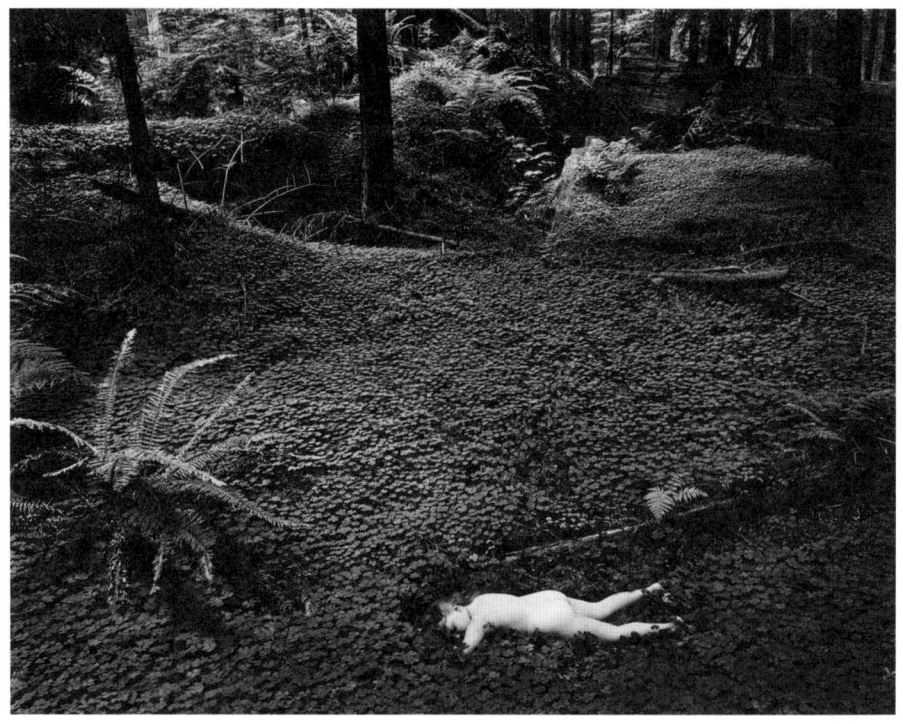

Wynn Bullock, *Child in Forest*, 1951

Our fixations are formed from the familiar, and we form them early. No memorial pantry could be more comprehensively provisioned than the shelves of our past through which we endlessly rummage. In the 1991 film *The Silence of the Lambs*, Hannibal Lecter enlightens Clarice Starling as to the origin of obsession: "And how do we begin to covet, Clarice?" he asks. "Do we seek out things to covet? . . . No. We begin by coveting what we see every day."

Our unique passions, our desires—for most of us, these do not tend toward the consumption of human flesh—derive from our everyday life, which is, as Janet Malcolm once remarked, "where the action is." Malcolm wrote that compared to her life at home, travel was a "pallid affair," and her ordinary days in her familiar surroundings were infinitely richer. Peel back the familiar, peek under its careworn covering, and you will find unsuspected creative possibility. You will find your story.

Sarah Payne, a creative-writing instructor in Elizabeth Strout's novel *My Name Is Lucy Barton*, makes it clear to her student that her story, her one story, is all she has, and she will tell that one story a thousand ways. God knows, that's proven to be true in my career, but you find evidence of repeated themes and fascinations in all forms of art. Beethoven established a signature use of fermata (the length of the holds) for emotional manipulation and punctuation, using it throughout his work, while Bartók is immediately recognizable for the folk melodies and spirituals woven within everything he wrote. Toni Morrison explored and developed consistent themes throughout her half-century career and, in doing so, expanded the range of American literature; a living Black woman pushing aside the established canon of White male American writers like Melville, Faulkner, Whitman, and Emerson, by telling her one irrepressible story, the story of her people. The lyrical work of Brice Marden is instantly recognizable, despite his many explorations and detours through minimalism, expressionism, and gesture, all of which ultimately refer us back to a singular sensibility. Rembrandt's palette hardly varied, only deepened, over his career, as he laid first dibs on the inventory of ocher, raw sienna, and umber pigments arriving in the Netherlands from Italy.

Regardless of our medium, we all tell our own story, the story we care about and the only story we can tell with conviction and passion. We tell it over and over again, and the proof of a successful creative career is how inventive and complex our variations on that story can be.

Sorry to interrupt, but while we are here, I want to reiterate this point: Our obsessions, our pain or desires, might well be manifold, our one story so incandescent it could light up a cave, but for god's sake make sure you have the skills to realize its expression artistically. Intent is not enough. What matters is the quality of the work, the deftness and refinement of the execution, the applicability of the chosen form. Without those, as Frank O'Hara wrote in a 1959 essay, our work is "just ideas"—and no idea, no impassioned defense in a classroom critique, no windy explanation, no prolix wall text, is going to make lousy art look any better.

And just this one last thing: In case it isn't obvious, git 'er done. Know when you are at the end, when you have given it your very heart, when every sentence you have written will provoke future students to uncap their highlighters, or to rotate their iPhones to selfie mode before your work on the wall. Then call it a day. As curators and editors all know (and mine is drumming his fingers right now), creative souls never feel the work is done to perfection—Mrs. Tolstoy copied *War and Peace* by hand seven miserable times for her ungrateful, perfectionist husband. But it is work that actually *got finished* that has found its way onto the walls or between the covers of a book. And, if that is to be your work, it will be your very best, *right*? Right.

It could be entirely possible that you don't even know what your story *is* until one day, maybe late in your career, you will realize how all the work you have made is tied together. Until that point, like a dowser's flexible switch bending toward the underground water, you will find yourself drawn to your own subconscious aquifers of desire and curiosity.

As so often happened, Ted divined this concept long before my willow branch had even begun to quiver—and expressed it in this letter from November 1976:

> Most photographers start with some ~~topi~~ core topic — Ozarks, night-landscapes-lit-by-car-headlights, suburbia, etc. — and slowly build up a body of work around that predetermined topic. Others start with some boundary — like what are the possibilities inherent in 3M processing — and proceed to fill in the space within that boundary.
>
> But there are some few people who photograph purely and simply <u>the things that move them,</u> and who think to catagorize and find a way to present them only after the fact of creation. And what it comes down to is that, rather than filling in the blank spaces inside a known preimeter, or building up around an known core idea until we ~~tier~~ tire of the process, <u>we</u> are working in an area where <u>neither</u> core nor perimeter are known until after the fact.

> But surely that ~~usxqq~~ is as it should be — in any <u>true</u> exploration, there is no way to know what you've discovered until you've been there. And so as I move forward in seemingly meandering fashion, making piles of unrelated images, I also occasionally make an image that provides a ~~likk~~ <u>link</u> between ~~kxxx~~ two or more other unrelated images — and what I ~~am~~ finally becoming aware of (I think) is that through these images I am involved in uncovering, or identifying, or simply being the transmittor of, a widely spread locus of visual points that are the boundary of my Spirit.
>
> *'Tis Late* — Love Ted

When Ted talks about the things that move us, the variety of those things is as infinite as the variety of human beings. Within each of us is a precisely tuned and personalized sphere of receptivity—think of it as a magnetic field—whose unique settings have been determined by our own life experiences. All the images, words, and concepts we encounter in our lives have to pass through this magnetic field, and some fluoresce for us, while for others they pass through unnoticed. Those that remain— our singular spiritual utilities—we scrutinize with the intensity of Amelia Earhart fanatics parsing out the garbled words of her final transmission, in thrall to the mysteries yet seldom the wiser. And they remain elusive until, unbidden and alien, they emerge in the art we make, revealing the story that we did not realize we had been telling.

The part of this process that depends on our memories is, of course, the least reliable. My brothers and I disagree about some things from our past that I have written, and I reply that everything I wrote happened— but that some of it may have happened in my head. I try to be as honest and true to the facts as possible, but like most everybody, my memories are spotty, a whimsical tangle of synaptic threads, some elements showing up in vivid detail, others lost in the weave.

In 1885, Hermann Ebbinghaus graphed out his "forgetting curve," a ski-jump-shaped line illustrating the dramatic speed at which our memories are lost, and none of it surprises me. He takes into account factors such as difficulty of learned material, and of stress and sleep, but the fact remains that within an hour, without deliberate mnemonic intervention, we will have lost nearly 70 percent of our just-acquired information or experiences. And there's no point in trying to commit something to memory by rote recall, because, as we know, our brain overwrites memories each time we revisit them. In fact, neuroscientists posit that through a process they call "imagination inflation," our minds, with the same galvanic spark as a real memory, can create durable and detailed memories out of complete falsehoods by simply revisiting them enough times. If you say the election was stolen and you saw the voting boxes in the dumpster and you repeat that enough times, soon you will lay down your life to defend your memory of this fabrication.

As we tell our stories, with each retrieval we create our multifarious and unique individual self. Just like the soldier after the Battle of Borodino (back to Tolstoy here) who described the heroics of other soldiers as if they were his own, we realize that each time we revisit memories, real or imagined, the distinction between the two becomes less clear; the truth, or "something close to it," becomes as mutable as our memories. Those memories, ambiguity-prone, recalcitrant, teasingly labile, are the unreliable scaffolding upon which we build our complex and unique story. Our one story. A thousand ways.

There's not a lot we can do to short-circuit this process—we discover who we are by being who we are and making what we make. Our past is made up of our infinite present, a palimpsest onto which each layer softly gathers; shifting, translucent, and mutable.

8

Why You Say Yes

Every limit is a beginning as well as an ending.
—George Eliot, *Middlemarch*

It's one thing to hew to the highest principles—for example to refuse to work for a company whose policies you abhor—but it's another to line up at the hardware store to buy the implement with which to spite your face. Or wait, maybe that's not the right aphorism. Maybe it's the baby and bathwater one. Whatever it is, I'm looking for the one that summarizes how misguided it is to say no when saying yes could make your artistic or financial life a lot better and enlarge your horizons in unanticipated ways. And more misguided still when the reason, deep down, is that you're too insecure to say yes. It usually has nothing to do with your convictions; it has to do with your fear.

For years, indeed right up to this minute, I have declined to do work for hire. On the face of it, it's because I want to appear elevated above the tawdry fray of commercialism and in the rarefied, ambrosial realms of Fine Art. But that's not the truth; the truth is that I am afraid I will fail and disappoint whoever is hiring me. I can't charge a fee small enough to reflect my profound doubt, my certainty that I will bomb—and indeed on the occasions when I have said yes, I have usually done the work for free.

A few decades ago, I got a call from a photo-world acquaintance, telling me he had an offer for me with some big money attached. Panic-stricken, I said no thanks and hung up. He and I had a difficult relationship anyway.

Of course, since he was likely getting a cut of the money, he called back.

"Look," he said, annoyed. "This is not the time to be dicking around and angling for a higher offer. I can't tell you who this is, but we are talking about a man you don't say no to, a man of great power, discernment, and wealth. He wants you to come take a portrait of him. He's willing to pay a lot of money. What's wrong with you?"

Breaking into a sweat, I said no, and didn't answer the phone for the rest of the day.

A few weeks later he called back and said that this unknown man of discernment and wealth had offered to double the—as yet unspoken—amount of money and for me to stop being childish and act like a competent, normal person. Didn't I want to know what kind of baseline money we were talking about?

No, I didn't.

Apparently, that didn't matter because he wanted to tell me. It was a lot of money. I hung up.

The next call came from a solicitor in London. He said he had been asked by the emir of the State of Qatar to convey the message that it was he who wanted his portrait made and that the previously tendered offer still stood, and he would be greatly honored if I would come to Qatar to take the picture. You know how it is with those plummy British accents—they intimidate the hell out of you. I screwed up my courage and said, again, no. I said, actually, no thanks, because I had trouble making pictures of people I didn't know, in places I'd never seen. We exchanged some pleasantries, I kept saying thanks, and that was that.

Until a few weeks later when the solicitor was back on the horn with this suggestion: I come to Qatar as the guest of the emir and just hang out a little. Take a look at the country. No obligations and, thank god, no money.

I said Yes.

When you come to a country as the guest of its monarch, especially a country newly catapulted out from the pearl-diving depths of poverty into vast oil wealth, you are handled as if you are royalty yourself. I asked if my sixteen-year-old daughter Virginia, who had spring break, could come with me, and of course she could—British Air first class to London, where we spent two luxurious nights to acclimatize and where we saw the unmistakable Julian Schnabel in his slippers and pajamas in the Heathrow lounge, and then on to Qatar. On that second flight, being so obviously pop-eyed peckerwoods and sitting right up front, we made friends with a chatty, unintimidating flight attendant. She came and sat on my armrest in the down time and jerked her head back toward our all-male, dishdasha-wearing, Muslim cabinmates and mimed the glug-glug drinking motion. I, too, had been surprised at the frequency of the cocktails passing by our seats, and the uninhibited enjoyment of them behind us.

Before we got to Qatar, we landed in Bahrain, just a few minutes of actual flying time from Doha, the capital city of Qatar. As we taxied toward the terminal, the plane lumbered off to the side and cut the engines. I didn't even know giant planes like that had stairs that could be lowered, but this one did and a few of the white-robed men rose to be let out the cabin door and down the stairs to a phalanx of waiting white Mercedes. No crowded corridors, no customs, no passport check. Whisked away. Then the engines restarted and we taxied back toward the terminal, where the arrivals jet bridge was suspended from the glass walls, its maw open for the remaining Bahrain passengers.

The flight attendant did her "thank you for flying with us" thing as the regular passengers prepared to disembark and then came and perched next to us while the luggage was unloaded. In a low voice, complete with a vocal eye roll, she told us how the airline wasn't supposed to do this, but for some high-dollar, fat-cat types, they stopped on the tarmac to let them disembark so they wouldn't have to endure the cattle-car treatment heading toward customs. It was a giant pain in the ass for her, and a paperwork nightmare, and always made them arrive late at the next destination. Sympathetically, we rolled our eyes, too. Those entitled rich people.

While she was off duty and feeling sisterly, I asked her if she could prepare a doggie bag of little airline gin bottles for me, since we were going to a dry country. She shrugged and said she could, but that they'd for sure get taken away from me at customs. I said I'd chance it, and she came back with a bag so big that it looked like Huck could have roped it to a stick for the trip downriver. I stuffed it in my carry-on under a stack of *New Yorkers* and she said good luck with that and went back to her station to strap in for takeoff.

Just after we landed in Doha and had begun to taxi in, the phone rang in the bulkhead and our flight attendant friend turned around to pick it up. She stood there with her back to us for a minute, then reached for a piece of paper that appeared to be the passenger manifest. She ran her finger down it to a stop, and then very slowly turned around and looked at us as the plane pulled alongside a phalanx of white Mercedes. As Virginia and I disembarked down the lowered stairs, she said, with more than a trace of betrayal, "No wonder you weren't worried about that bag of booze."

That's not quite correct, it wasn't really a phalanx this time, it was a trio—as I recall, two white Mercedes and a Land Rover. We got in the Land Rover with its driver, Khalid, and the Mercedes fell in behind us. I'm not sure what happened to the other sedan, but both cars pulled in and parked outside the giant ziggurat of a hotel in which we soon occupied the top floor. For most of the first week, one of the vehicles remained outside the hotel twenty-four hours a day, its driver, usually Fazal of the Mercedes, waiting in the hotel lobby in case we might want to run out for some late-night photography. When it became clear that wasn't happening, he stayed home until dawn.

I had brought my 8 × 10 view camera, regular black-and-white film, and twenty-five sheets of color negative film. And not a clue as to what I wanted to do with it. The thing about having no pressure on you to produce work for money is that now there's a different pressure; you're oppressed by the freedom to do whatever you want. Which of course is to create great art (my computer, in trying to correct my misspelling of "great," inexplicably changed this to "grey dart," which is probably how I should refer henceforth to the little somethings I make). My particular problem was, and is, that I only want to make good work. When I make bad work (I almost wrote "If"!), the little homunculus of malevolent self-doubt within me raises its flipper arms in a triumphant gesture of Ah-ha! See, I was right!

And I always believe it—no babble of competing voices can drown this one out. I don't always see bad work as holding the seeds of, or as being the road map to—whatever metaphor you want—*good* work. I see it as bad work. The shriveled lifeless seed, the pale blue dead end on a tattered old map. If perfection is the enemy of the good, it is also a surefire guarantee of artistic paralysis. Those first few nights I stared out at the lights of Doha Bay, dreading the daylight, sensing the expectations of Fazal, sitting patiently, 2:00 a.m., in the hotel lobby.

Freedom is the scariest thing of all—when I encounter a blank calendar page, I will needlessly transplant the philodendron to avoid picking up the camera and making new work. But the discomfort of not making work eventually becomes so great that making pictures is less painful than not making them, even considering the looming uncertainty each time I pick up the camera. That looming—and, I believe, essential—uncertainty is the unshakable companion for all of us who want to make art. *Grey dart.*

Like Penelope, each day we make our work, weaving into it our fears and hopes, only to unravel it the next morning and start again, sleying the reed on the beater bar (don't you love weaving terminology?). The unraveling and the uncertainty are part of the process, and, paradoxically, how well we can tolerate this uncertainty, how inexhaustibly we return to the loom (the looming loom?), will determine our success. Having such a low tolerance myself, I had made a big deal about not doing work for hire in Qatar, but the problem with that stance—rarefied, safe, and unaffordable—was that I now had to act like I had something of my own to say, something to make: dart, grey or otherwise. At the very least I had to fake it for Fazal.

At dawn I went out for a run, wearing leggings, a long-sleeved shirt, and a hat despite the heat. All the women on the Corniche were enveloped head to toe in black abayas, with stiff, beak-like attachments called battoulahs, especially prevalent in Qatar, covering their faces below the eyes. Several hissed at me as I passed. I concluded that it might be difficult to make portraits in Qatar, which was all right, as it seemed both Fazal and Khalid were eager to show me the desert.

Doha was still relatively undeveloped back then, and as we set out later that morning to take pictures of who knows what, it took mere minutes to achieve the open desert spaces, punctuated by large walled compounds, raw, newly built, out in the middle of nowhere. I had never spent time in a desert, but it was immediately clear to me that this light was like nothing I had ever seen before and that anything photographically familiar wasn't likely to show up before the Second Coming. If there was a landscape more alien to my experience, it would have to be lunar.

I think that Fazal sensed I was demoralized and did his best to show us places he thought we would want to see. He was one of the emir's personal chauffeurs and had an unsmiling, lopsided rigidity to his face, like his jaw had been wired shut. He practically clicked his heels as he opened the back doors for Virginia and me, then spun around smartly and with a practiced gesture swept his fine white robe out of the way of his softly closing door. For the first several days he did not say a word, although once I detected a rightward shift of his head when Virginia and I chatted in the back seat.

That was all the opening I needed: I asked him if he spoke English.

The story of Fazal, and of the emir, is why you say Yes. The capital-letter kind. You say Yes even when you know, to your very bones, that you can't do what is expected of you and that you are in way over your head. You say Yes because you will grow in ways you could never expect. And you might just luck out and get a photograph despite everything.

Fazal did, in fact, speak English, though far from perfectly and not nearly as well as Khalid, but well enough. Somehow a hierarchy had been determined; if we were going deep into the desert, we rode with Khalid in the Land Rover, often unnecessarily trailed by Fazal in the Mercedes. Fazal was proud of this car, buffing off the desert dust when we stopped, and proud of his position in the royal court, of the emir, and of his rapidly developing country.

He delightedly showed us the children, Pakistani like so many of the workers in Qatar, strapped to the camels at the racetrack. When I noted their precarity, he reported that since one of them, badly secured with ropes, had swung upside down under the camel and been thrashed to death by the churning legs, they had updated the security straps with Velcro. No problems since! He was equally proud to show me the emir's stable full of purebred Egyptian and Polish Arabian mares, none of whom had ever seen so much as a blade of grass and who, we were assured, were sent out to a happy back pasture in this desert country when they grew old or failed to become pregnant.

I've always been a rules bender and mores tweaker—in my long life I've tweaked some mores that you could hardly find a pinch-hold on. In Qatar, of course, I had more than a little to grab ahold of, but I tried hard to restrain the impulse and to respect the local traditions and beliefs. I dressed in long pants and long-sleeved shirts and covered my head when in public. Still, I chafed at Fazal's insistence that Virginia and I ride in the back seat, and it didn't take long for me to move up front. I plopped myself into the incubating white leather and placed my bare feet on the dashboard for the long, unvarying trips through the desert, refraining from twiddling the radio dials with my toes, as I did in my high school dating days.

While we drove, Virginia and I would get going with stories and the giggles, and once, glancing over at Fazal, I realized that something very much resembling a smile was cracking through the lower part of his face. At least it seemed he intended it to be a smile, but one assembled not quite well enough to uncurtain the teeth. And this, as it turned out, was because my first impression had been correct: his jaw *was* wired shut, more or less. Over the course of many days, struggling with the language, we learned that Fazal had been in a terrible car accident, had not been expected to live, and was held together by staples, wire, and steel plates. We gathered that he was often in pain, and because he seemed shy, we suspected he had a limited social life. We asked constant questions and occasionally he would become animated, his head turning in Tin Man fashion to make eye contact. The day he showed up with gifts for Virginia and me—mine, a piece of petrified wood on which he had shakily inscribed my name—was the day I decided to say Yes more often.

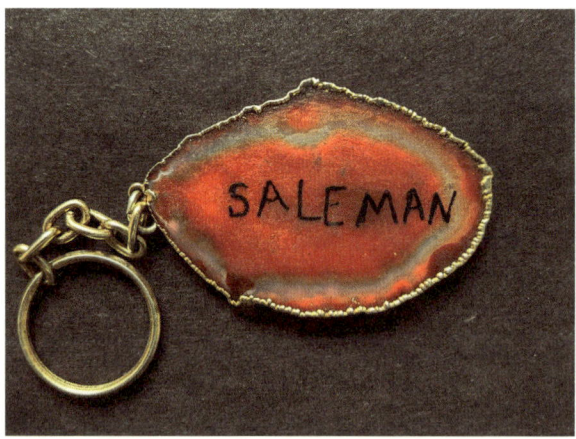

Fazal was deeply conservative, and I wondered what he thought of the party that Khalid had arranged for Virginia and me to attend. Single-gender parties are popular in the Muslim world, and this was a fancy one, held at a newly built gold, glass, and crystal hotel. It was what we now call a bachelorette party, although mercifully that word had not inserted itself into my vocabulary at the time. We swept through the lobby within a uniform mass of black-robed, veiled women, fought our way through several doorways hung with multiple layers of thick velvet curtains, and emerged into a crystal-chandelier-lit ballroom, decorated with exotic trees and flowers that wouldn't last a minute outside in the Qatari landscape. The room was packed with women of dark, sloe-eyed beauty and, once they had removed their robes, eye-popping sexuality, dressed in stiletto heels, jewels, and designer outfits right off the runway.

After a multicourse dinner, American music began blasting from behind us. A lacquered screen rising out of the nearly impenetrable rain-forest of leafy potted plants in the back of the room prevented the male DJ from seeing what was happening on the dance floor, where all but a few of the women had begun doing an erotic, bump-grinding slow dance with each other. I felt I should cover Virginia's eyes; this was something I hadn't really seen since high school, and then only late in the night when the chaperones had all gone out for a smoke. I was as mesmerized and uncomfortable as if I had been a pimply-faced Calvinist looking at a peep show.

Seeing us emerge, blinking, from the curtains into the bright lobby, Fazal jumped to delighted attention, then after looking more closely at our faces mantled with a blush of embarrassment and excitement, made that disgusted teeth-sucking Pfffft noise to show his disapproval. It was hard to tell what upset him: that Khalid had allowed his charges, guests of the emir, to be exposed to something unseemly, or that we might have enjoyed it.

I got the answer several days later. A visibly nervous Fazal reported that I, without Virginia, was to have my ten minutes at the palace with the emir, and he had plenty to say about it. Starting with no riding in the front seat. No bare toes. No giggling on the way over. Car would be washed, vacuumed, and there would be absolutely no snacks. I already knew the rules about clothing, but as I was dressing on the day of the appointment there was a knock on my hotel door. I opened it, expecting Virginia, and there stood Fazal. My surprise must have been evident; this was violating not only those Muslim social strictures regarding women that had been drilled into me but maybe also just old-fashioned propriety.

Unfazed, Fazal creaked in and asked to see what I was planning to wear. When I showed him a white linen tunic and pants, he pawed through the clothes draped over the chairback and suggested a scarf to go with them, then demonstrated with his kaffiyeh exactly how to knot my hair into a demure bun. Satisfied, he produced a contortion of his facial muscles resembling something very near a grin, twirled his forefinger jauntily in the air above his head, and spun to leave. I stood with my back to the door for a minute, trying to grasp the giant cultural leap we had just taken.

The old Fazal was waiting for me at the car. He made no eye contact, mechanically showed me into the back seat, did the whirly thing with his robe, and drove me in faithful-retainer silence to the palace. Under the portico, he practically goose-stepped to my door, which he had told me not to, under any circumstances, open myself. I wanted to do something typically crass, like throw my chewing gum into the shrubbery, but when I tried a funny little Groucho eyebrow wiggle, he glared furiously at me out of the corner of his averted eyes. Which, I am telling you, is possible. Ask Bertie Wooster.

I was escorted by a couple of robed men through a palm-edged entry and down a number of marble halls into a perfectly square white marble room into which you could practically have crane-dropped my entire house and had plenty of room to run the Derby on the outside. Around all four walls were gold chairs, one after another, just begging for some statistician to translate them into a measurement like, "If these chairs were put in a line they'd reach from the Washington Monument to the Pentagon." Countless identical gold chairs.

The men vanished in a swirl of white, leaving me standing alone in the cavernous room. I tried that thing you can do in St. Paul's Cathedral to see if by some sonic quirk my whisper would travel around the chairs, but it was immediately lost. Feeling that way myself, I looked to see if there was any chair that looked more emir-y than the others, but they were all identical. I chose one and sat down, leaning back and placing one sneak-ered foot on the opposite knee in a debonair, confidence-boosting mascu-line stance, wrists dangling insouciantly off the lion-headed chair arms. I was terrified.

From across the marble expanse, a distant billowing white figure emerged, tiny and indistinct as if substantiating from a mirage. It was the emir, looking pretty much like every other man at the palace, only more billowy. As he approached and grew larger still, I lost all my posturing bra-vado, uncrossed my legs and ankled them together, sitting primly upright like a schoolgirl at pledge-of-allegiance attention. I had no idea what I was supposed to do; Fazal hadn't told me this part. I had never met royalty before, unless you count Luci Johnson, Lyndon's younger daughter, at the Clover Creamery, where I still regret not being the one to steal the chewed wad of Juicy Fruit she left on the side of her bread plate.

I stood up and stuck out my hand. A beat. He shook it and sat down in the chair next to where I had been sitting. It felt like we were a pair of shy, side-by-side losers sitting out a school dance. Staring out across the room, he asked, "How do you like my country?"

Taking a breath, I got up and lifted my chair out of the line, turning it so that I was now almost facing him. He looked startled. I sat down again and said, "You know, I want to talk to you about this. I'm worried that it's not being cared for."

I grew up on the photographs of Edward Weston, the view-camera king of the sweeping sand dunes of the American West. Sometimes they had naked women splayed out postcoitally over them, probably hot and itching, but the ones I remember the most are the ones without his girlfriends. Undulating, eternal, almost liquid—and pristine. Not a used Pamper, not a hubcap, not a trace of plastic-spewing, grubby humanity. But the dunes that Khalid drove us to were stippled with litter—in fact, much of the landscape was awash in trash. The most striking aspect was the abandoned cars—sometimes on the main road, or perched on the sides of the mountainous dunes, or upside down at the bottom, their windows broken out by the tumble. These weren't junkers—these were brand-new luxury cars. Pulled over by the side of the road, their doors were often open to the breeze, as if a family had just stepped out to enjoy a scenic overlook. Some had been vandalized, most just discarded. "Ran out of gas," explained Khalid reasonably.

The country was so oil-rich that not only did no one really work, but everyone in the country received a guaranteed income that I seem to recall was close to a quarter million a year. Gas was just pennies, there was no income tax, and education, housing, utilities, medical care, and loans were free. The work was done by immigrants. Halfway through our stay there, Qatar won a decades-long case before the international court against Bahrain involving the rights to a vast reservoir of natural gas in the ocean off the coast. To celebrate, Doha's young men drove their brand-new cars into the streets for several nights, pressing simultaneously on the accelerator and the brake so that once the tires burned up, some of the cars burned, too. The main street was black and stinking of rubber smoke.

I went to Qatar expecting to be Edward Weston and turned into Robert Adams. The closest I came to a Weston image was this one:

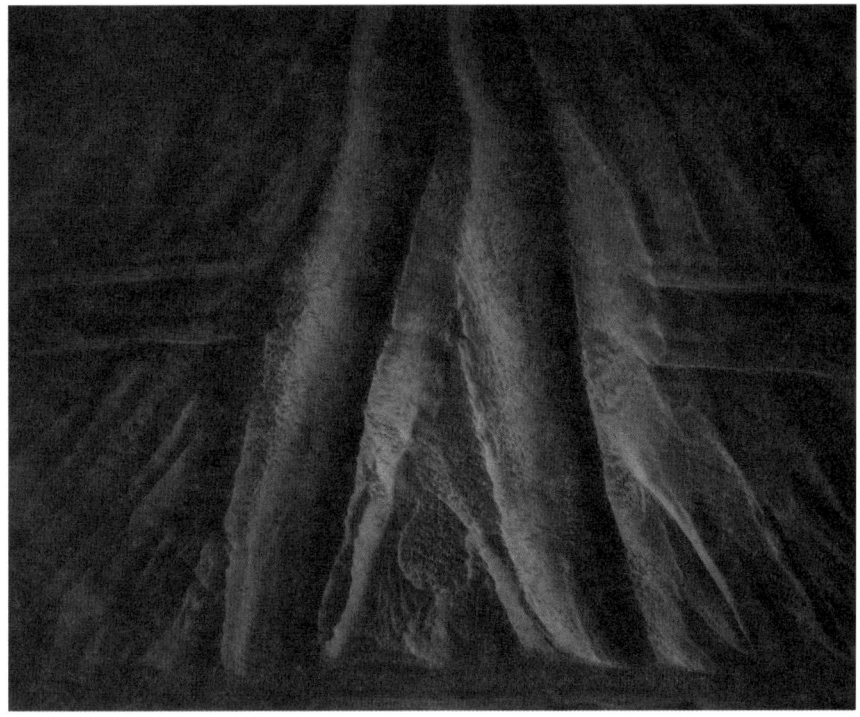

And even it was a sand formation caused partly by car tires.

The rest of the pictures are Robert Adams writ large—of a landscape despoiled and degraded. I had found my subject. The fear I had of going to a strange land and not making a single good picture melted away the very first time I set up the tripod and looked through the ground glass. Out there in the desert, with not a moss-draped live oak anywhere, without a poetically kudzu-mounded hillside, without the glowy humidity of the American South that almost guarantees a good picture, I still found something to say. Just as I always do, just as I believe I never will.

All I had to do was put my head under the dark cloth and my face to ground glass. That is all any of us ever have to do; pick up the paintbrush, the welding torch, the ball of moist clay, fire up the computer and start pecking. To defeat fear, I occasionally just set up the camera wherever I am, pull the dark cloth over my head, and look. Sometimes, by excluding outside distractions and creating aesthetic limitations, even artificial ones, I ease my fears that I will fail, perhaps in the same way Temple Grandin found relief from her anxiety by being pressed between two mattresses.

Often, I keep the tripod head slightly loose so I can rotate it around until I find something that was completely invisible to my un-cameraed eye just two minutes before. (This particular swiveling maneuver once nearly cost me a camera, as, hopelessly circling for a good picture, my 8 × 10 unspooled off the tripod bolt and crashed to the ground. You are way smarter and would never do this.) Unless I have the camera to my face, be it a 35 mm or an 8 × 10, I often simply don't see the picture; the only way I have found to make good pictures is to make pictures. Many, many pictures. Most of them not very good. Then weed out the duds and start over again—like Penelope, deliberately unweaving, improving, making better work the next day. Even in Qatar, in the most inauspicious, barren landscape, as alien and bleak as the moon, I found pictures to take. But first, I had to stomp my fear into a mudhole and say Yes. Then, the next-hardest thing, I had to take the tripod out of the car and set up the camera.

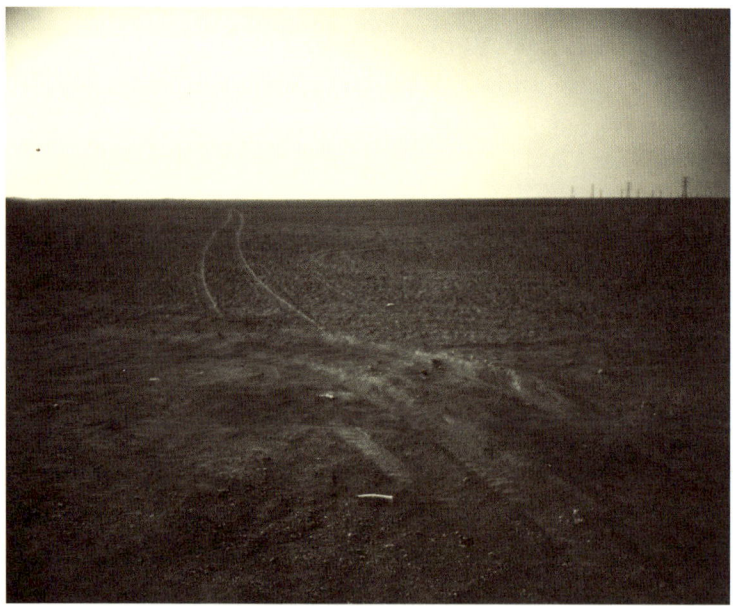

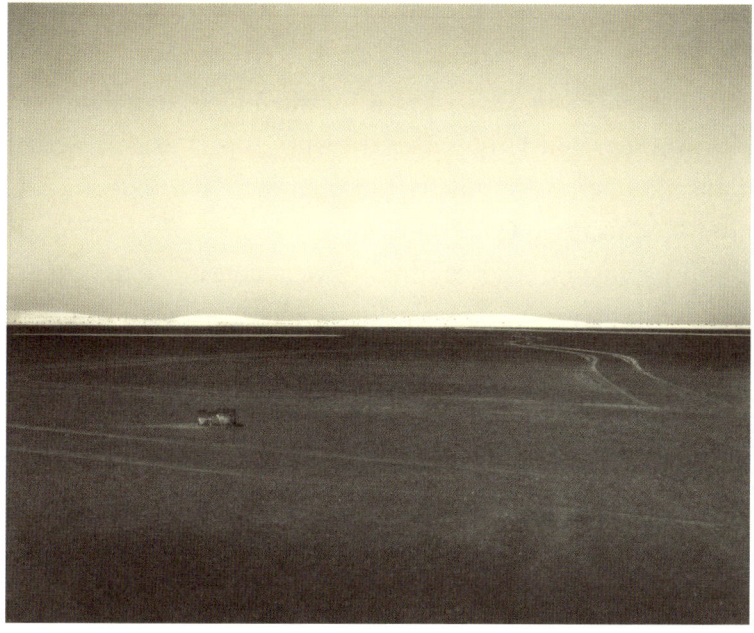

You take that first picture exactly as a writer bangs out that first line. Hemingway wrote early in *A Moveable Feast* about gazing out over the roofs of Paris and exhorting himself to write. Basically, it's simple: You have always written, you will write again, just write the one true sentence you know. Once you write that simple, declarative sentence, and ruthlessly cut out anything resembling what he called "that scroll-work"—in his case, a word possessing more than two syllables—you go on from there. Not one to send anybody rushing for a dictionary, Hemingway made that blockage-busting creative formula work for him, and you can make it work for you. Pick up your pencil, your camera, your paintbrush; find your story, keep it simple. Or, let it find you, but keep going. As a writer, you may have no idea what possible role, say, the death several weeks ago of a woman named Anna on the railroad tracks of your hometown might play in the subsequent five hundred pages of your book, or how the Marabar Cave you have explored since childhood might figure in the narrative plot, but if you don't type that first line, you will never find out.

Years ago, our neighbor Sam asked if I wanted to go morel hunting with him. I had photographed him a decade earlier as part of a project for Hospice. It was his wife who was dying, but what we talked about most was the recent death of his fifteen-year-old son.

Like all parents of dead children, Sam was haunted and grief-riven, so, being out in nature, and especially if there was a possibility of eating some of it, was curative. I said yes and we set out on a sunny April morning to shuffle along under a stand of poplars, trying to beat the turkeys to the mushrooms.

Within minutes Sam had discovered dozens of morels, and I was still stupidly swiveling my head, my woven bag hanging limp and empty. Triumphantly he would pounce on a morel just feet from the tips of my Blundstones, where I was in danger of actually treading on the mushrooms. He wasn't above humiliating me for being so blind and began playing that "you're warm . . . you're warm . . . oh so hot it's going to burn you!" game. For the life of me I couldn't see a single morel anywhere, until—I could. I found the first one. And then, they were everywhere! It was as if a switch flipped and magically I could see the hideous, unappetizing brown heads emerging from the forest litter.

For the artist, starting to make work is like spotting the first morel; once you see the first good picture, or find the first good words, they are everywhere. That first moment of radical seeing shines the essential light on all the rest of the creative landscape; images multiply, generate kinships and metaphor, become inevitable. Once I had taken the first of those ravaged desert pictures, I couldn't stop—I saw them everywhere, excitedly shrieking to a mystified Fazal or Khalid to pull over, *right there, right there!* along a stretch of featureless desert absolutely indistinguishable from the miles of equally featureless desert we had already traversed. Everywhere there were power lines, rusting oil barrels, tires, pipelines, old fences, fallen stanchions, abandoned blockhouses, refineries behind razor wire, and all of it punctuated with plastic bags, discarded clothing, diapers, soda bottles, flip-flops, and, of course, the abandoned cars. Seeking respite, we went to a remote beach, and even there:

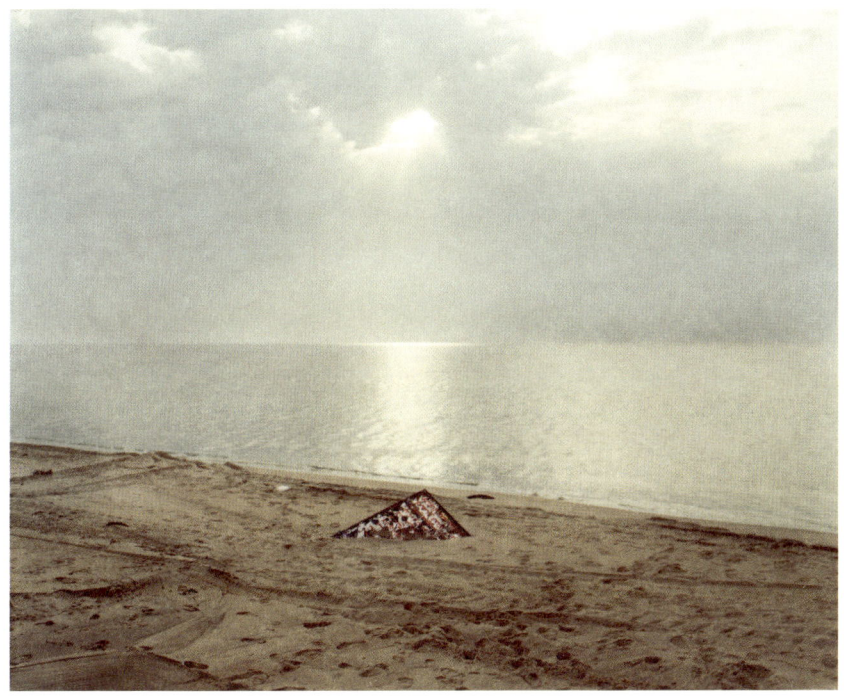

The landscape of Qatar was about as far from the deserts in the photographs of Du Camp or John Beasley Greene or the Edward Weston dunes of my roseate expectations as you can get. And so, sitting in that gleaming, marble hall on the edge of the gold chair and practically knee-to-knee, I told the emir what I had expected, and what I had found. He took it pretty well, protesting that there were beautiful, still pristine, parts of the country and that his intention was to set aside a large area for a national park. He proudly described an inland sea, wild goats and oryx, his ambitions (since realized) for a major art museum and Qatari presence in the art world, and he promised to make arrangements for me to watch his Arabians race from his royal box. He asked a lot of questions.

I told him how my father, describing himself at the time as "a brash, naively exuberant young man just out of medical school," had traversed the desert landscape in 1938. In his journals he adopted the poetics of his stylistic mentor, Gustave Flaubert, writing, possibly about Qatar itself:

The ancient, low-lying lavender hills.
The luminous waves of the desert sands.
The joy.
And costumes and customs and camels.

The grey mud-brick huts of villages that huddle together every mile or so, surrounded by beautifully attended small plots.
The families who tend them, sturdy, cheerful, hospitable.
The gracious, tender care I have received from them.
And, always, the desert, the ponderous, windblown movement and mighty weight of it.

I did not, however, tell the emir of my father's next, less poetic journal entry, in which he expressed dismay at seeing a woman, covered head to toe in black, getting hauled like cargo over the side of the freighter in a flimsy straw basket, forty meters above the gray water of the Persian Gulf. We did not talk about women and certainly not about the bachelorette party.

My appointment with the emir had been scheduled to last ten minutes, and when we were well past that I would see a figure off in the distance, stepping into the room, pausing, and backing out again. After about thirty minutes the emir reached up and loosened the top three buttons of his gold-embroidered thawb, the traditional long shirt. I tried not to show my astonishment. In all the days in that country I had hardly ever seen a man not buttoned right up to the Adam's apple. It was as though he had just slipped into something more comfortable. He raised a large hand, and from who knows where a staff member materialized with a small gilt table on which he ceremoniously placed glasses of iced water and thimble-sized porcelain cups of bitter Bedouin coffee.

We took a minute to drink the coffee and some water. Then we began to talk again about the stark beauty of the landscape (despite the debris), the quality of the desert light that I had come to love and was unlike anything I had ever seen, and the windstorms that sometimes threatened to blow my camera over and turn it into more trash tumbleweeding across the landscape. He was right to want to protect a great swath of the country from his own subjects, who took it for granted in the same way that Americans throw their McDonald's trash out the window on the beautiful Skyline Drive. I told him so and how much I had enjoyed my time there.

After a companionable pause, he began to describe in almost sentimental detail a spit of land on the ocean that was special to him, where he went with the sheikha to relax and enjoy the sea breezes. He described what I imagined to be a gazebo, all four sides hung with fabric, the plangent ocean breezes at nightfall causing them to suspire like giant, pale lungs. As he talked, he made gentle, almost balletic, waving motions with his arms and a dreamy, distant look came into the dark eyes that had once been characterized as raptor-like. The light as he described it, especially in the early fall, seemed to be exactly the Josef Sudek-through-the-rainy-window light that I loved for portraiture. He asked: Would I photograph him there?

Of course, I said Yes.

But no money for taking the picture. That was my deal.

As I have said, we all have a different needle setting and our own unique magnetic fields. Artistic true north is variable and we each, in our own way, navigate the ambiguous territory between purity and sellout. My position was neither, really, the needle trembling somewhere in between in a manifestation of my own uncertainty. I had decided I could try taking the picture in the fall—what did I have to lose? If it was terrible, it would simply confirm what I suspected all along. If it was brilliant, then it would prove some arcane corollary of a coin-flip law, or the guarantee of the twice-daily correct clock. Or something along those lines.

I told the emir I would come back. I had enjoyed getting to know Khalid's family and another young woman, Fatima, who allowed me to make several pictures of her, although she was disturbed to realize her face was faintly visible under the chiffon of her veil in one of them (not this one).

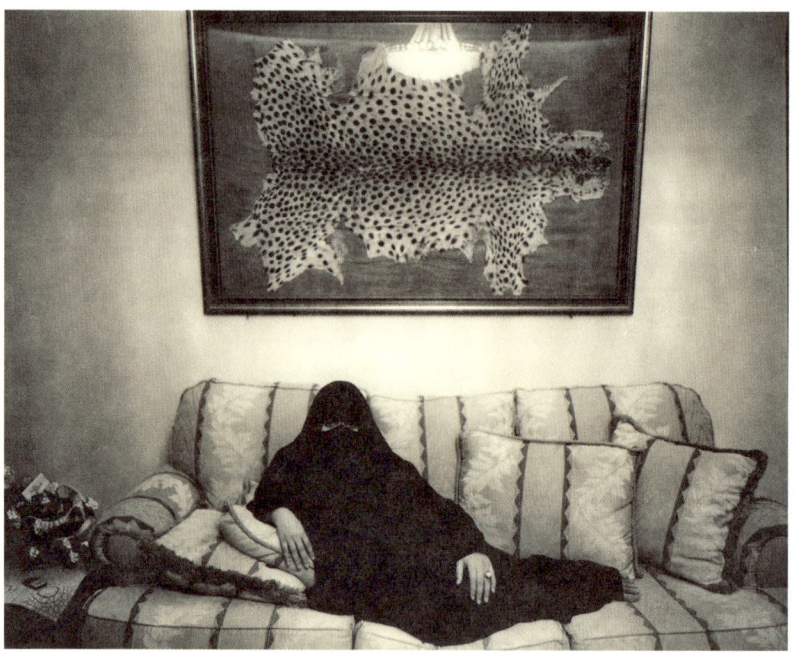

Everyone I met in Qatar displayed an innate hospitality and generosity that I have also found in the equally paradox-ridden American South. I had come to love the ponderous and luminous desert in a way that I never thought possible, just as my father had, and found a connection to him there. And most of all, I had grown fond of Fazal.

These connections are the keystone that Wallace Stegner describes in *Angle of Repose*: the intersecting lines of our cross-cultural human relationships in Qatar could have merely propped each other up, leaning together from the vertical, the optimistic geometer of my brain suggesting an intersection at some distant vanishing point. But this would have been a false arch—one that Stegner argues will not hold without the essential keystone: the Yes of trust and faith rising from the human heart. This is why I went and why I would go back again. It is the Yes of friendship, the Yes of faith, even faith in my creative abilities, the Yes of the inexplicable. It is the single most difficult utterance, and perhaps the most important.

When, after ninety minutes or so, I emerged from the palace, the old Fazal was gone and Fazal my friend was frantic. Ignoring all protocol, he rushed to me, searching my face for signs of what had happened. When it became clear I hadn't been detained in some imagined palace dungeon for impertinence and that in fact I had been whooping it up with the emir, his joy was that of the proudest parent at the school recital. I had not failed him; I had behaved; his emir was pleased. He let me back in the front seat for the ride to the hotel to pick up Virginia. We took one last drive in the desert before the flight the next day.

In the weeks after Virginia and I returned home, there were handwritten faxes in phonetic spelling and awkward phone calls from Fazal. His English was worse over the phone. He had been to Jordan and Syria. It had been cold. He was getting a new falcon. He missed us. He missed us. He missed us. He was crying.

A month later, I received an invitation to return—with a proposed date of the second week of September 2001.

Needless to say, I did not go then, and even the Yes of the inexplicable has not yet brought me back to Qatar, to my great regret. I still love the pictures I made of the desert there, the unlikely aesthetic offspring of Robert Adams and Edward Weston. When asked last year for an unseen body of work to be published on the cover and in a twenty-page spread in an important literary quarterly, I suggested the pictures from Qatar. I've experienced some censorship in my life, but this was a new one on me. They refused to print them because of Qatar's questionable human rights record. One wonders how any landscape photographs taken anywhere could ever survive such scrutiny, and it made me sad to think that mine of Qatar now join the boxes of other work too controversial to be shown, hidden away on my studio shelves. The emir's portrait will remain the best one I have never made, because, of course, it shimmers only in a mirage, in a gossamer dream across a fiery chasm that separated me from that world.

9

Monkey on a Road Trip

If at first you don't succeed, try, try, again. Then quit.
There's no point in being a damn fool about it.
                              —attributed to W. C. Fields

I sat down the other day with an Agfa photo-paper box Sharpied with
"DS" on the orange top and pulled from it a dishevelment of maps, notes,
travel books, and candy bar wrappers. It's been several decades since I
began my series of photographs of the Deep South, and to get my bear-
ings I started with the unpoetic and candid account I had written of the
three road trips in the late 1990s. As I read, I pulled out and sequenced the
hundreds of unsuccessful negatives that had been packed into the cabinets
along with the other losers.

Why do I insist on believing that every other working artist has it
easier than me—that they are out there effortlessly producing good, new
work while I am stuffing my cabinets with rejects? Or, more to the point,
that good work is inevitable at a certain stage in a career? That once you
get past that hurdle, the good-work minimum-height requirement, from
then on you will be buoyed by the inevitability of continued success?

Just the fact that it took three arduous trips to eke out a few dozen
good pictures undercuts that pernicious perception. It is assumed that
each good picture, every resonant poem, each uncracked pot, eases the
path for all the subsequent ones, that you get better as you go, not repeating the mistakes of the past and finding inspiration at every turn. But that
is not always the case, and I include in these few pages of travel chronol-
ogy some of the failed pictures that form a dense constellation around the

stellar successes. Tucked within that Milky Way–like mass of clunkers is a perceptual phenomenon that possesses, at least for me, a potent force field that you may recognize from your own practice.

Mercifully this phenomenon comes into play when you can best accommodate it, like a tax tariff that takes effect only after a certain level of income. It was not until I was pretty far into my career that I first began to feel the effects; I'd taken some good pictures, mostly of people: some local women, the twelve-year-olds, and my own children. And I had made editorial choices that were slanted in a certain direction, for better or worse, and had a career-defining trajectory that seemed immutable. The lessening of the gravitational power of the family work and the gradual seduction of the landscape sent me off into completely uncharted territory, but I eagerly harnessed up for the liftoff. And immediately flew smack into the paradox of success.

Dusting myself off, I discovered that what I had smacked into was the surprisingly—gratifyingly—solid edifice of my own past work. No matter how hard-won or painful at the time of their production, by the time they were on the walls or the pages of a book, my pictures had begun to take on the smug patina of predestination.

They were now cocksure, with an incipient dignity, like an old rocker with a Brylcreem ducktail whose sideburns are just beginning to gray. Where they were once transgressive, they now began to seem mainstream. Where they had required repeated attempts to tease out a success, filling me with frustration and uncertainty, they now were invested with a decisive Cartier-Bresson-like certitude. Just as we mothers are said to forget the pain of childbirth, it seemed I could no longer recall exactly how difficult it had been to make the old, established work, and now its self-confidence was subtly subverting my efforts to make new work. Because if I'm so good, why is this new work so damned hard all of a sudden?

As a friend once remarked, you can always prove to yourself that good pictures are elusive; but you can never quite assuage yourself with the faith that they're also inevitable. Emphatically unassuaged, I set off for the unknown, south to the dark soil of the Mississippi Delta and the bruised skies of Louisiana, with modest faith in the certainty of good pictures and, so the quip goes, much to be modest about.

Below, I reproduce excerpts from the casual chronicle of my trips, written some time afterward, which eventually got condensed into the romantic blue highways account in my memoir, *Hold Still*. I say condensed because during the writing of the Massey Lectures for Harvard, which I expanded into the book, I didn't take the time to dive deeply into that Agfa box of memorabilia and notes that would have revealed some of the minor, unromantic inconsistencies. What I wrote in *Hold Still* was not dishonest; let's just say it was *soft-focused*, as if I'd put a diffusing nylon stocking over the lens of reality.

And this brings me to another point: Retracing my travels through the South would have been so much easier if I had saved my receipts. Which I did, for a long time—I saved every paper receipt from about 1972 until 1999, when, inexplicably, I decided those were the boxes to toss from my capacious attic, losing thereby all records of what photo paper and chemicals (now mostly extinct) I had used to make that early work, the manufacturers of these materials (now long bankrupt) and, germane to this, the itinerary and dates of my otherwise unremembered travels, traceable from gas station receipts. This inability to anticipate the importance of such ephemera springs, I suppose, from my abiding lack of confidence that it could ever matter enough to justify occupying what I thought of as valuable attic space.

It was the same bone-deep disbelief that back then had me grabbing up test prints and using them to write letters on, as if simple stationery wasn't available to me—notes to everyone: the paperboy who delivered my *Washington Post*, babysitters, the arresting officer for my speeding ticket, and most memorably, furious notes to critics (great idea: send them a *Candy Cigarette* on the back of which you tell them to go fuck themselves and that a strong letter will follow)—all written on my own, now often valuable, prints. Not for a moment did I anticipate that they would ever be worth something to anyone, so deep was my insecurity (and now, of course, I seethe when I find the letters on eBay).

You smart young artists probably already know that you're going to be famous some day and are prepared for it. Ted Orland describes an instructor struggling to teach the most basic aspects of the writer's craft to a class of as-yet-unpublished hopefuls who peppered her with questions about bidding wars, royalties, movie rights, and sequels. That cart is so far ahead of the horse in this case that the poor nag turns around and goes back to the stall. But perhaps you're right to anticipate; fame has come to be expected and can be shockingly easy to come by these days. You, being children of the Influencer Age and entirely used to confidently asserting yourselves, will not be as unprepared as I was when the mantle of fame descends on you.

I should have saved receipts is all. If paper still exists, you should, too.

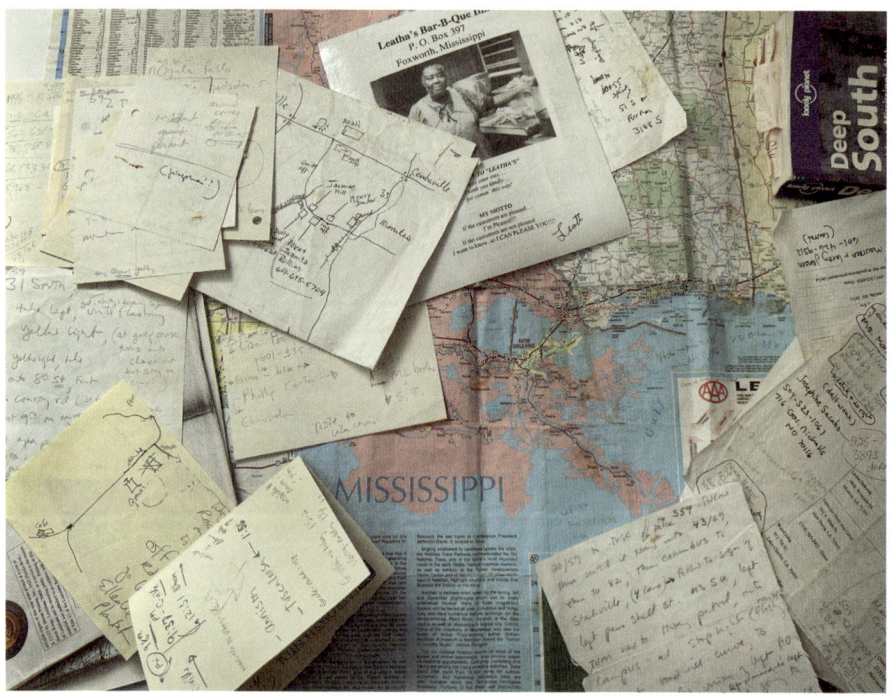

Here are my notes from those travels, pretty much verbatim:

Trip One:
April 9–19, 1998
Suburban, no collodion outfit in back. Ortho/silver film. Changing bag. Used that a lot. No pistol.

I was a little anxious about setting off on a road trip with just Virginia (age 13) for company, so when a friend of ours, Dave M, said he needed to go see his aunt in Baton Rouge, I asked if he wanted to go with us. He knew all those back MS roads and liked to poke around. I proposed this first trip during Easter vacation for V, although it meant I was missing Jessie at George School Parents' Day. Emmett was at John Dewey and almost ready to graduate; straight As, healthy, beautiful, funny and showing such emotional maturity we had agreed to let him go on the class trip to London that same week. Which seemed extravagant given the tuition we were paying for the place. It turned out to be a calamitously fateful E. moment, in certain ways defining the rest of his life, but we couldn't have known that at the time.

Anyway, we strapped on the cowhorns and left on Thursday April 9. I drove the first 5 hours and then Dave and I switched at a gas station and I mixed a gin and tonic, unwrapped my honey-sodden PB sandwich and kicked back in the passenger seat. We had all 10 James Lee Burke audiobooks featuring Dave Robicheaux and Clete Purcell, which I had gotten through interlibrary loans; listened to damn near every one. Love the early ones with the original reader, Mark Hammer. New reader, Will Patton, not as good. Anyway, stacked in the floorboards were all those big boxes of cassette tapes, each one the size of a lunch-box, about the same size, in fact, as the portable telephone we would rent for the trip.

At around 11PM, halfway through Heaven's Prisoners, *we were closing in on Huntsville, AL. Dave was still driving. I was dozing (maybe there was a second G&T involved) but was jolted awake when D skidded to a halt on a 2-lane road. The winds were bansheeing and the rain was horizontal. V, sleeping in the back, woke with a cry—we both were trying to be heard above the turboprop roar outside.*

The Suburban kept lurching forward in huge jolts, like a lunging horse, and I thought that D was having a heart attack and stomping on the gas and then the brakes. He was gripping the steering wheel with a death-like clutch and his face was straining in a demonic, teeth-baring rictus. I was panicked because I didn't know what to do about a heart attack, he didn't respond to any of my shouts, and the car was galumphing in giant leaps all over the road, first one side, then the other, lurching from ditch to ditch.

Gradually the wind's fury subsided enough so we could be heard over the noise. I shrieked at Dave, "You're having a heart attack!" and tore at his death grip on the wheel. He was like a man that had grabbed a live electric wire and couldn't release it. By this time, the Suburban was canted into the ditch on the right side of the road.

No heart attack, he gasped, a tornado.

You know how you read about those cars that get lifted up and dropped in, say, a trailer park 10 miles away? That was nearly us. The 5,500-pound Suburban, packed to the headliners with people and equipment, had been repeatedly lifted off the ground as if being tested for flight-worthiness by the tornado.

Dave was rigid with fear and exhausted from wrestling the car from the roaring vortex. He had a lot of knowledge about tornados, having grown up in MS, and a huge fear of them (therefore).

Because I didn't have that experience, and because I didn't realize the dimensions of our danger, I wasn't quite as shook up as D until he began telling me how mortally close we had come to biting it in those moments. He said he had been within a second of telling V and me to roll down the windows and dive into the ditch by the side of the road, the winds being too powerful to open a door. Apparently, that would have been good advice, going for the ditch, if we could have gotten to it without being sucked up.

We sat for a while and waited for things to calm down, then drove to a motel, not a chain motel, a little vestigial 2-lane-highway motel. The next morning when V & I came down to the lobby, Dave sat at a Formica table reading the local paper that reported, in 40-point bold type, that 12 people had been killed by that tornado right where we had been.

After breakfast, we soberly fired up the Suburban, appreciating its leviathan qualities as we drove through the branch-strewn roads, avoiding the downed power lines—headed toward the Natchez Trace. We picked it up south of Chero-kee, AL, and lumbered along at the speed limit. Mile after mile of boring forest. I was beginning to think that maybe the tornado had been an omen of some sort, pulled from the biblical grab bag to warn me off. I stared dully out the window at the sameness scrolling by. Not likely to find a good picture here anytime short of Elvis's return, although I hoped I might hasten that along by setting up the camera at the Chickasaw burial mounds that showed up from time to time. Waste of film. What was I doing down here, anyway, that I couldn't have been doing at home? Oh, right: transporting D to his aunt. Showing V the Mighty M. At least there was some reason.

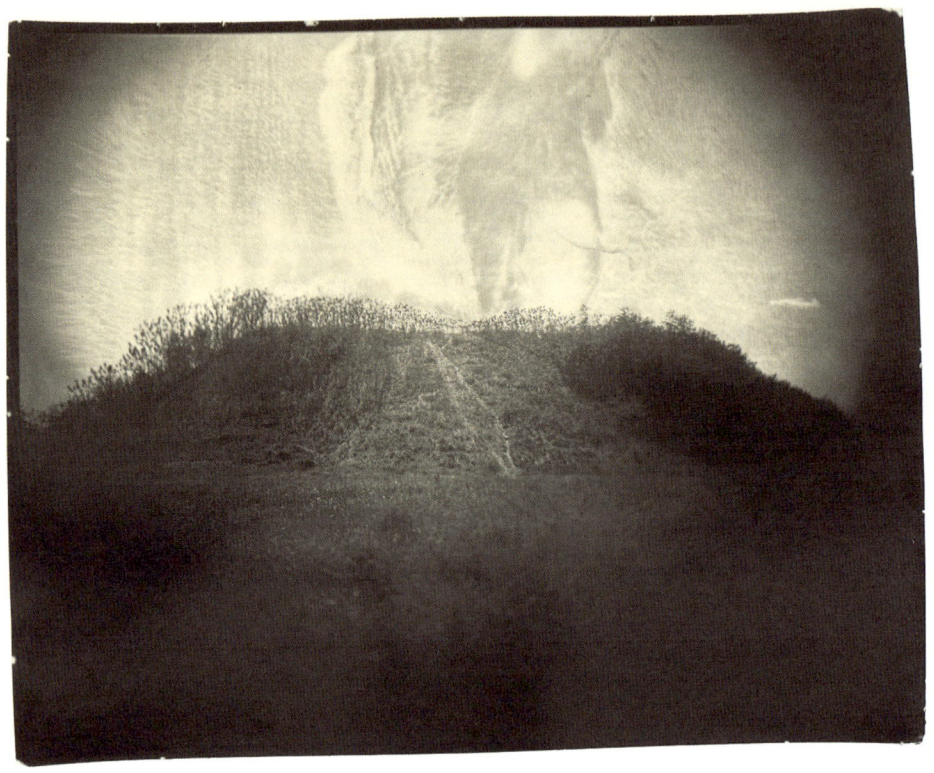

After entirely enough time on the Trace, we turned west, probably at Tupelo. D was keen on finding a graveyard where a Confederate relative had been buried and my heart lifted at the prospect of romantically drooping, moss-draped branches and ancient, lichen-covered tombstones. Who can't get a good picture in a cemetery?

Apparently me. Hardly worth bringing out the camera. I was discouraged, the 2nd long day of this trip and so far, three gas stations, a weed-covered hill and Stalinist blocks of stone instead of tombstones. No moss. Blazing sun, no gauzy atmospheric haze. Regular old trees.

Of course, since I was there and all, I hauled out the camera and the heavy bag of film holders and went ahead and took some pictures in that scraggly-ass grave-yard. And of course I can't resist a good tree picture. Which, looking at it now, I realize weirdly foreshadows the emblematic Scarred Tree *of my third and final trip. When I guess I finally figured out how to take good pictures.*

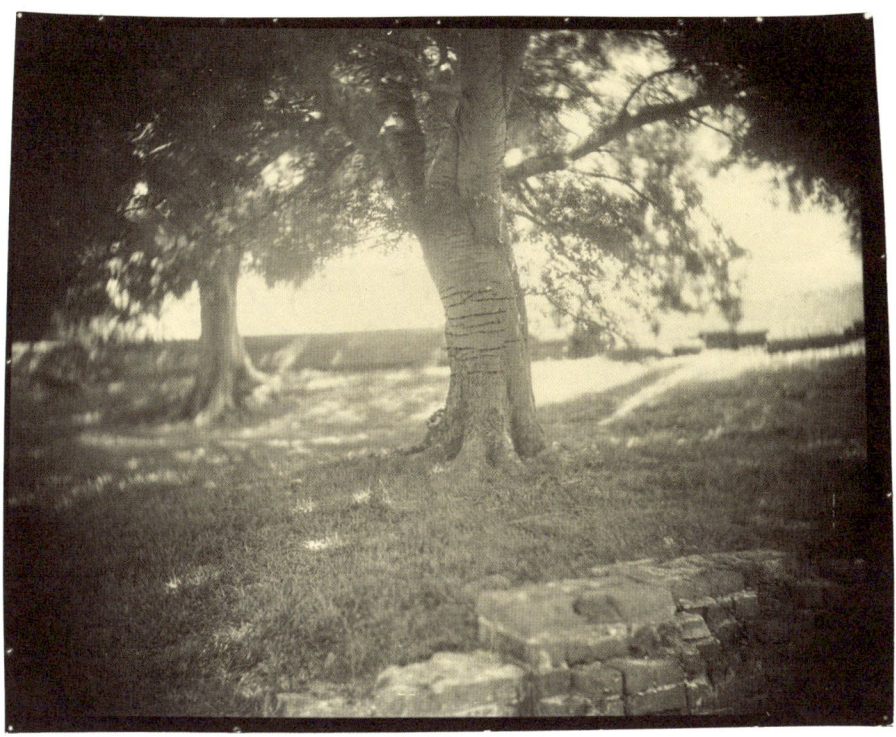

Maybe if I'd been able to look ahead and see that good pictures were, in fact, in my future, I would have felt better, but at that point, I was just taking dumb pictures and I knew it. But better dumb pictures than no pictures I reasoned, as D wandered around spitting on his shirttail and rubbing the carvings for a better look, while V read Rebecca *under the magnolias. But dumb pictures beg the question: Why do I bother? I began to doubt the wisdom of the whole enterprise. I could have stayed home in Virginia. There are magnolias there too.*

Packing up, we headed on down toward Oxford, where, on the outskirts Dave pointed out a house where he thought the Grishams once lived. I didn't photograph that, of course. So far, not a single good picture. Not even close. After craning our necks for Atticus in the Oxford town square, we headed out to Faulkner's home, Rowan Oak where I was positive I would finally get a good picture. V took the house tour while I tried to find something to photograph. SOL. Just more scarred tree practice.

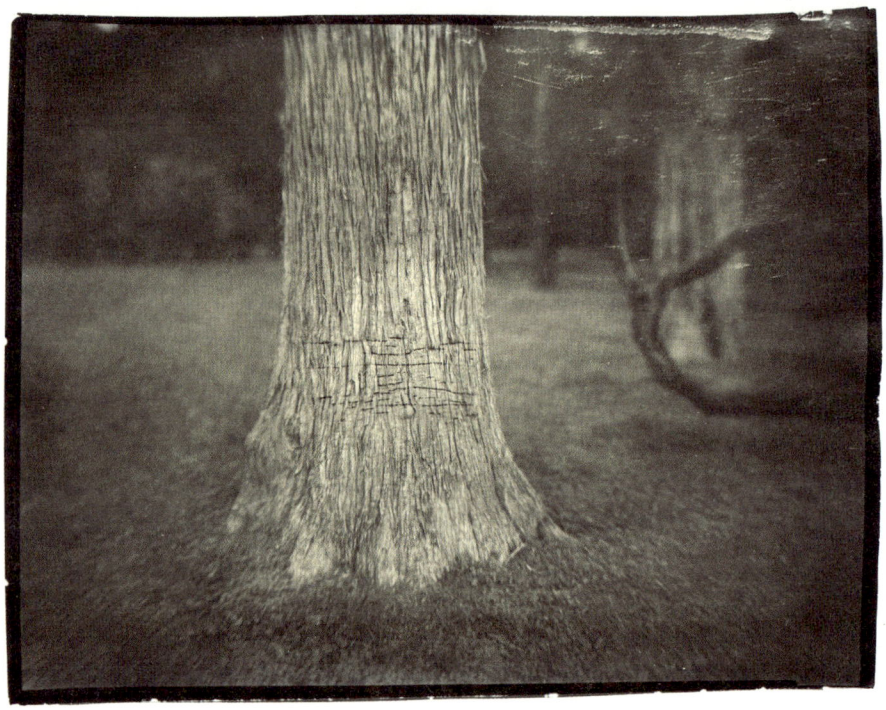

Everybody had now joined me in the slough of despond. I announced there were no pictures anywhere in this god-forsaken landscape. Needed to get to the river. Pissed at everybody. Everybody pissed at me. We loaded back up and pressed on southwesterly: Pea Ridge, Prophet Bridge, Eureka (if only). Then, appropriately, Dummyline Rd. From there to Bobo and across the Little Tallahatchie into Sumner, where my friends Maude and Lang live in a great ancestral pile they call Grey Gardens South. Could be Edie Beale's winter home.

When we gloomily disgorged at GGS, Lang made me a strong drink and I began to feel better. After a while, Maude, who I didn't know well at the time, swanned into the kitchen, cool, thin and elegant in twill riding jodhpurs, the old-fashioned kind with a slight balloon at the thigh, and I delightedly asked "Oh, do you ride?" She looked pityingly at me: they were Paris couture.

Typical of trickster memory, based on Proustian imperatives of smell and taste, I can recall almost nothing about that visit except this: Lang produced a sizable pork loin roast seasoned with a creole rub that he tied together like a pro, without consulting the directions, done it all his life, and roasted it. Superb red wine. No good pictures after 800 damn miles, but I almost felt OK about it.

I was determined to get to the Mississippi where I knew all the good pictures would be, and maybe this is just another instance of an unyielding expectation that gets in the way of a manifold vision. Rather than actually looking out the window at the ravishing Delta landscape, I single-mindedly pursued the evocative riverine image I believed was, mirage-like, just over the horizon, stopping to pull out the camera only occasionally when a plaintive, mongrelly tree or some irresistible spectacle of kudzu would siren-song me out of the Suburban.

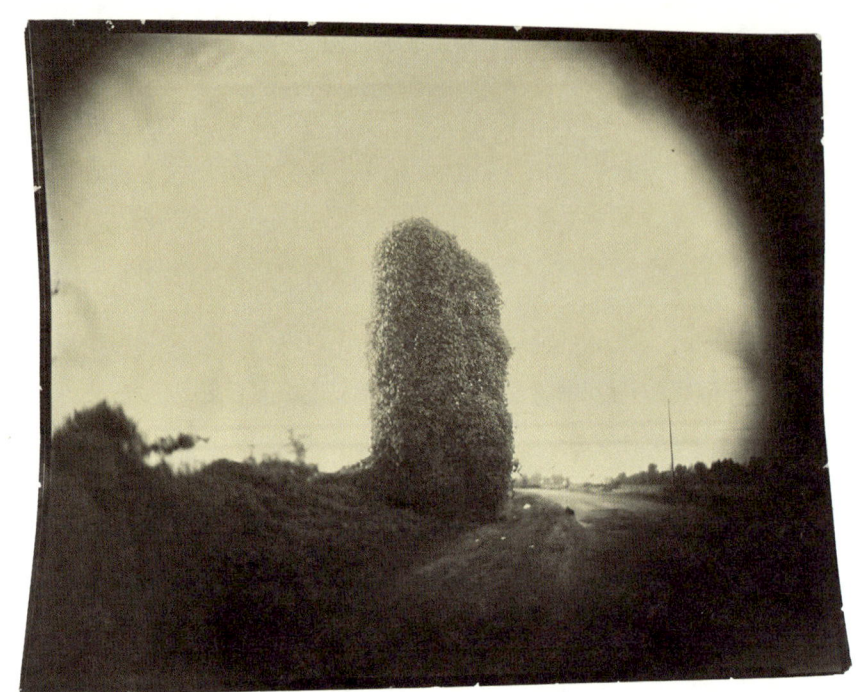

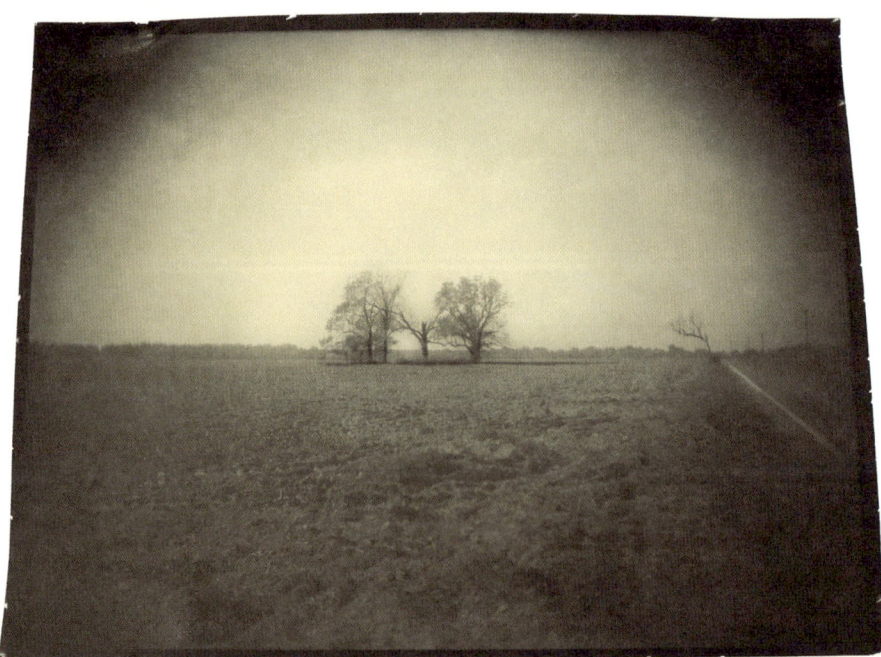

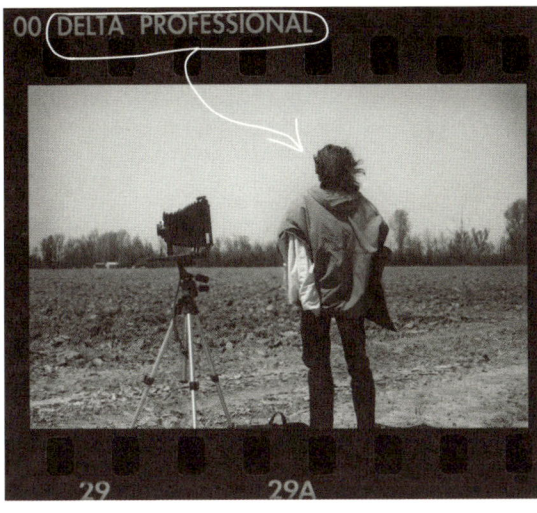

When, a bit above Vicksburg, we finally spied the uninspiring, blowsy, aptly named Big Muddy behind some cottonwood trees fluttering with plastic Walmart bags, I was so disappointed and peeved that I didn't see the point of setting up the camera, but because I had raised such a stink about getting toot sweet to the river, I made a show of taking a few pictures.

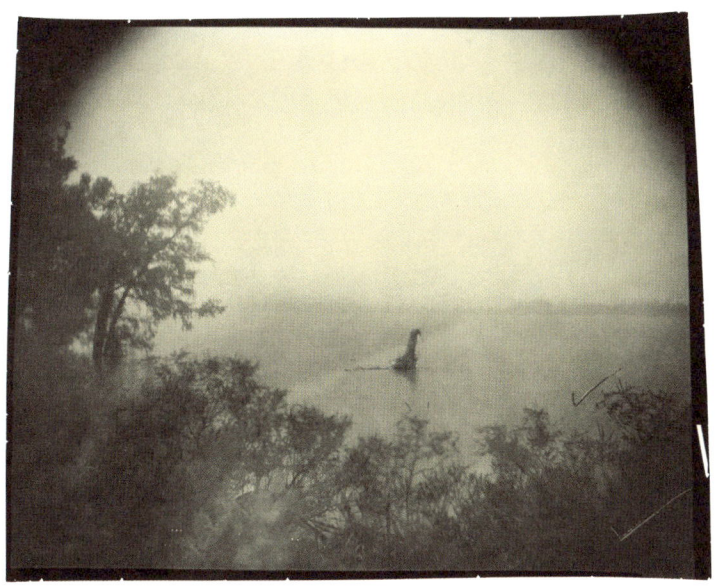

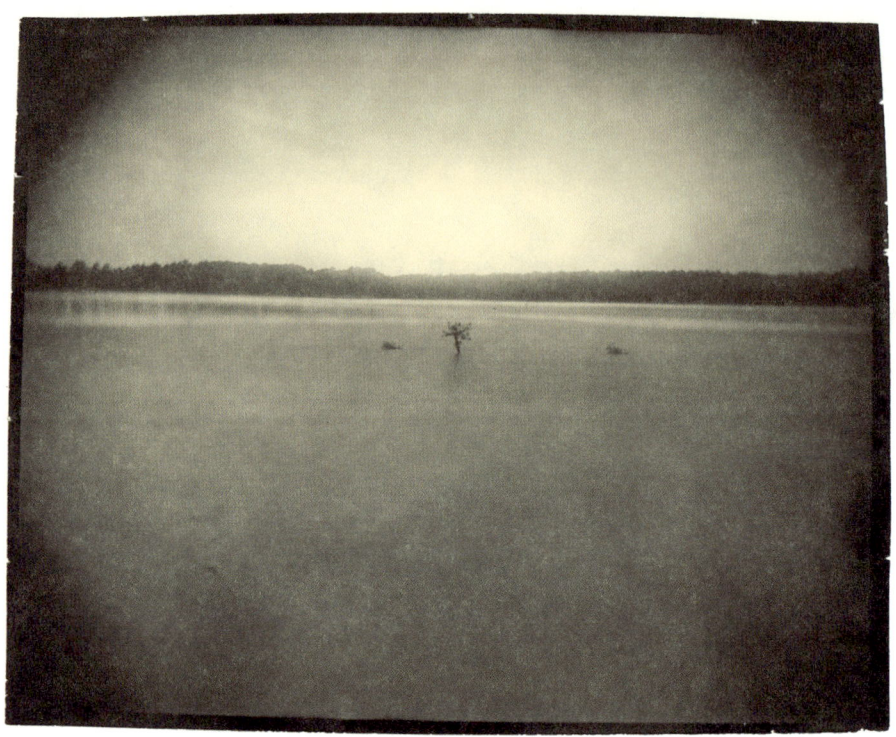

Climbing back in the car, I wasn't going to argue with D's suggestion that we go to the Vicksburg Battlefield. Where I got exactly no good pictures, either. Scowling dispiritedly at the wall carved with names of the dead, I imagined pen-knifing my own among them.

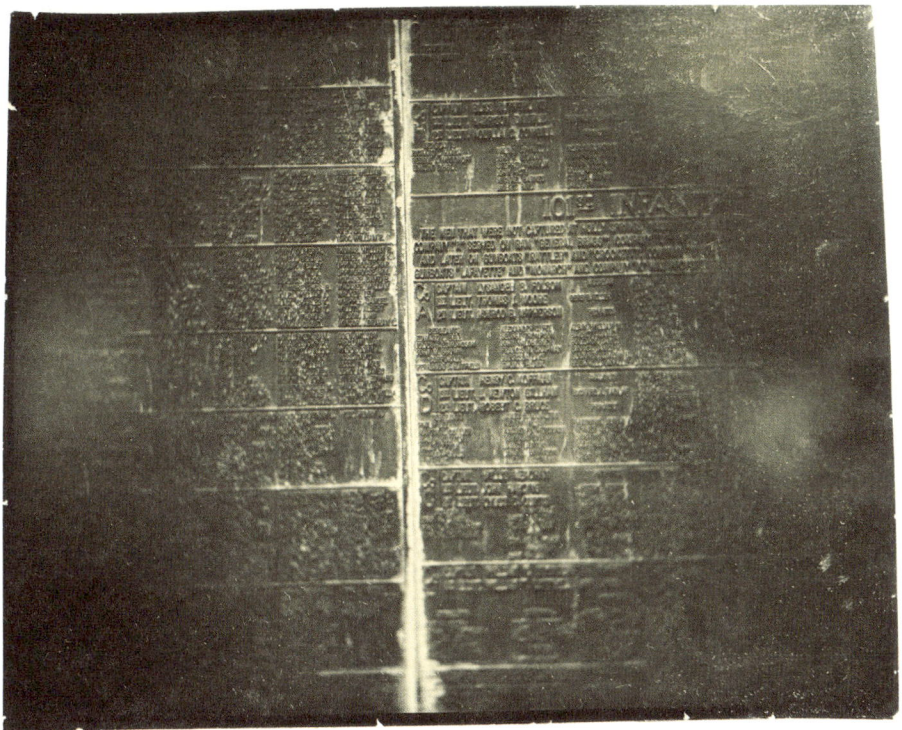

I guess that's about all you need to read of the self-pitying, Byronic despair in which I indulged for those first few travel days, because in truth it didn't get all that much better for a while. Susceptible, as ever, to opportunistic and self-indulgent sorrows, my spirits sank to a depth unplumbable by any line and took everyone else with them. I have wallowed in those depths many times before, even in the early years when ebullient optimism should have catapulted me back up into the oxygen. Here, for example, is a letter written to Ted in 1978, which pretty much could have been written yesterday.

```
and I waste hundreds of sheets of film because 99% of the pictures
I take are shitty. So, I am left with the hard fact that I don't
know my ass from a hole in the ground from a photograph and it's
sheer LUCK that I get an image that's printable. Out of 1500 images
last year I have 15 that are worth printing. Maybe.
I really DO feel tnat I'm NOT great, that I'm mediocre ¢ but not
quite mediocre ⵗ enough to iกgore  that the well never
############̸######  exactly runs dry but that it's a shallow and
listless flow, ....It's a terrible feeling, I look around me and
```

But I kept taking pictures. Perhaps the most important concept in that journal account of the trip south (and even in the 1978 letter) is that even though they were *dumb pictures*—and I knew they were—I kept taking them. Monkey at a typewriter. Sooner or later, there was going to be a good one, the monkey was going to get lucky, even if it was by accident.

Which, in fact, the first one was; a happy accident immediately after a bizarre encounter I now view as a portent, perhaps a tornado-reversing portent: Having stopped by a muddy stream, red with bulldozed dirt from a subdivision, I heard the unmistakable chords of Beethoven's *Pathétique*. What the hell. Following the music to the open window of a fake plantation home, its unfinished portico held up by Styrofoam columns, I discovered the source was the pianist Simone Dinnerstein, assisted by a man disfigured by leprosy. Feeling as though I was stepping out of a Fellini set, I tiptoed away and returned to the predictable: the Suburban, my camera, the dumb pictures. Like this one, taken right then:

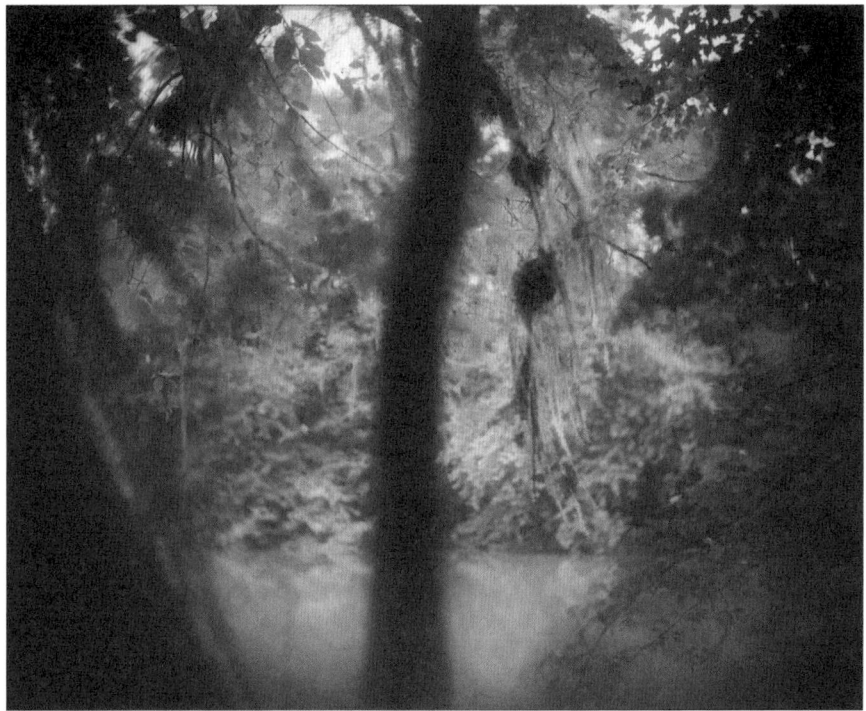

Not so great, right?

Yes. I know.

And I took it not just once. *Six times* I took this picture, or variants thereof. In case you wondered, 8 × 10 film is not cheap, but the old spend-thrift monkey just pecks away. And—guess what? A miracle.

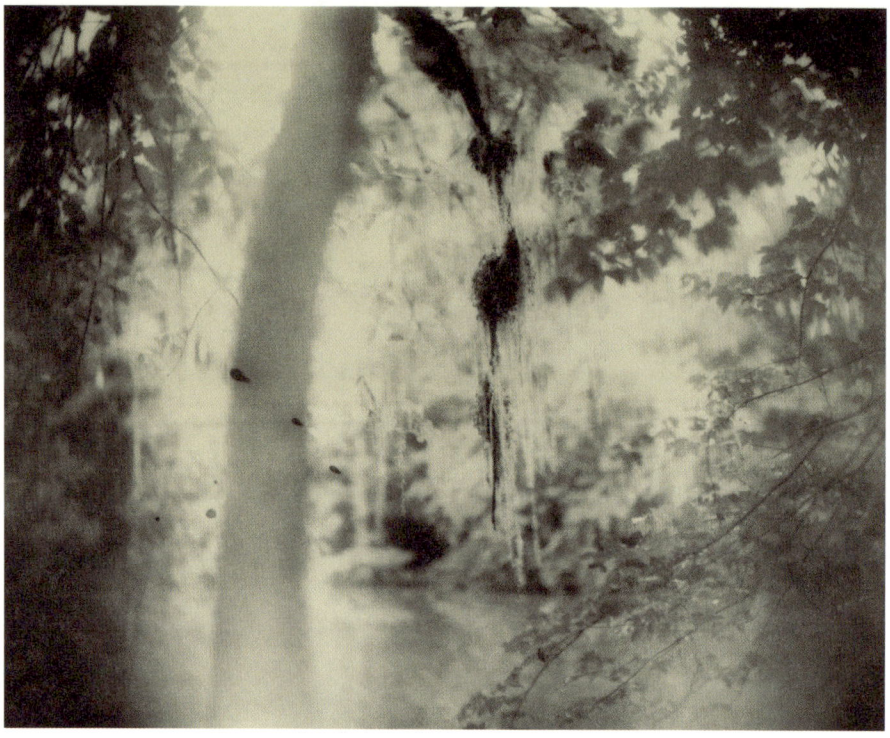

A miracle of incompetence; a sloppy chemical moment in the processing.
Luck, in other words.
Bad luck that turned into good luck, for the monkey.

What   I feel about Mann's work is best summed up by that old
saw: give an ape a portable typewriter and it **might** come
up with "Moby Dick." Mann uses expensive equipment
and if she shoots long enough and learns about cropping
and composition and lighting and self expression
and, oh, yes, subject selection, she may **yet**
come up with a poor man's Weegee.

Yours truly

RETIRED NYC HS ART TEACHER

This retired art teacher busted me, and my simian process, in his letter to the *New York Times* way back in 1992. His self-reported experience
with photography, beginning in college in the 1940s and later as a photo
teacher at a local boy's club, sharpened his eye for fakery in all forms.
But he was wrong about the expensive equipment and dead wrong about
Moby Dick. No monkeys, no matter how dexterous or numerous, could
ever write *Moby Dick*, one of my favorite books. They'd be lucky just to
get the title. And, likewise, sometimes no amount of trying, no amount of
good old stick-to-itiveness, will get you a good picture. It pains me to say
this and it didn't happen all that often to me, but sometimes, in fact, you
just have to give up.

Like this damn dead duck I was obsessed with. My friends John and
Leslie raised fowl of various kinds, slaughtering and freezing them.
This was before I had chickens myself and I was still charmed by their
deranged chaos. I knew that a chicken dustup was virtually guaranteed
if I brought feed and tossed it into the background of a picture with a
kid in it. Bound to get something interesting. For one whole fall, I'd pick
the kids up after school several days a week and go out to my friends'
farm, where I'd set up the camera among the feathers, manure, and dusty

scratchings, hoping I could get something good without anybody getting raked by a rooster's spur.

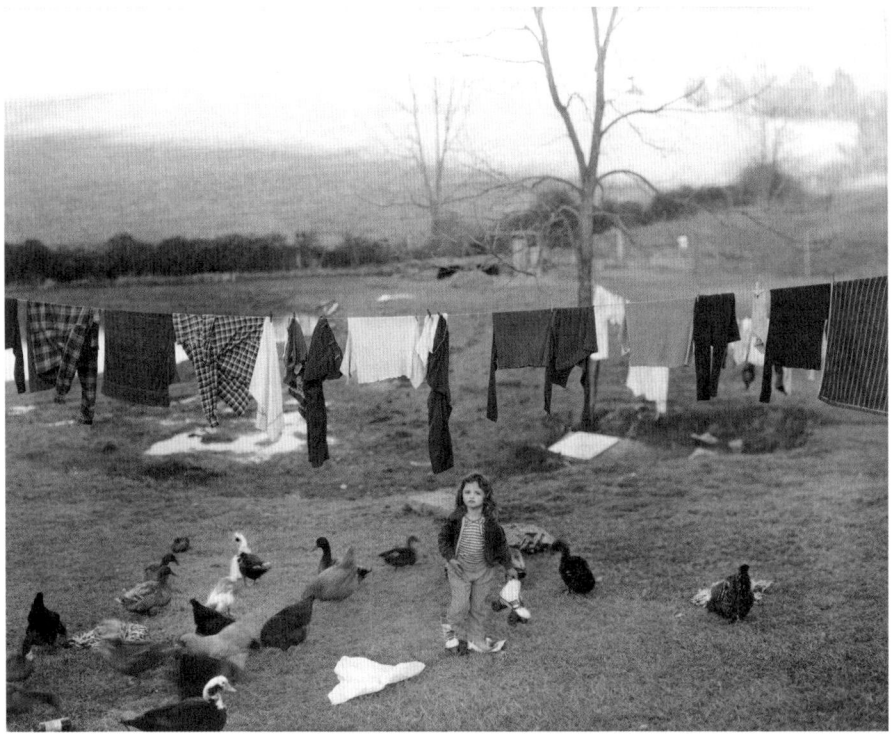

One day when we arrived, Leslie had grabbed up a flapping, honking, dander-spewing duck and was holding it upside down by the yellow feet. We watched in fascination as she fed the head and long neck down an aluminum funnel-like contraption that was affixed to the fence post. As the duck was squeezed into the funnel, the flapping diminished and pretty soon out of the lower cone-hole emerged the beak and head, then the neck of the still-squawking bird. One quick flick of Leslie's knife at the touchingly vulnerable throat and the bird was silenced, blood pouring into the bucket below.

By that time, of course, never one to miss the photographic opportunities at an execution, I had run back to the car, grabbed my camera, and had it set up at the ready. The kids were backing away, staring in horror and fascination as the yellow legs began to droop. Brightly, I inquired, "Who wants to be in this picture?" and three pale faces swiveled to me in disbelief.

It ended up being Jessie, my brave girl, with Emmett willing to play his part a safe distance away.

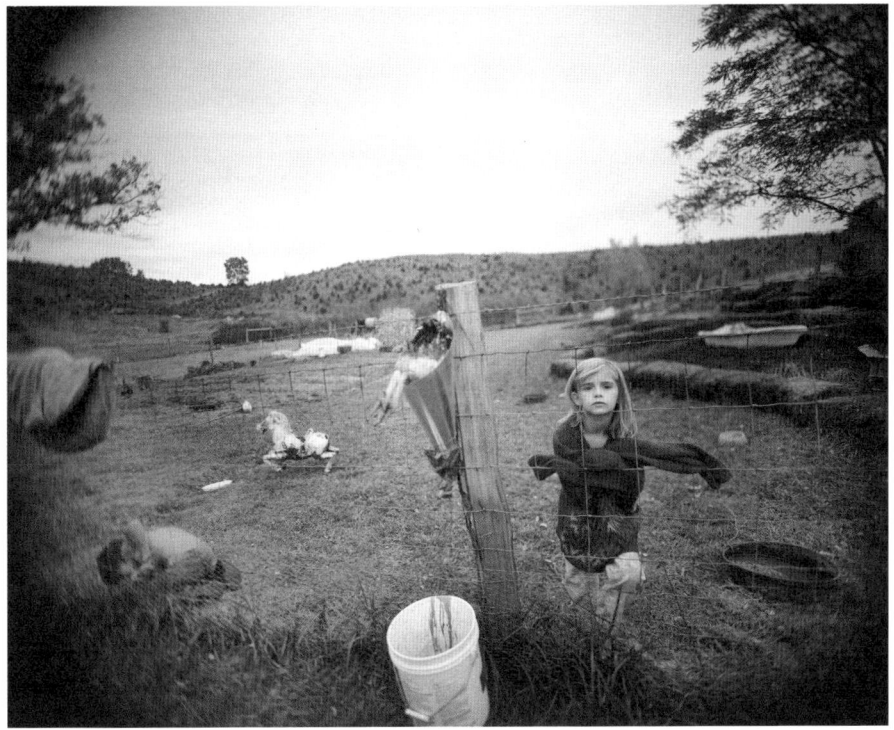

(In a notable supporting role here is the ex–carousel horse that Leslie was only too happy to get out of her yard and that has made guest appearances in many of my pictures over the years, living now as a double amputee on my studio porch.)

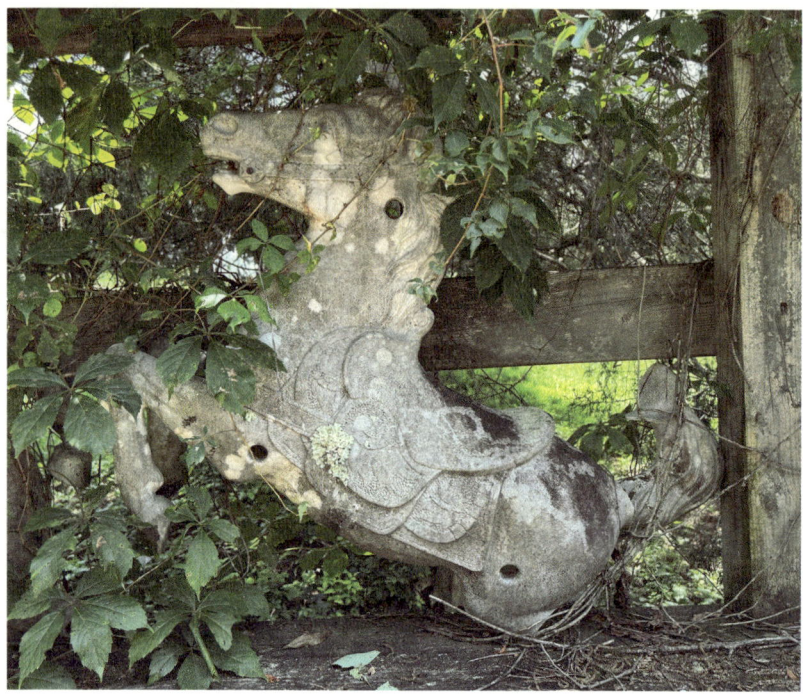

For whatever reason, I didn't think the original picture was any good—although almost forty years later I rather like it—so I asked Leslie if the next time she was slaughtering she would be willing to set aside a duck for me so I could try to reshoot the picture. She obliged, putting an exsanguinated carcass in the freezer so that I could come get it any time for a repeat picture.

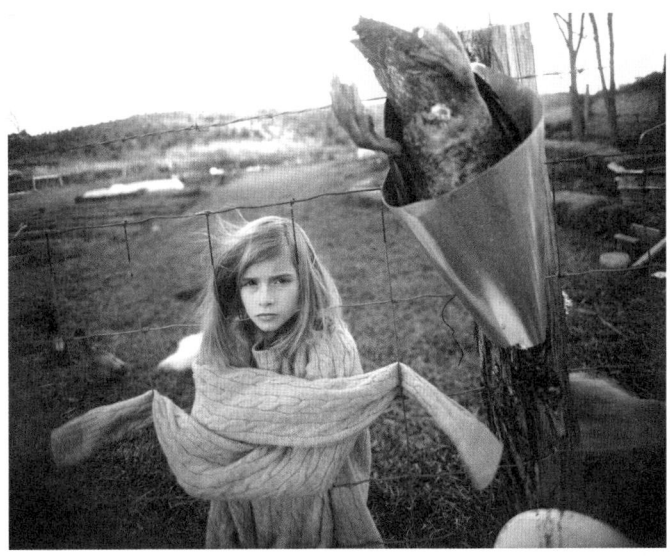

Or, as it happened, dozens of repeat pictures. I tried taking that damn duck picture so often that its wing-feathers snapped and the jagged, hollow quills threatened to stab Leslie every time she reached into the freezer that winter.

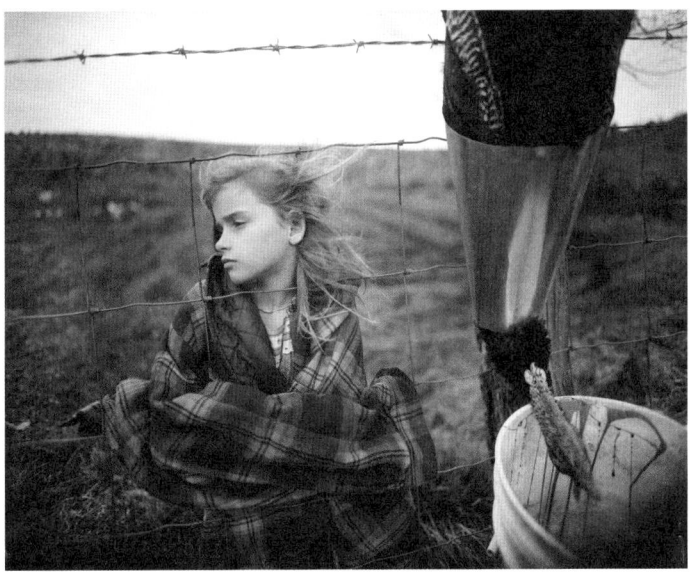

Even the indefatigable Jessie flagged.

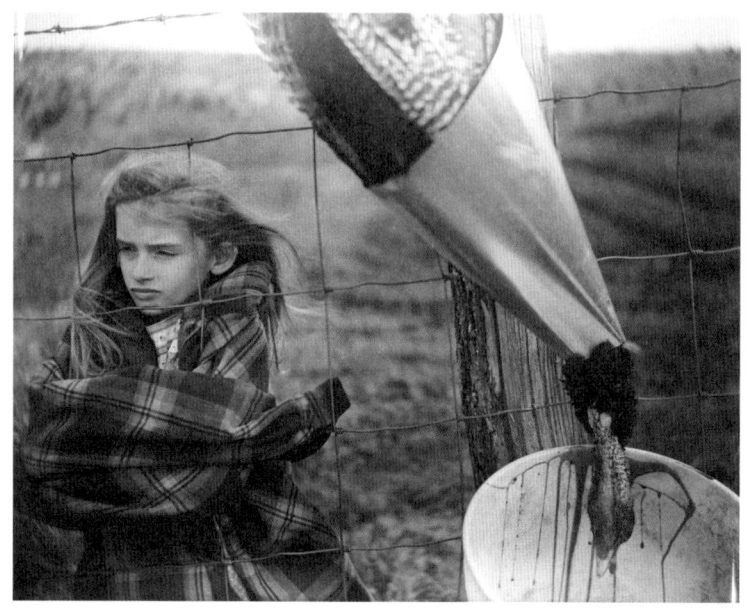

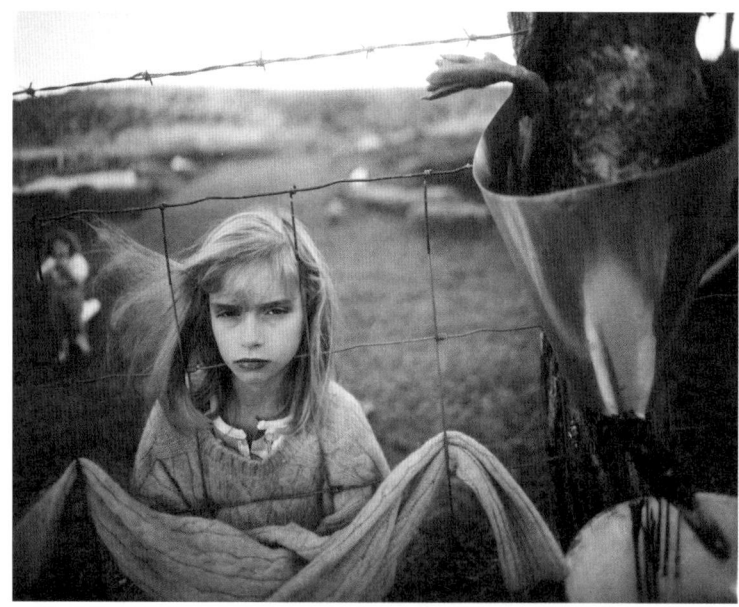

A few times I had to call in the understudies.

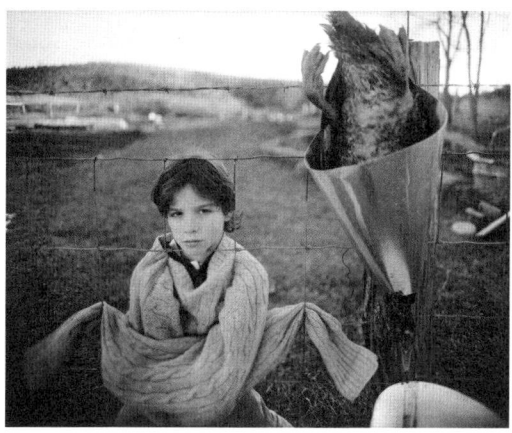

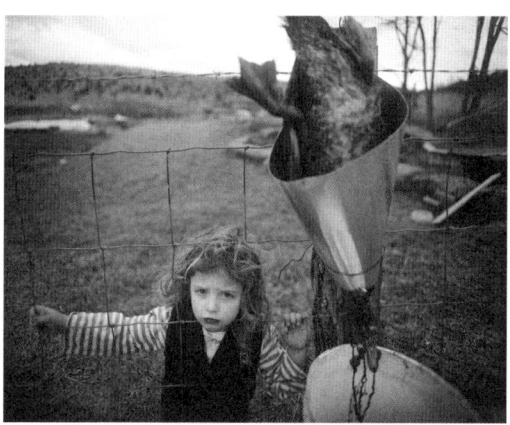

Of course, I had to bring my own blood each time, having found the Karo syrup I tried the first few times unconvincing and that I once hastily stuffed back into my camera bag loosely capped after dripping it onto the bucket—with a predictably bad result. At least it wasn't the jar of blood.

As winter turned to spring, and we were still ramming the rock-hard carcass into the cone, and likewise ramming this dumb idea into the dead end where it clearly was headed, Jessie put her foot down and asked for a reward: a red taffeta ball gown she had seen at the Stonewall Jackson Hospital Thrift Shop the week before. The afternoon we were to take our last trip to the cone, I dashed to the thrift shop and grabbed it, standing across the card table from the Pink Lady volunteer as she tucked the handful of dollars into a metal box and expertly rolled up the red dress in a spread of newspaper. No matter how briefly I was in that shop, I always seemed to run into one of our local nutters—you know how a small town loves its characters—most memorably once seen lugging two brown paper grocery bags full of cash from his sale of a Twombly painting he had kept behind his sofa for forty years. And sure enough, he swaggered down the ramp, yelling his usual question: "Who's died? Anybody in my size?"

This man had been a scourge of my young life, having fallen in love with my father, who was his medical doctor, and becoming enraged by the rebuff he received. It was doubtless a kind and courtly one, as befitted my father's nonjudgmental personality, but a rebuff all the same. He then sued my father, saying he had fallen off the swivel stool used for examinations, and when that didn't work, he burst into the office and threatened my father with a gun. My Texan father was no stranger to guns and began concealing them in both the house and the office, and installed a warning buzzer beneath his secretary's desk at the office. I have a clear memory of his little derringer once lying casually beside him as we ate dinner.

But even with the gift of the red gown, this duck picture couldn't be saved. Not that it was Jessie's fault, mind you; it was 100 percent my fault. The more times I tried, the worse it got. In the end, the first picture was probably the best, just not good enough. Mila Sevo, my archival-studies summer intern (who as I write is struggling through the boxes of negatives) reported to me last week that so far, she has found some *fifty-eight* negatives of dead-duck pictures. I suppose that knowing when to stop is just as important as knowing when to push through—although perhaps it's only the difference between the unvanquished, determined monkey typist who happens to be stone-blind and the equally tenacious seeing monkey who thinks he may discern a hidden pattern and attacks the keys in a frenzied search for it.

So often I would feel a great picture *just there*, teasingly close, with skittish, floating elements—the insolent cast of an eye, the pert lip-curl—that simply needed to lock into their divinely determined slot. Those times I also stuck with it—most memorably, and successfully, with the picture of Emmett in the river I described taking in *Hold Still*. The first time I saw Jessie holding a candy cigarette, looking like something out of a 1920s Hollywood movie still, I knew there was a story there and I began corralling the supporting elements for a picture that I built as carefully as a mason knits together a stone wall. I returned to it over and over again.

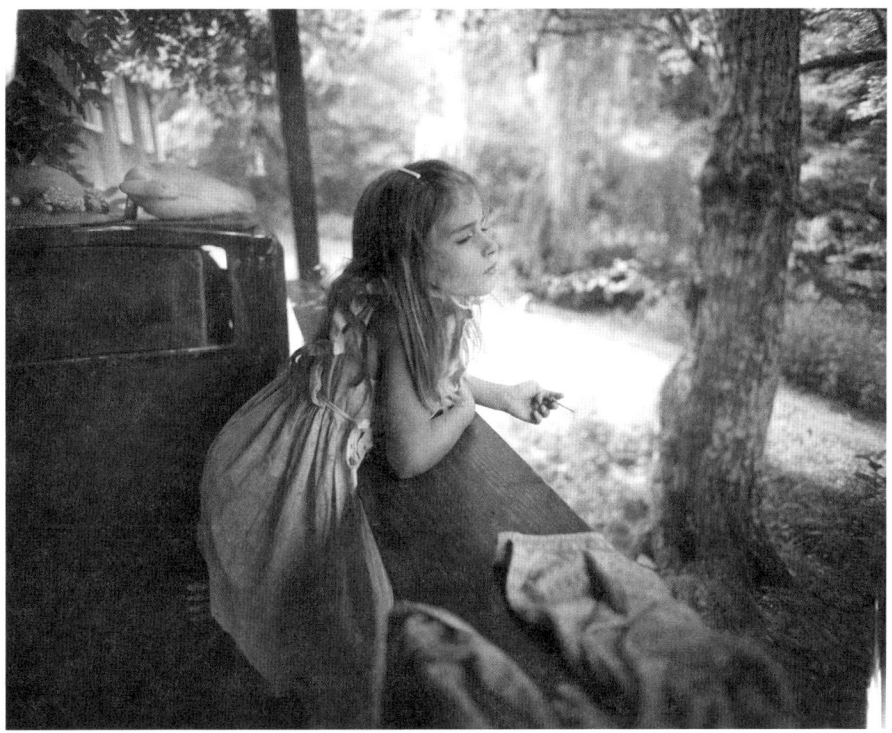

Many boxes of candy cigarettes.

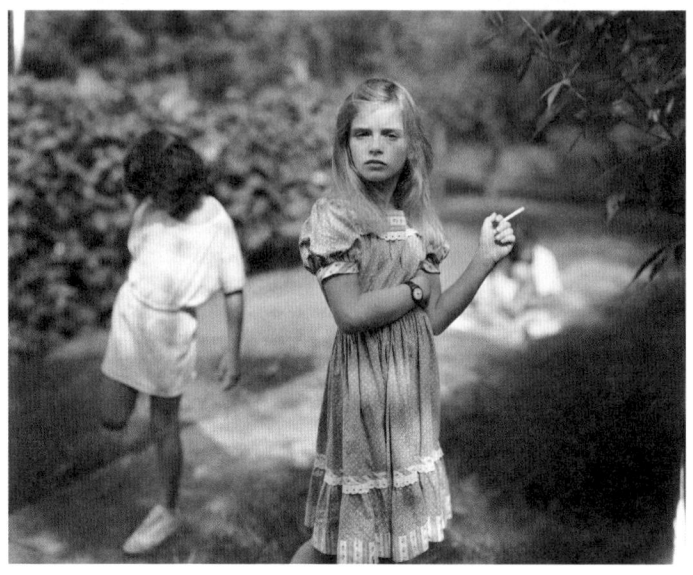

Many annoyed extras: Jessie's friend Rachel, my mother, Emmett,

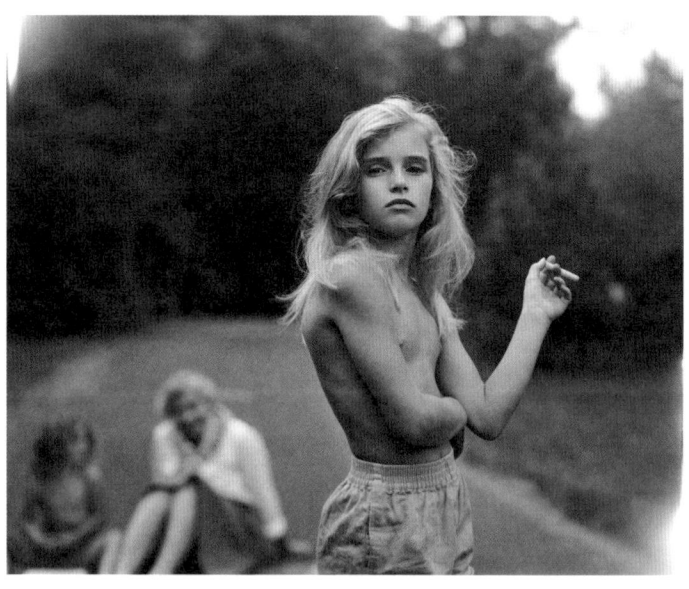

and especially Virginia.

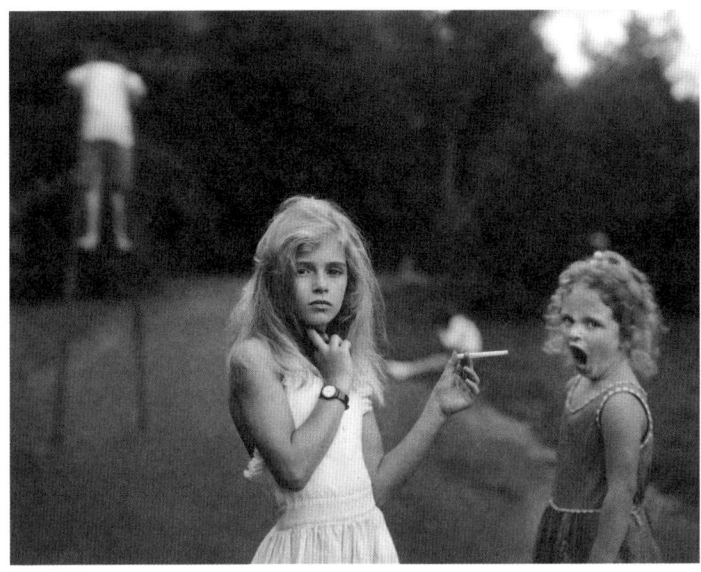

And then, the right keys were struck, at the miraculous right time:
M-O-B-Y-D-I-C-K.

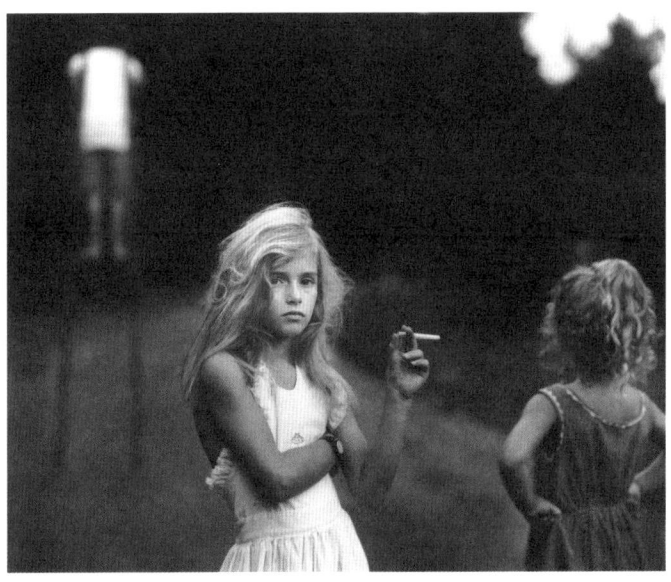

I went to the Deep South two more times, despite that frustrating, minimally productive first trip. Or, because of it. *"If at first you don't succeed . . ."* should be carved on my tombstone. And, so that I could share in the sentiment he expressed on his, I should be buried next to Gustave Flaubert. He beat me to the best epitaph of all, and one that basically sums up my life as well: *"He stayed home and worked."*

I had gotten just enough good pictures on that first trip to make me believe that it was possible, if the film factories worked overtime to make 8 × 10 Tri-X and I used every existing sheet of it, to get a few more. To cover my ass, I took along my collodion darkroom for those times when it was too cheerfully sunny to get a picture that had the murky, crepuscular, bad mood I was after.

I also packed my father's adorable, Lilliputian derringer, and I see now that my pretravel notes suggest that I should "learn to shoot." The gun is so tiny that Virginia was shooting it at age five . . .

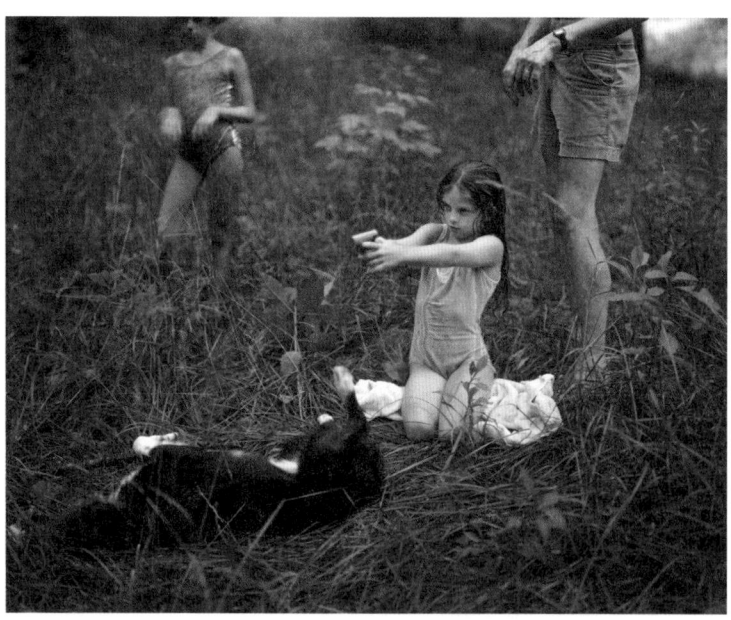

but that doesn't mean that I couldn't have done some damage with it, as long as my assailant was a refrigerator no more than ten feet away.

For travel listening, I had rented more audiobooks, among them, fittingly, *Moby Dick* and Joseph Conrad's *Heart of Darkness*. The days were long and lonely, the distances, though not watery, were vast, and the social, racial, and historical complexities unavoidable. *Call me Ishmael*, I thought, kneeling in the back of the Suburban and banging my head as I folded my bedding, still damp with the night's sweat. Stepping outside into whatever skeezy campground, I would study the maps, which revealed an expanse of distressingly unlimited possibilities, and randomly choose the day's destination.

My high school English teacher, Ray Goodlatte, once assigned a Wordsworth poem with a line about cloistered nuns not chafing at their confinement and hermits contentedly chilling in their cells (I might be misremembering this: Do hermits have cells? I thought it was caves). The point was that they accepted with equanimity the limitations imposed on them, which paradoxically encouraged their creativity, just as Wordsworth himself embraced the restrictions of the sonnet form in which he had chosen to write.

Ray had asked the class what the Wordsworth poem meant to us and we rebellious teenagers heaped scorn on the capitulation of the captives— we wanted freedom: no limits, no strictures, wide-open creative territory. And indeed, that was the landscape I explored for years, promiscuously taking pictures of almost everything that crossed my path, just for the sake of seeing what it would look like—in a photograph. And that is how it should be: Most creative people need a period, or a lifetime in some cases, of unfettered artistic exploration.

But, in my case, despite being an unregenerate rebel most of my young life, I began to feel what Wordsworth called the "weight of liberty." Without quite realizing it, I began to give myself assignments; parameters within which to work. Like using just one shutter speed or one lens, or only taking pictures that had chiffon in them, or limiting my subjects to the age of twelve, or, most memorably, insisting on hand-holding my large-format view camera, making me the butt of jokes for years.

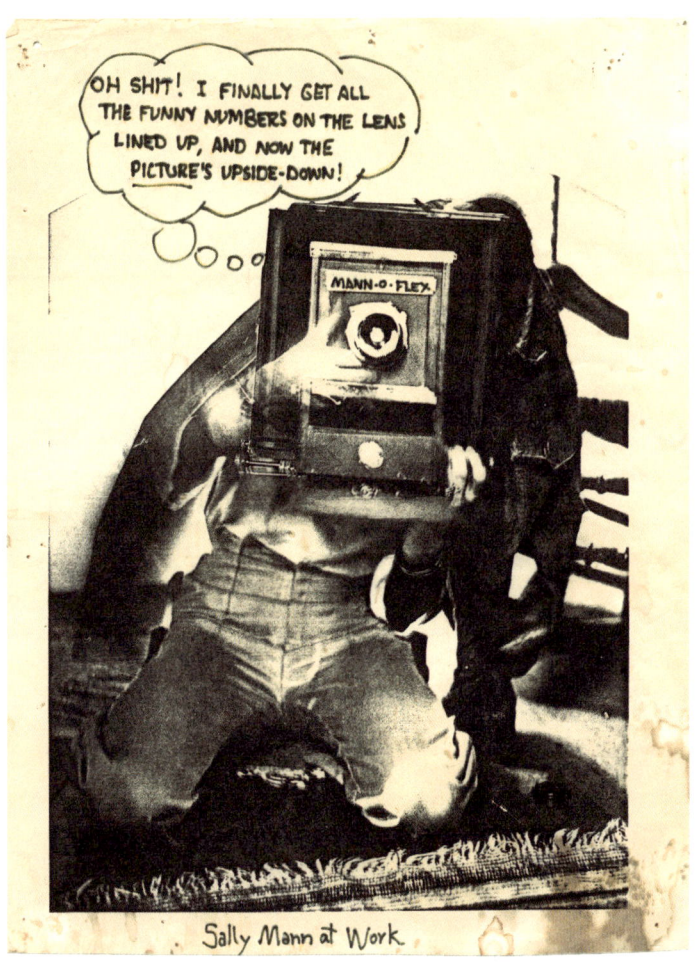

Sally Mann at Work

For a personality like mine, perhaps best visually represented by the ball of boisterous scribble that floats above the head of a cartoon character, there was freedom in constriction. I once remarked that I would be happiest making work in an airplane bathroom, rather than choosing among the insurmountable opportunities outside it. Henry James in

The Aspern Papers describes this as "that odd law which somehow always makes the minimum of valid suggestion serve the man of imagination better than the maximum." I was pleased, sometime later, to read that Frank Gehry, a man not known for his artistic restraint, once said that his hardest project was one in which the client said: "Just build whatever you want."

And, whatever I wanted, photographically, was right outside the Suburban those mornings—a lot of it. In fact, maybe too much of it. Rereading the notes I wrote on the first trip down south, I think the root cause of my fretfulness was option paralysis; I was trying to home in on just one thing—at the outset, the Mississippi River, which proved to be not the shimmering poetic subject I had hoped—while being presented with an array of anxiety-producing aesthetic possibilities. As Dave and Virginia sat patiently by the side of the road in those first few travel days, I reverted to my original practice of indiscriminate shooting, which over the years I have found to be the best way to discover your true subject, and fast. It will draw you to it like a magnet.

What I was drawn to, irresistibly and ineluctably on each subsequent trip, was the deep melancholy of the solitary, and believe you me, there's plenty of that down south. I had my subject: vine-covered sugar furnaces; an abandoned shotgun cabin surrounded by acres of cotton; a lightning-split remnant of the primeval forest that had been ripped from the rich soil of the Delta; one charred upright that was all that remained of a torched wooden church, with, weirdly, a greasily red tampon at its base; a wire-enclosed cemetery in the middle of goddamned nowhere. Always a cemetery. Always the souls of the dead. Always a reminder that on the pain-haunted, cruelty-haunted soil on which I planted my tripod legs had been "groves of death," like the burial grounds of the enslaved that Conrad found along the Congo River.

Eerily, I found the voice of Conrad speaking to me as I drove, and with one hand on the wheel, I scrawled out this quote on the title page of my Lonely Planet guide:

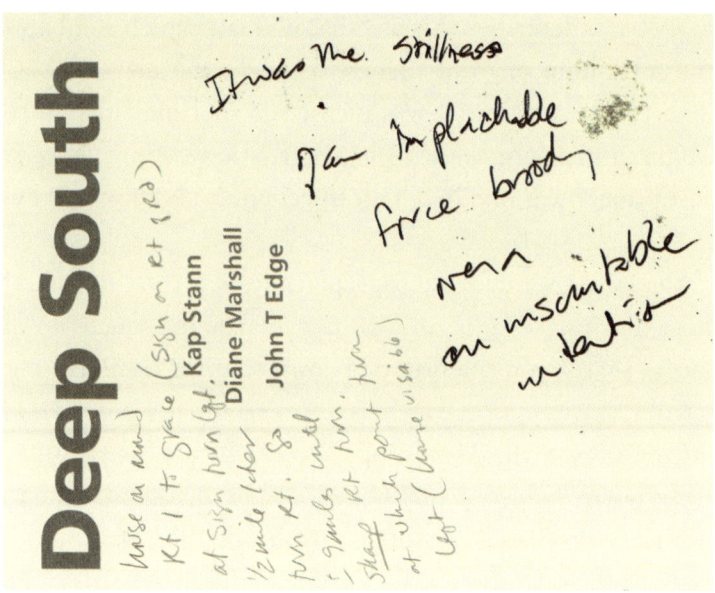

"*It was the stillness of an implacable force brooding over an inscrutable intention.*"

Good one.

I had the brooding going, implacable and fierce, and god knows the intention was occasionally inscrutable, but as I traveled, it became clear. I was taking the same picture, over and over. It was that same tree, the one I took in the dead-end magnolia cemetery while I waited for Dave to conjure his walrus-mustached ancestor, the same one as the Rowan Oak cypress on that first day in Oxford. I shot tree after tree, screeching to a halt at the sight of a lone specimen, a grueling, camera-hauling mile across a newly tilled field, each picture almost right, but each one not quite the unassailably definitive picture, emblematic of both those travels and, metaphorically, the South itself.

I've written before about the miraculous, furnished house that was loaned to me at just about the time I thought I would lose my mind with what my father referred to as "the loneliness of the long distance" (he wrote that in his journal after he had spent five scary nights hoofing it on a jungle trail from Burma to Siam in 1937). My nights weren't necessarily scary, and after all I had the derringer, but damn if I wasn't ready to have a shower and sleep in a real bed. And who, of all people, had washed up that same day and in that same backwater of Louisiana as I had? The California photographer Richard Misrach, whom I had first met when we were both instructors at the Ansel Adams Workshops and who also worked with an 8 × 10 view camera, albeit in color.

Once in the 1990s, Richard had passed through Lexington, staying over with us a few days, and had marveled at the beauty of the area. When he suggested that he might stay a few more days and take some pictures around my county, I bristled with possessiveness. This was my territory, my postage stamp, my Hale County, my own Yoknapatawpha. He had no right to swoop in here from his territory, the Western deserts, and start taking my pictures. It was partly in response to his visit, which Richard, sensing my defensiveness, graciously kept to a social one, that I began taking my own 8 × 10 pictures of my beautiful home territory. And yet here we both were, Richard and I, interlopers in the lifelong territory of the Mississippi photographers Maude and Lang Clay, as well as, of course, Maude's uncle, Bill Eggleston, in my case ripping them off just as I had feared Richard was going to rip me off years before. Aesthetic territorialism, I guess. Richard and I spent the whole afternoon taking pictures together. Of all the lonely places I had been on this trip, most of which I had reasonably described as backwaters, there are few that answer so completely to that description as the dirt roads we drove that day, and I was glad I had Richard with me. That deep melancholy of the solitary gets a whole lot deeper, and sometimes a whole lot scarier, when you're alone.

Here are my notes from that day:

We met at noon on the 28th (Jessie's birthday!). I know we spent that whole afternoon shooting—I took the Tree with 2 Streaks, *several dusty roads, those bowed grasses . . . nothing brilliant but can't say I didn't try.*

Richard wasn't shooting, except maybe some digital color, but was gracious and patient with me while I labored along, always thinking that this one would be it. And of course, it never was. I worked until night fell and the ground mist rose, which I also shot, but, of course: all duds.

Went back to the house, had several many drinks, as we say. Richard is a light-weight, apparently; he staggered up the stairs by 9, in full woozitude. I stayed up a while longer to unload and reload film, a job I hate. It involves sitting legs splayed out on the bathroom floor (and I've been in some hotels whose floor you really don't want to sit on) and twisting my sticky arms into the elasti-cized holes of the changing tent where they heat up to about 200 degrees. My back hurts like hell, hunched over the armholes. My hips too. It takes a long time and when the mosquitoes land on you and start their evening feast, you can do nothing about it, or risk ruining the film. Good thing I'd had those gin and tonics.

When I got up in the morning there it was: Right outside the back door, the barbed-wire-scarred tree in the fog, lifting fast. So glad I had taken the time before bed to reload my film holders. I was ready to go, quick, quick, quick!!! Grab camera, lenses, film holders, set up tripod, struggle with that stupid screw attachment, make all the decisions: which lens, which angle, how close, what's that damn thing on the fence behind the tree, shitshitshit, is it a plastic bag? well, nevermind, get the picture before the fog lifts, ortho film or Tri-X? OK some of both, what's the exposure, where is the light meter, lost as usual, well, I can just guess . . . no, here it is, my old Weston meter from 1969, who knows if it's even right, should I use incident or reflective when it's foggy like this? Deci-sions, decisions, decisions . . . I shot so many frames, my hands shaking with excitement, you'd think it was the Zapruder film I was making.

It must have been entertaining for Richard watching this frantic, inept performance. He photographed the aftermath, the camera still set up, the sun shining in. The fog drifting away across the field. Me probably collapsed inside with a washcloth over my forehead, feeling like I had done a day's work. After a while, we went for a run, he peeled off, and I managed to gut out my 3 miles in some really serious Louisiana heat.

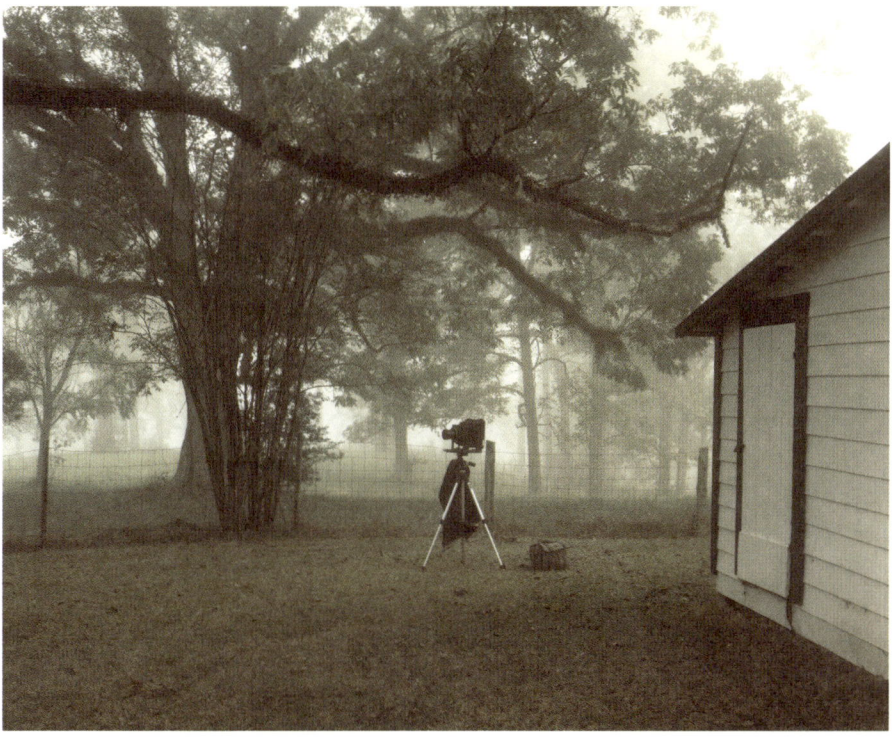

At that point I was pretty sure that I might have gotten a good picture, if I didn't screw it up unloading the film holders or developing the negative or by contriving some other way to ruin it. For a die-hard pessimist like me, that's a rare and exhilarating feeling, however ephemeral. When you get a good picture, after taking so many that you know will end up with the other duds in the Loser cabinet, the scene is charged for just that instant with a numinous shimmer—no longer commonplace but instead alive with a transformative razzle-dazzle. I am far from spiritual, but I have experienced, convincingly, the ineffable magic by which obsession, frustration, repetition, and serendipity miraculously transfigure that thin, Nabokovian slice of time, that tenth of a second, into something eternal.

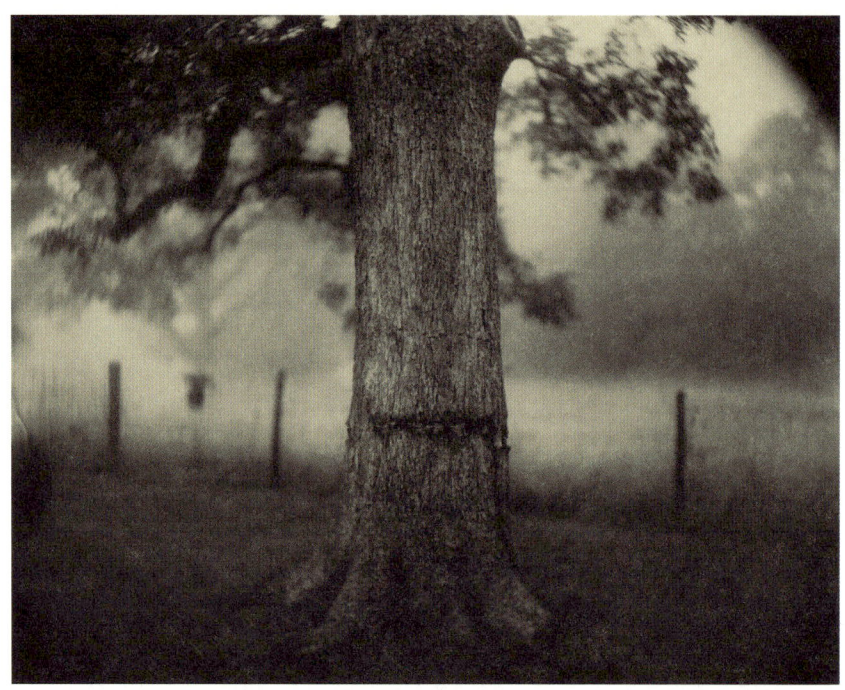

By the time Richard pulled out for his drive back to the airport and I began packing my stuff for the rest of the trip, the sun was up and the scarred tree was just an ordinary tree, no shimmer, no razzle-dazzle magic. Just a tree that had an unfortunate encounter with the great American scourge, barbed wire.

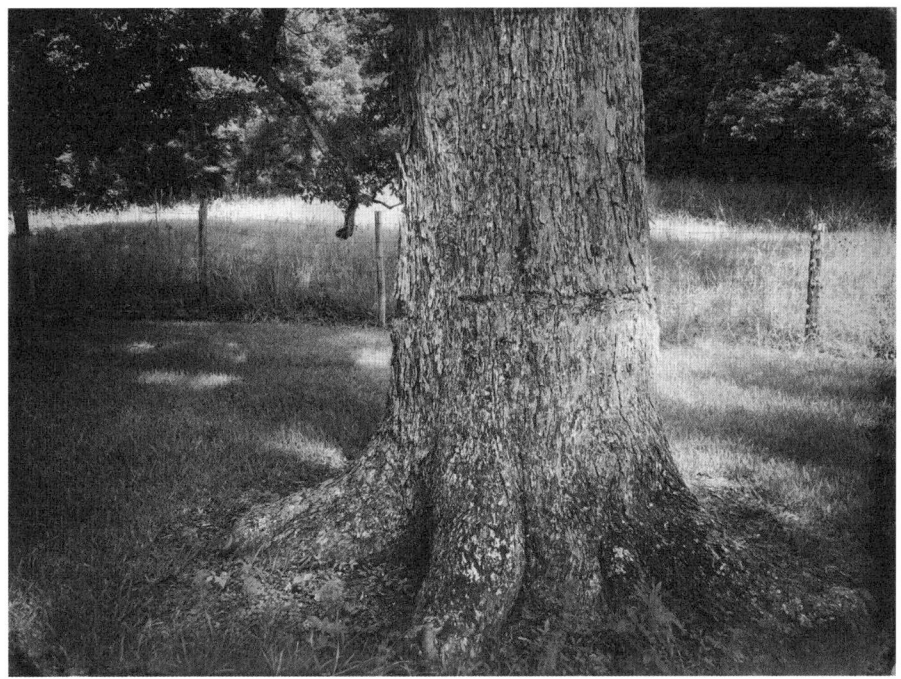

I am a very lucky monkey.

10

Your Darlings

In writing, you must kill all your darlings.
—William Faulkner

Sometimes other people kill them: They're outright censored, like the Qatar pictures, or they're ignored; not included in shows, not published in anthologies, and not collected by museums. I've had my share of that. But in other cases, you have to do it yourself.

Sure, they're your darlings, but if they're not good enough, send them straight to the choppy-chop. Faulkner was right about that, even if he wasn't the originator of the famous quote (it was a Brit with the positively Wodehousian name of Sir Arthur Quiller-Couch) and didn't necessarily think he needed to apply it to his own writing; if one thing in your creative career will define your work for all time, it will be your editorial rigor.

The perplexing refusal by an otherwise reasonable quarterly to publish those Qatar desert pictures, and other instances of censorship throughout my career, have often been easier to accept than my own self-imposed censorship, sometimes protective, often a result of commonsense editing, or, to my chagrin, just bad judgment. But on balance, I should have done a ton more of it. A ton.

It is hard to be at this stage in my career and find myself cringing as I page through my own books, mentally razoring out the occasional page. But I do, and frequently ask myself what the hell I was thinking. Sometimes I know the answer—I thought those faces would look good if the eyes were all at the same height, like an eye horizon, across which you could hop visually, brow-to-brow, as you turned the pages (*What Remains*, pages 103–129).

Too clever by half. Or I thought (*Immediate Family*, 1992) that it might be amusing to take a glancing kick at the buzzing cultural hornet's nest of the time and populate that book with especially provocative pictures, even if those sixty-five images didn't necessarily reflect the overall feel of the Family Pictures project, which had many times that number of negatives. (In fact, 4,338 black-and-white and 1,919 color, most unpublished to this day.) One can take only so many stings, even when they're not unexpected.

And sometimes what I was thinking remains a mystery to me, like when I discover pictures that I never let sail out into the world and should have. But more frequently, I wonder at my judgment when I see work out there that never should have made it out of dry dock, at which point I give a defeated mental shrug, assuming that, at the time, I was hoping to make the image fit into an aesthetic or a now-forgotten concept.

Which we all do. But perhaps we should do it in private, like going into the dressing room to try to get those expensive pants to button, at which point we should take a long, hard look and imagine living with them ten years and ten more pounds down the road. If something you are working on is iffy, on some level, usually the gut level, you will know it is. Don't ask for anyone else's opinion ("I'm sure those jeans will stretch out, but they still look great on you"). Always trust your ambivalence. Set the work aside for a while and when you come back for it, you will know.

I'm pretty sure everybody has these moments; nobody makes consistently brilliant work. But the impact of what little brilliant work we do make will be diluted by the mediocre work if it's out there too, like a drop of India ink in water. You want only the full-strength, high-test stuff in the world. Wait until you have a lot of it, even if it's decades, ruthlessly cull out the mediocrities, even if you love them, then slip the winches and set the good stuff out to sea.

In my case, it was easy to wait out those early decades, because nobody wanted to see my work anyway. I adroitly protected myself from rejections with a tissue of lies, and I can recommend this as an effective strategy: People don't care to see your work? Doors slammed in your face?

Convince yourself that it was you who did the slamming and there you are, leaning against the door to keep the clamoring crowd of dealers, collectors, and editors *out*. You wouldn't let them hang a damn show or publish your book even if they got down on their knees and begged you for it.

I had this defensive technique figured out as early as February 1979—having at that point never taken a picture worth anyone banging down even the flimsiest door—when I wrote this to Ted (large-format geezers will recognize the paper as the yellow tissue Kodak used to put in-between sheets of 8 × 10 film. Ms. Frugality here was never one to waste a perfectly good piece of paper!).

> attitude toward GREAT FAME. It has proven so successful, in the trial runs that I've given it, that I have taken it to heart: Absolute indifference, absoulte calm, absolute confidence. It worked well until I treed to plug in that third element....Indifferenee and calm came easy, but the confidence comes hard.

Not that anyone was offering me "GREAT FAME," mind you. But just in case anyone tried to press it on me, I was ready to fight them off. Absolute (or "absoulte") indifference, calm, and confidence. Don't you be trying to make an art star out of *me*!

We all ask the big, existential questions ("What are we doing this for?" "What do we really want?"), but my tissue of protective lies grew to encompass my insistence that I didn't care about any of it, not even selling prints. The letter, below, is from 1985, when, with three children to feed and educate, I most emphatically *did* care.

> what I see is: taking down the show and carrying it home and putting it back in it's dear little box and, well, now what? What are we doing this for? Do you ever ask yourself that question? What do we really want? What is the thing that gives pleasure? What is the goal, after all? Where are the rewards when it's all said and done, wouldn't we rather be sitting out on the deck with a fresh gin and tonic in our hands surveying the kids gambolling in the sunset and patting the dog? I mean it? Do I care about New York? Shit,no. Do I care if I sell prints no and even more emphatically np. What I care about and what gives me the most pleasure is that instant, when you turn on the lights and lift the film out of the fixer and turn the music up real loud and do a little crab step across the darkroom floor. I would just die for that feeling, that is it, for me, that is what matters and in the end, all work becomes "old work" from that moment on.

And, in 1986—thank god I had gotten a computer by then with which I could correct my two-fingered typing—I had further protected myself by accepting the inevitable; my "minor star" status in the vast galaxy of art stardom, rhapsodically insisting that a fully lived life and the joy of blessed motherhood were all the reward I needed.

```
                            You know, Ted, I'm glad
that fool show is over. I'm glad it's all behind me because I
had to do it but I sure don`t want to do much more of it. It
actually was several years ago that I realized that there would
never really be any blockbuster shows for me and that I would
always just plod along on the edges of the art world's
consciousness, never quite becoming famous, never quite drifting
out into space either, always just remaining like some nagging
little minor star, some small, unnamed planet out there. There
are times when I'd love to see some cashier's face light up in
recognition or see a kindly review in the Times but honestly
Ted, my life is just so full right now that those rewards seem
skimpy. Do you know what I mean? I feel somehow already pumped
up, already full of the wealth of living, sometimes I look at
these lithe, lovely, spirited children of mine and I wonder why
I ever even bother to take pictures. Then, of course, I remember
```

The whole thing was disingenuous, to say the least, but especially the part about the "skimpy rewards." It was an undeniable thrill when I gave my credit card on a phone order a few years after this protesteth-too-much letter and was asked, "Not Sally Mann, the photographer?" I mean a real thrill.

But it is not disingenuous to make the argument for holding back your work, even if that means a long period of artistic obscurity, deliberate or not. If you are willing to accept that your success, if it comes, will be later in your career, you can make your art or write your books without regard for the all-consuming, and often fickle, marketplace. Being unrecognized and especially not being identified with a particular style allows us to make the work that matters to us, irrespective of whether it would sell.

For me, staying home and enjoying the simple life of a nineteenth-century Flaubertian recluse, which is what I do 99 percent of the time, helps with this approach, and perhaps something like it could work for you. Nevertheless, even today I find that I need to employ that still-serviceable protective covering, spun from the mendacious pluck, false confidence, and timeworn lies I wanted to believe, especially when I suffer rejections that sting. (Yes, I do, and yes, they still do.) All the while we keep working, making our art, whatever it is. It's our job, just like any other job, only with longer hours.

So, double bolt that mythically bulging door, send away all the art-world impresarios and agents, do not succumb to jealousy or study the auction results, go back into your studio, sit at your desk, make your work, and ruthlessly toss out whatever isn't good enough, for whatever reason. Do that for the next twenty-five years.

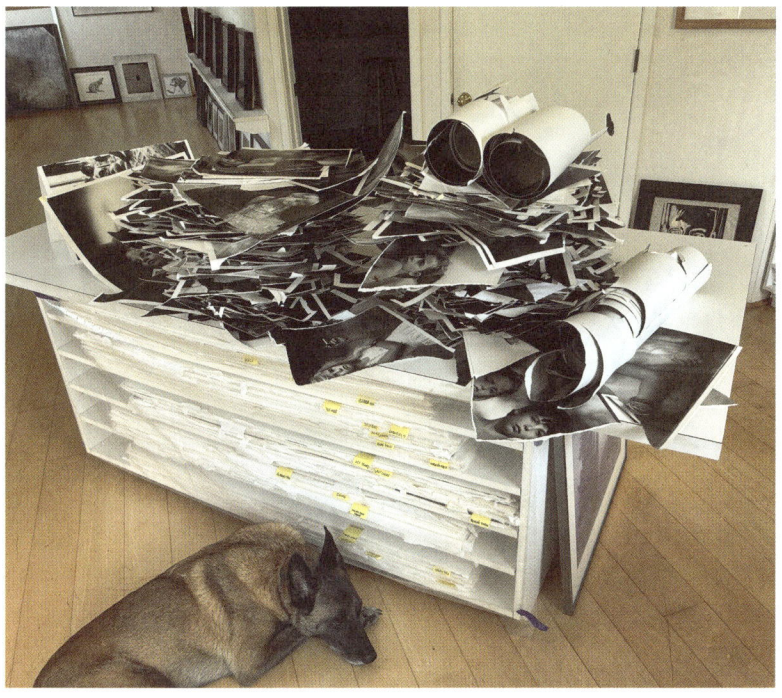

(Like so: 643 imperfect Family Pictures prints torn up and headed for the landfill, and one perfect dog.)

Once you're a few years into that quarter century of hard work, how do you decide what to keep and what to toss? Back in the old days, the way I would decide if an image was going to work or not was, as we have seen, to make contact prints and pushpin them on the darkroom bulletin board.

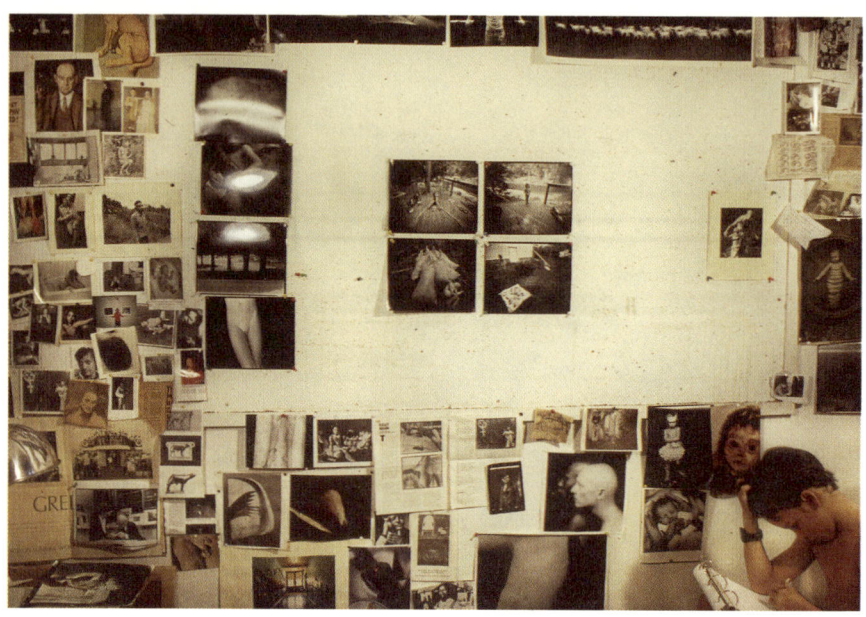

Walking by twenty times a day, it was neither my conscious brain nor my avid eye that determined the good ones; my viscera did that. And only when I wasn't asking. The trick is to eye things askance, in passing, in the liminal moments while thinking about your failed car inspection, and maybe, if you're lucky, one of the images will give you an unmistakable gut-flutter, an internal vibration like a tree full of starlings.

That's the one! Don't second-guess it. Don't stand there and make a long, windy case for why the other ones might be just as good. Reason and analysis don't work, but you can't mistake that punch to the gut, or the diaphragmic zephyr, or Robert Frost's immortal wound to the soul. Your gut language, to whatever degree emphatic, is the first, and last, word on the subject.

Immediately take the losers down and put more prints up. In the snapshot above I was having one of those especially lucky weeks—of the four in play in the center of the wall, the bottom two I kept, they're in *Immediate Family*; everything else was tossed onto the reject piles. Emmett, oblivious here, does his math homework. Occasionally the kids and sometimes a few select friends would chime in, but I'm so completely gut-dependent that I usually didn't listen to them. There were exceptions. My friend Peter C. Jones once passed through for a visit and has never tired of reminding me about his role in bringing to light one of my now-iconic Family Pictures.

He was pawing through the disorganized piles of reject prints and negatives that typically covered my counters and came upon the five failed pictures I'd made the week before of Jessie with spent flowers draped across her shoulders. With a triumphant exclamation he snatched one out of the pile and bellowed, "What the hell is wrong with this one? What were you thinking? Why on earth is this in the junkheap?" while indignantly waving *Night Blooming Cereus*. It chagrins me to report that he was spot-on correct, that I had missed it and thrown the good one out with the four duds. He has rightfully dined out on that story for eons, describing himself as the godparent, if not the actual creator, of that photograph.

Nope.   Nope.

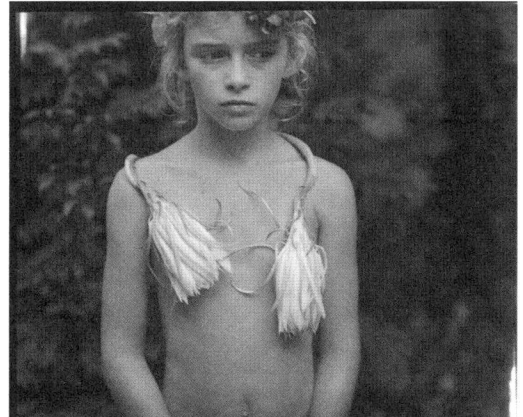
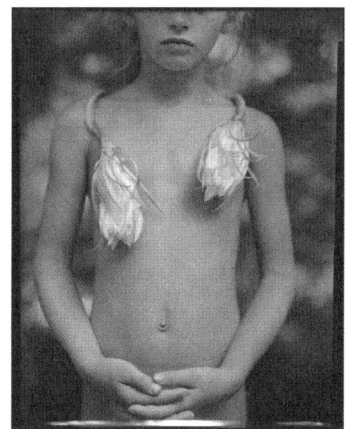

Yes!

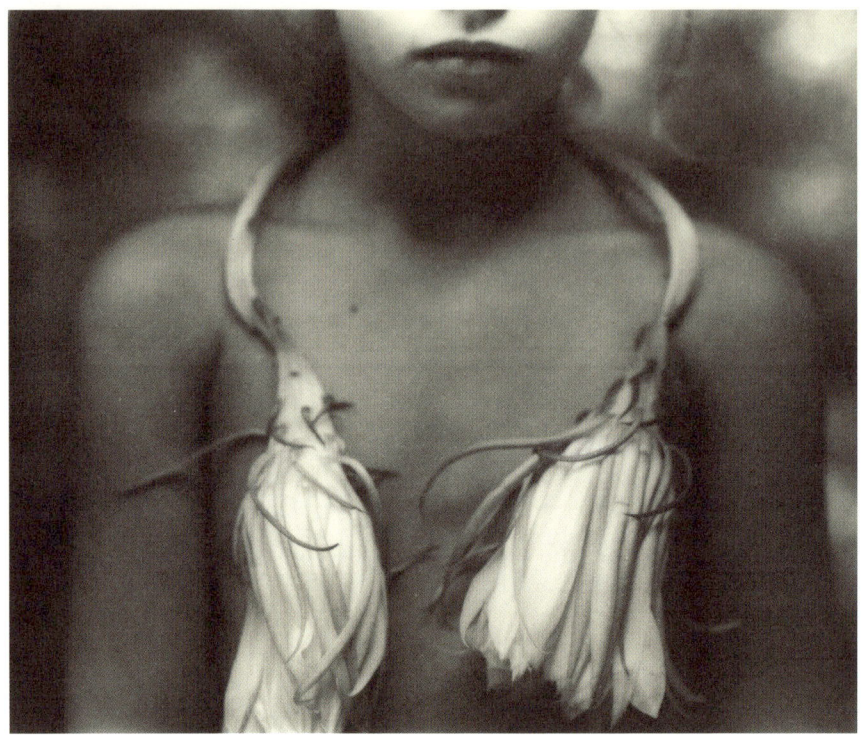

And now, years later, I don't need the distant but still-audible echo of my friend to know that I missed some other good work in my early edits. Thinking back, it isn't so much that I missed a few good images, although that is true too, it's more that I lacked a level of subtlety and critical vision that would have benefitted the whole body of work. With the images I chose to publish in *Immediate Family*, I was sledgehammering my way into the edifice of visual consciousness, when a ball-peen tap might have sufficed. And might indeed have made my entrance more welcome. No matter what I said or wrote (*vide supra* the "Do I care about New York?" letter), I wanted attention for the work, and the easiest way to get it was obviously to put forward the most attention-grabbing imagery. That's just how it was, and I'm not necessarily proud of succumbing to that impulse.

I remember my friend Maria Hambourg handing me a book of photographs by Helen Levitt, open to the page of children running after soap bubbles, and dryly advising, "You need more bubbles." What she meant was less of the drama and more of the sweet quotidian. More Helen Levitt and less Larry Clark.

That's why those twenty-five years are important. Give yourself time to sort out what you are trying to say with your work, and whether you are saying it the right way, by which I mean the way you want it seen for all time, and, for that matter, if what you are saying is worth a damn. Your work will always have ups and downs, as this 1984 letter to Ted acknowledges, but "it <u>always comes</u>." (This sunny optimism was not normal for me. I must have mixed a particularly strong gin and tonic before I sat down to my Olivetti that night.) For sure, one thing that doesn't change is this assertion: "I just want more good work."

```
and I think, on balance, that we've done alright. I try to figure out what
I want next out of life and I just want more good work. I just want
diversity and quality, that's all. And the longer I work and the longer I
push the limits of what I think I am capable of doing, the better I
feel about being able to achieve that. Each time I sort of arbitrarily
wrap up a project and begin to flounder about, wondering what on earth
I'll follow it with and will I ever do work that is as good, it always
comes. Maybe not right away and maybe not without a few false starts
and enormous doubt but it's there and eventually I begin to hit my
stride again and that feeling of elation and power and confidence takes
over and the good flows. It's true that some years' work is better
than others, and that as time goes by I look back on some of the work
with a little embarrassment or chagrin but in the main, I think that
the stuff is strong and it just keeps getting better. ( you can tell where
I am right now in the cycle--on a real roll...let's talk about it again in
about a year when I'm lost again...) In any case I wonder from time to time
```

But even then, when I was at the very beginning of my career, I knew enough to admit to embarrassment and chagrin at work I had allowed out into the world that I shouldn't have. Of course, it's a hundred times worse now. Being presently in the process of trying to get my *soi-disant* archive in order, I have frequently gone back to those early years and fanned out a fistful of prints from the At Twelve and Family Pictures series, standing before them like a puzzled primate struggling to decipher the Tablets of the Covenant. To echo Peter: What *was* I thinking?!

Like what was wrong with these?

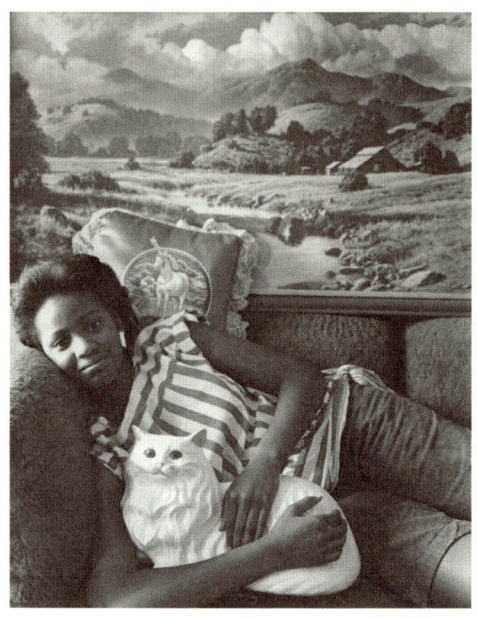

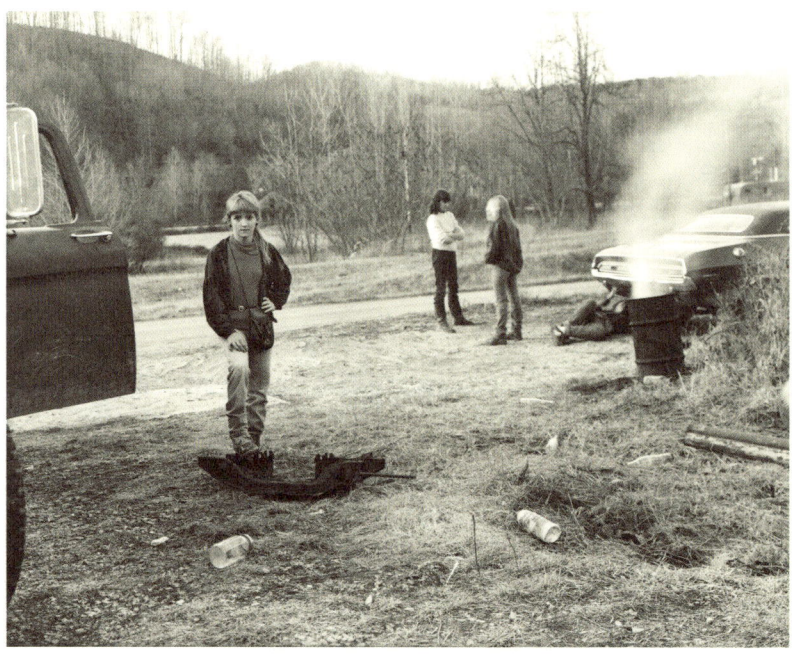

Easily distractible horses are often fitted with blinkers, cupped pieces of leather fastened to the bridle in such a way as to keep the horse from seeing anything other than what's in front of it. As I maneuvered the local roads with my 8 × 10 view camera in those tentative early days, I kept the blinkers metaphorically clamped to the sides of my head, preventing me from seeing, and then taking, pictures that did not fit whatever it was I thought I was looking for.

I don't remember now why I didn't pursue the random detour or shrank from the idea of a possibly fruitless dead end, or, god forbid, of losing my way. I stayed right in my lane. Where was the fearless iconoclast of my high school years, when I was given the nickname "Reb" for breaking every rule with the deliberate calculation of a half-wild dog measuring the backyard fence. Working along on the At Twelve project with earnest, Prufrockian caution, I made long lists of the traits or characteristics I was seeking in my girls (freckles, confidence, athleticism, height, wealth/poverty, etc.), loaded up the cameras and my kids in their car seats, and let off the clutch. It wasn't an adventure; it was a cold-blooded pursuit that allowed little deviation from the plan.

In addition to the two At Twelve pictures shown above, I have found a few other treasures that I passed over when it came time to print them for the eponymous book, but not nearly as many as I found among those 4,338 8 × 10 negatives from the Family Pictures stored in boxes, three layers deep, on shelves in my darkroom, resembling nothing so much as a forgotten cabinet in the Collyer brothers' attic. (They break down this way: Emmett: 804; Jessie: 1,068; Virginia: 1,147; Group: 894; and Miscellaneous: 422.)

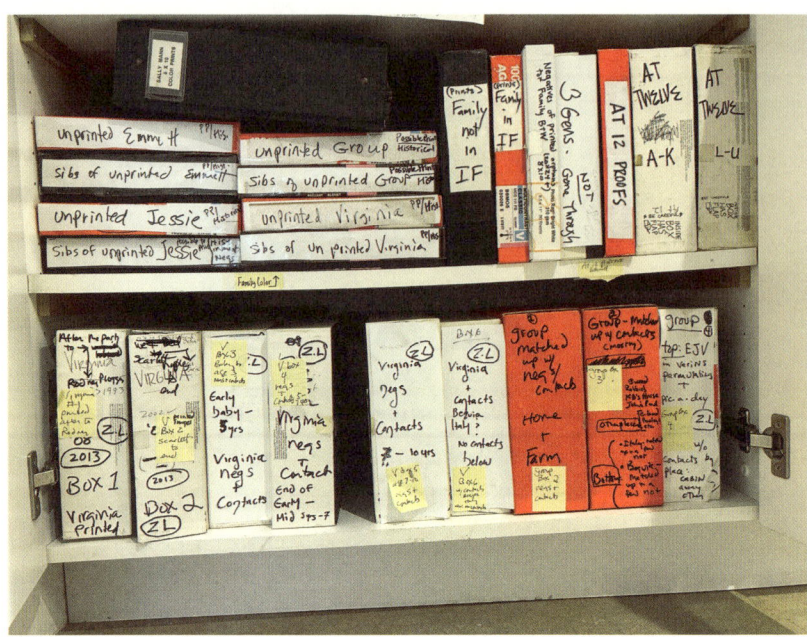

Without Peter or anyone else to go through them, these beauties have been sleeping there undisturbed until just now, when my summer assistant Mila began sifting through them. The old chorus of "What the hell is wrong with this one?" has begun to rise out of Snow White's forest, as one by one the negatives are awakened by the light.

Something that happens over the course of a career is that you develop an aesthetic persona with each editorial choice you make, and each subsequent choice tends to diminish, rather than enlarge, the options for the future of that persona. You hone your look. You find your ideas running along an increasingly narrow-gage ideological and aesthetic track. You are making your distinct, recognizable imagery, the pictures that everyone will come to identify as, in my case, a Sally Mann. But just as the narrow-gage tracks converge with distance into the singular, so, too, will your vision. Many of the negatives now brought onto the table and kissed with light resemble not a Sally Mann but a quieter persona; a Judith Joy Ross or Francesca Woodman or Judith Black. But, because I had an immutable course laid out in my mind, I discarded those images, perhaps to the detriment of the overall body of work that would, I now believe, have benefitted from a more catholic approach. In a word, more bubbles.

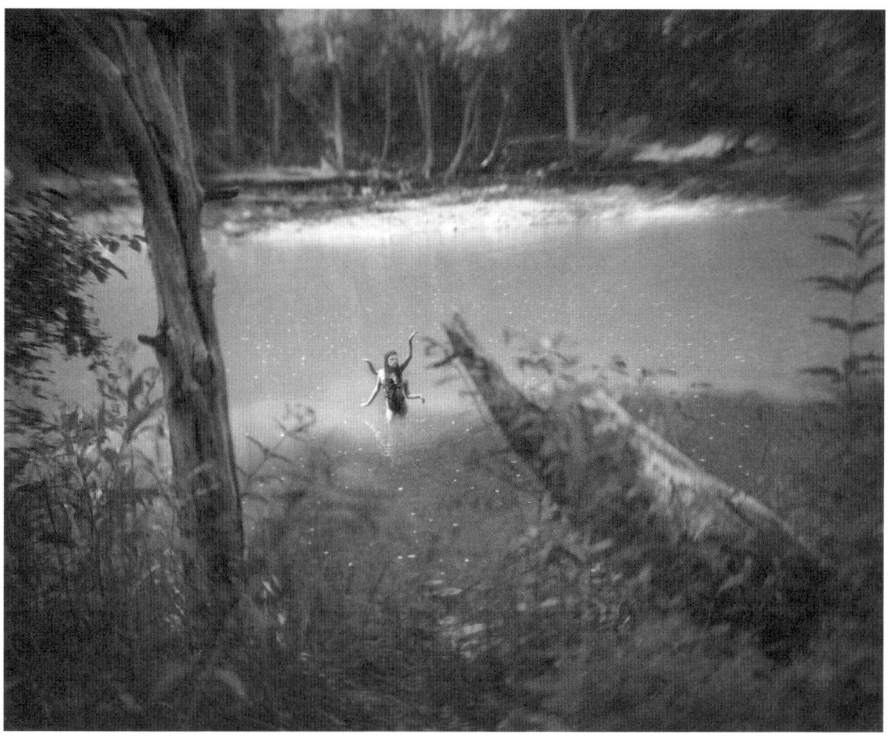

The bubbles, literal and metaphorical, definitely do the trick, but there is something else about this picture. It illustrates that after hewing to straight photographic practice for many years, I inexplicably careered off into unfortunate and alluring aesthetic thickets, like when I discovered an ancient lens that gave a zoom-like edge effect, and I began to take what might have been exceptional pictures had I not used that regrettable lens. Over time, but not soon enough, I came to dislike the edge-rushing, vertiginous look and now see it frequently in the work of other people who have been similarly ensnared. If that's you, throw the lens away. It's a cheap trick.

I first tested it on Virginia, lying in the grass outside my studio, and damn if that test wasn't pretty good, with a few blades of grass sharp and everything else mysteriously woozified. A bait 'n' switcher if there ever was one:

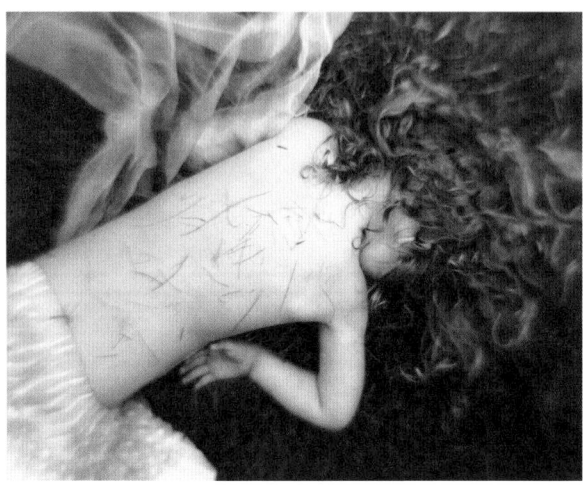

And so, the next day I went on to make *Fallen Child* with that same lens, which, well, you have to say isn't such a bad picture in spite of the lens. (You can see the echo of Emmet Gowin's image here also.)

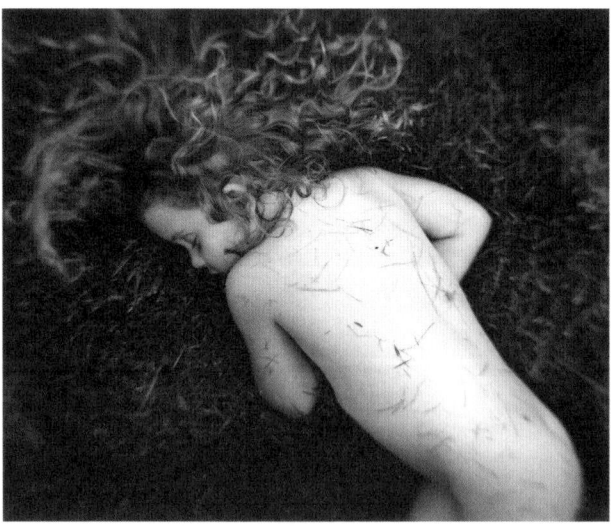

I should have quit while I was ahead, but instead of cutting my losses, I kept taking pictures with that funky lens, pictures that probably would have been much better if they'd been made with a regular old mostly sharp Dagor. Wouldn't it be nice if Larry wasn't all blurry in this one?

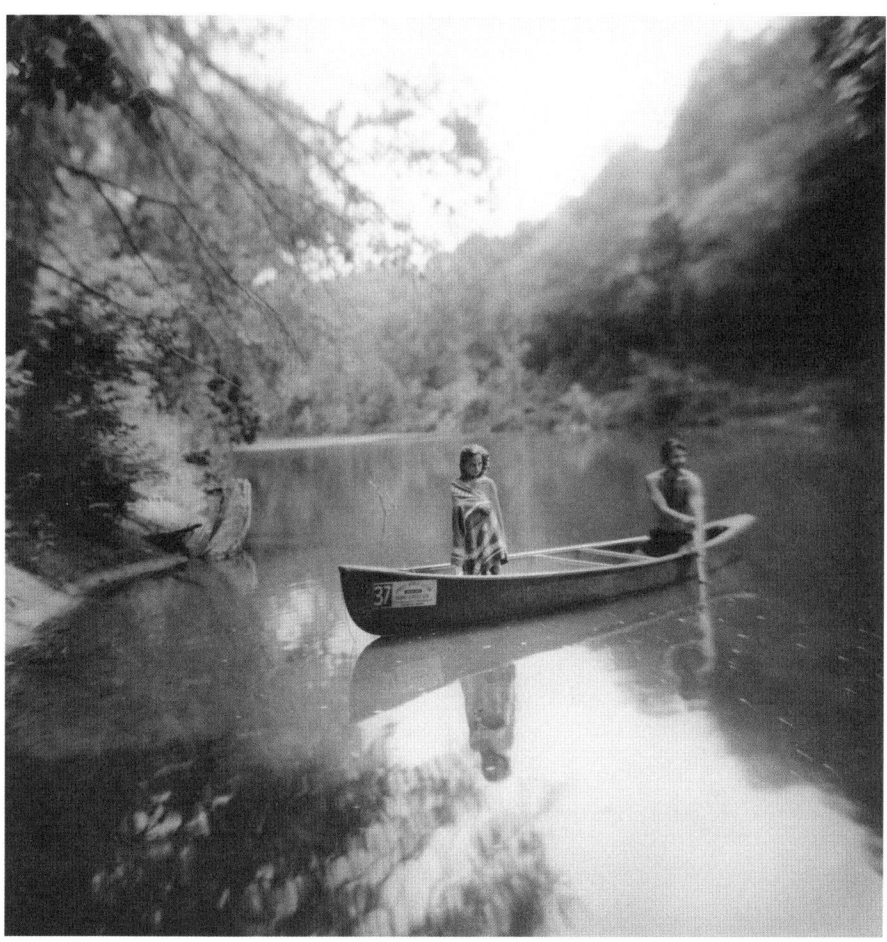

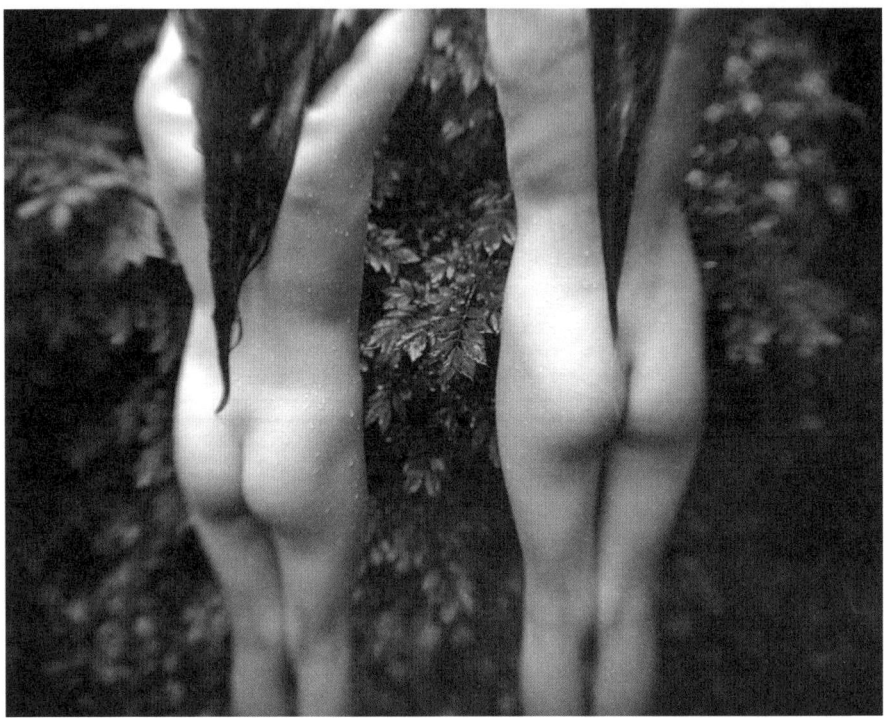

And here, there are exactly three drops of water in focus, which simply isn't enough to hold your eye, once you're done amusing yourself with the *Where's Waldo* process of finding them in the first place (hint: just off the dead center sweet spot). Isolated focus with a spinny edge is a seductive gimmick that works maybe once or twice, but stupidly I kept messing with it, unnecessarily distracting the eye from what would have been pictures rich with visually interesting detail, if they'd been sharp. Looking back at it, I think of this lens as the visual equivalent of the literary device known as magical realism—its most canonical and perfect incarnation being *One Hundred Years of Solitude*. García Márquez should have somehow slapped an airtight patent on it to prevent the subsequent overuse by a generation of epigones.

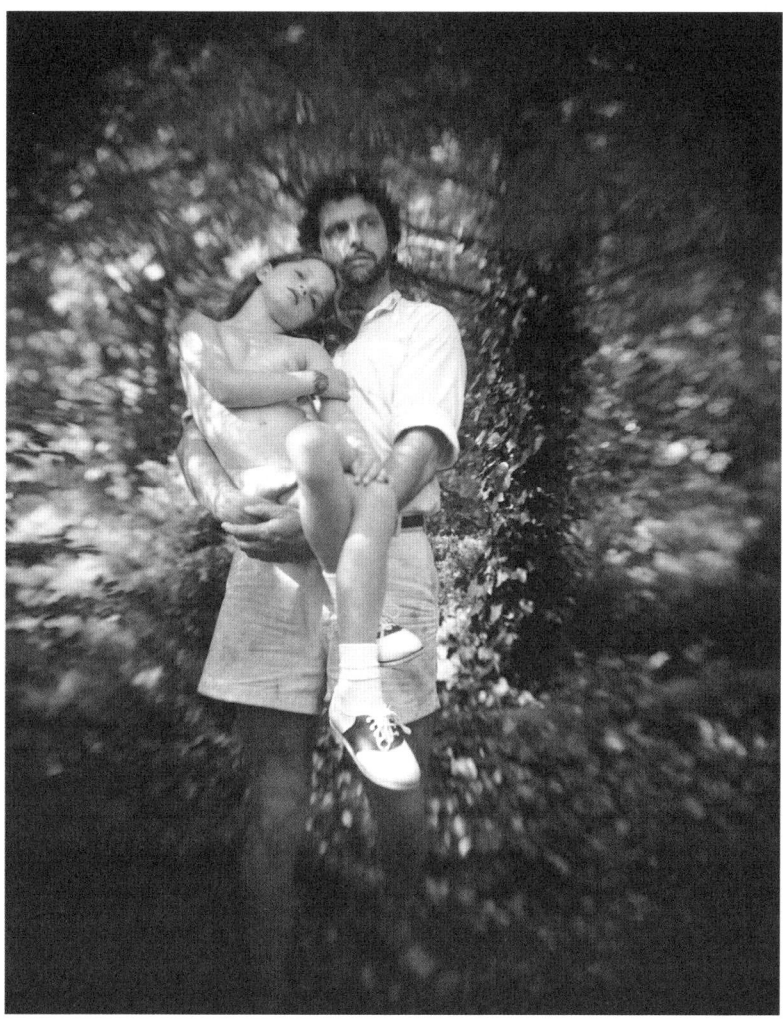

Apparently, in the case of this lens, I was not one to miss an opportunity to compound an error, because I then threw that same infernal lens into my Suburban when I went down south and compromised a few other pictures before I was released from its spell. You can see how easy it was for me to believe the lens was leading into a magical realm as I looked at the scene from under the dark cloth, a place where there is a numinous shimmer on the edges of the everyday—look at the way it makes your eye go right to the sweet-spot focus, the vine in the fork of the distant tree. Talk about punctum!

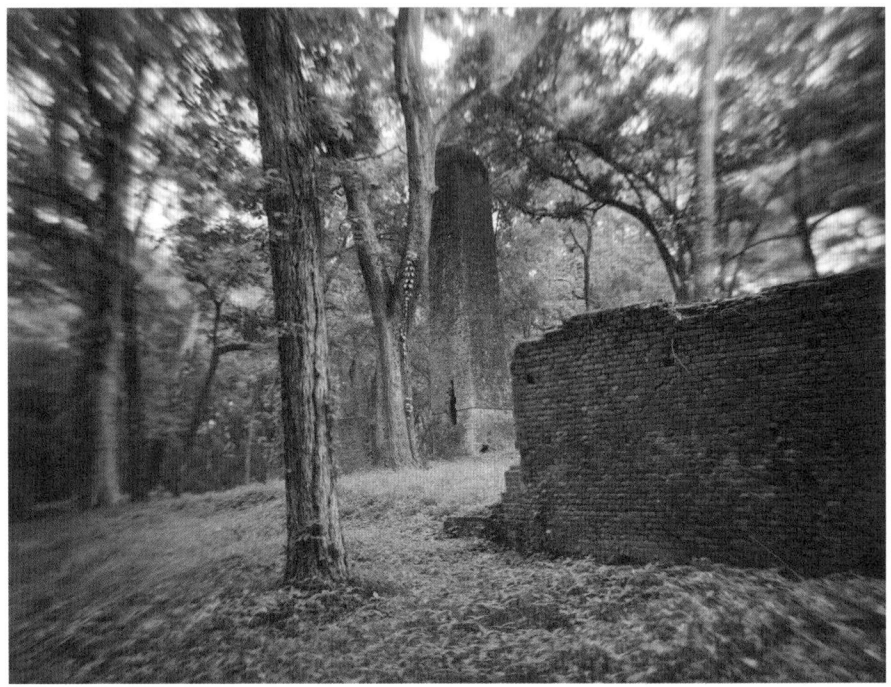

This lack of confidence in my unadulterated vision—I mean not trusting that it's going to be a good picture without some visual contrivance or serendipitous accident of the process—is present from the beginning. In my twenty-second roll of film, at age eighteen, I discovered Vaseline, I mean for my lens, and marking my contact sheet with a bold, blue X, designated my inexplicable preference for the mysterious, but utterly unreadable "portrait" of my then-fiancé Larry. Having rubbed the Vaseline off the lens with my T-shirt, I then made a far better portrait but didn't even bother to uncap the pen for that one.

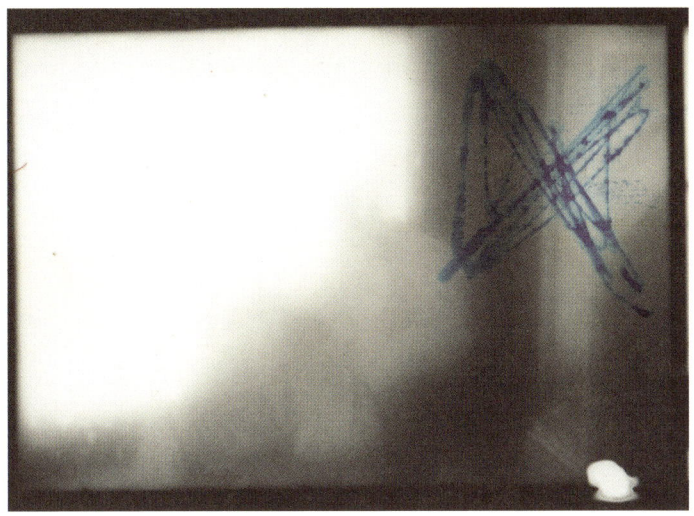

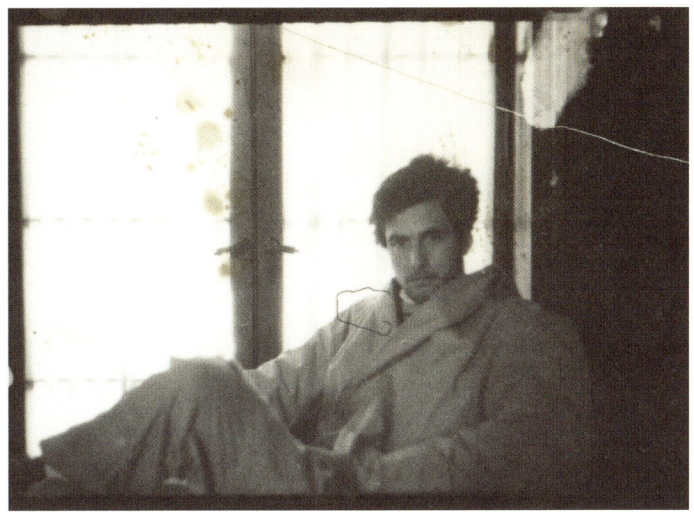

After the Vaseline came the stocking-under-the-enlarging-lens trick, which was just what it sounds like: in my case a flesh-colored—which in those days meant Caucasian flesh—nylon women's stocking stretched across a metal coat hanger and held under the lens to diffuse the image before it reached the photo paper. This technique was practiced primarily by early twentieth-century portrait photographers hoping to minimize wrinkles and was revived in the 1970s quite evocatively for record covers and even landscapes, by Norman Seeff. Having learned to practice soft-focus moderation (in general, moderation does not come naturally to me), I still use that technique for enlargements to this day.

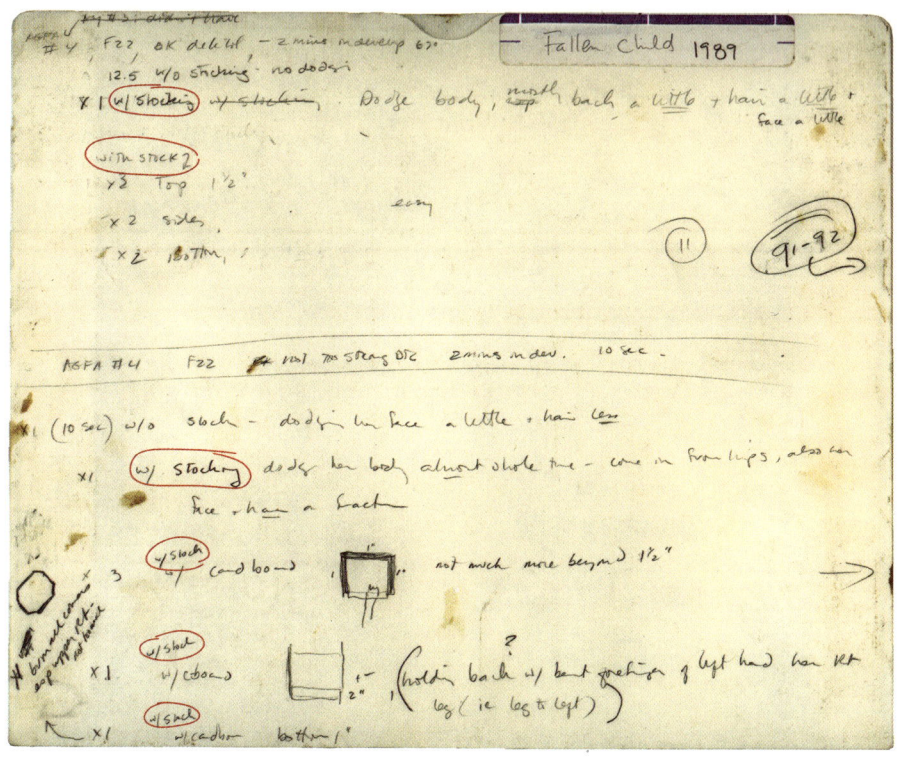

For the sake of consistency here, I have used for this example the printing directions for *Fallen Child*. Frequently some percentage of the enlargement time on the Family Pictures, and even the landscapes, would have a gossamer touch of the stocking, often so old they had double-thickness at the thigh for the garter-belt clips. And yes, I remember wearing those.

The goal of all this artifice, which worked only some of the time, was to imbue the image, or the print, with the feeling that you were not quite in the immediate world, but rather still haunted by an elusive, enigmatic dream that didn't fully dissipate when you woke. John Loengard, a long-ago editor of *Life* magazine, once said that a dash of the peculiar in a photograph is as necessary as Tabasco in a Bloody Mary, and if I could slightly amend his entirely accurate statement, I might say a whiff of the smokily mysterious is equally necessary. This sounds like a really good idea, this concoction, which, as I think about it, I'd love to be drinking right now as I reverse out of the soft-focus cul-de-sac to continue down the dispiriting highway of my photographic failures. (That was a metaphor. Even I don't drink and drive.)

Many of those failures back then can be summarized in a few words: more bubbles and fewer misbegotten, effortful gimmicks. I needed to study what I was doing more carefully; toss aside the blinkers, derail the train, cut through the knot, shortcut the Knossian labyrinth, pick your metaphor for whatever it takes to prevent an artistic conceit from completely hijacking and determining your work. Looking back at my choices, I see now that there are so many ways I could have improved the work I did.

But it's not too late for you! This applies to everything—if you are so lucky as to be able to write like Hemingway, don't tart it up with magical realism gimcrackery; keep writing that one true sentence (but, I agree, he could have used an adjective here and there). Or if you paint like Giorgio Morandi, just keep doing it. You don't need to come over all Jeff Koons. Sometimes the hardest thing of all is to keep the work simple. Our best work has a casual Noël Coward insouciance about it, Nick Charles in velvet slippers at the bar cart. It's not facile; it still needs to do art's heavy lifting, but it must never be seen to break a sweat; paradoxically, its authenticity depends on the impression of effortlessness, on the nonchalance of a miracle; the candy cigarette held just so.

Does it matter that you now know it can take countless tries to achieve art that appears so self-assured as to be inevitable, that does art's hard work but appears unfazed by the effort? Of course it doesn't: Get to work! Keep trying until you get it right. Trust what your eye and your hand and your gut are telling you. Think of your artist's vision as liquid intelligence, separate altogether from your solid-state brain; allow it to find its own level, to penetrate a psychic stratum deep within you, permeate and carve its trace.

Remember Rilke: Look to what is simple and seek solitude. Above all, make your work. Take your time. Make sure it's good. Then make a lot more of it.

In the long arc of a career, through experimentation and deletions, your good work will remain, and some you didn't know you had made will emerge. Your spavined fingers will one day be flipping through the discard pile and you will discover a totally unseen treasure of a picture, like the one below found yesterday, an un-darling from thirty-five years ago. You will edit work out because you think you know where the work should be going. But your perspective changes, and just like the shifty gallery owner, the very things you liked before are the things you don't like anymore. Time does tell, but you have to hang around to hear what it says, even if it says you're a dumbass. After all those solitary, despairing, rapturous, exhausting, and entirely ordinary years, your surviving group of durable darlings will remain, like hard stone impervious to the glacial scour, untroubled by the relentless churn of the cultural current.

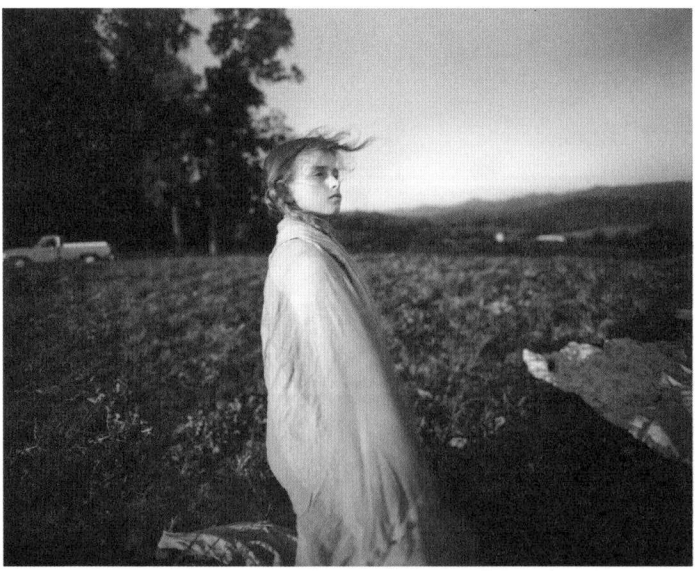

11

Challenging Work

All serious daring comes from within.
—Eudora Welty

Of course, at each stage of your career you will make mistakes. Lots of them; we all do. Artistic mistakes, but life mistakes, too. Sometimes big ones.

In the late 1940s, my parents moved from New Orleans, where my father was teaching at Tulane Medical School, to Lexington, Virginia, and found a dreamy spot to build a house. It was not just the 180-degree view of the Blue Ridge Mountains, or the proximity to the town that drew them to the property, but the dozen mature American elm trees arching over the invitingly flat space on the otherwise rolling thirty-acre property.

Painstakingly measuring and plotting out each tree on graph paper, my father designed a visionary one-level house that angled and contorted itself among the elms, making sharp turns between living room and bed-room wing, between kitchen and study, workspace and breezeway, look-ing like a snake that had swallowed an erector set. Each segment of the house had a giant elm spreading protective and cooling branches over the leak-inviting flat roof, while much of the interior design had to be custom-chiseled to accommodate the tortured angles.

And then, within two years of moving in, every one of the great trees perished in the Dutch elm epidemic of 1953–54, leaving the house naked and exposed, inexplicably lurching across the landscape and broiling in the Virginia summers. It was as if the stream feeding Fallingwater had dried up and with it the rationale for the cantilever, and, for that matter, the name itself. My poor father was slapped down by the hand of natural caprice and, ruefully acknowledging his too-human arrogance, began a self-directed crash course in landscape design. Basically, he stuffed the dog in the umbrella stand and pressed forward, making still more mistakes, fixing them, then making others.

In *Speak, Memory*, Nabokov recounts how he, as a first-year student at Cambridge, entered the darkened rooms of his university tutor for the first time, wearing his academic gown and mortarboard, nervous and uncertain. The august figure of the tutor is seated in his wicker chair, before a crackling fire. Young Vladimir takes a breath, marches with mustered, almost military confidence into the room, and steps smack into the center of the tutor's discarded tea service, which had been placed on the floor to the side of his chair. Everything is shattered. Nearly the equivalent of the white room in the Los Angeles mansion and, indeed, there is a brown-room sequel: like the now-successful Robbie, seventeen years later the confident and successful Nabokov goes back to see the same tutor, mounting the stairs to his dimly lit room like a sleepwalker. He knocks and enters, saying to the aged, hunched figure of the tutor, "I wonder if you remember me . . ." and, sure enough; the same dismal clatter and crunch of shattered china as he again steps into the middle of the tea tray. Turning, the tutor wearily responds, "Oh, yes, of course. I know who you are."

The tea services I have repeatedly stepped upon, the brilliant concepts I have had to abandon because of an intractable natural truth like my poor father, have not been just artistic; I have made major life mistakes, too. There are many ways to screw up; big ways, little ways, keep-you-awake-at-night ways. You will have your ways too, but mistakes are not all bad; if you haven't made any lately, go out and make one. It will move you forward. Dog. Umbrella stand. Seven strides. Down the drive. And through it all, you will keep making your art, perhaps almost unconsciously, as if sleepwalking, because art is what you do.

It happens when I work, when I am taking pictures and my vision, even my hand, seems guided by, well, let's say a MUSE. There is, at that time an almost mystical rightness about the image: about the way the light is enfolding it, the way the eyes have taken on an almost frightening intensity, the way there is a sudden, almost space-like, quiet, as if suddenly there was a weightlessness and an absolute vacuum. These moments nurture me through the reemergence into the quotedian...through the bill paying and the laundry and the shopping for soccer shoes...

Although I am finding that I am becoming increasingly distant, like I am somehow living full time in those moments. I find my children's faces turned inquisitively up to mine, floating almost like underwater plants distant and unrecognizable, the spoken question unheard, the answer impossible.

This was written to Ted in 1988, trying to explain how taking some pictures seemed almost, well, *spiritual*. Or as close to that as I'm likely to get, short of an out-of-body session with my local Holy Rollers. There have been times when it seemed that my hand moved as though possessed—setting up the camera, arranging the subjects, toning or manipulating the final image—guided by an invisible force, not unlike the description by philosopher Ludwig Wittgenstein of his uncannily autonomous hand, which seemed to write without the courtesy of consulting his brain.

Not to come over all woo-woo, but maybe we artists are merely a convenient vehicle for our work to express what it needs to say. We carry it like a self-replicating virus, or like that species of Hymenoptera, the burrowing wasp described by Proust, which guarantees the survival of its offspring by providing them with their paralyzed host's living flesh upon hatching.

Another way to think about it is to situate creativity within the Platonic doctrine of recollection, which asserts that we do not "create" so much as provide the vehicle for the release of knowledge that came bundled with us at birth. In this scenario, the work exists within a universal reserve of latency, of inchoate and unformed possibility that awaits the artist's hand to be physically realized. We can only hope that what our work wants to say is worth the many sacrifices we make for it to do so.

Despite being a person who generally likes to be in control of both my body and my mind, I relax that control where art-making is concerned. Trancelike, I allow myself to be ensorcelled as surely as Odysseus by Calypso and welcome the diversion for as long as the enchantment will last. It's possible this only works with art. In almost any other enterprise such a high level of uncertainty would be ruinous; you would never begin a statement in court without knowing how you were going to close, but when making art, a tolerance for uncertainty is almost essential. Walker Percy once remarked that if he knew when he sat down to write a novel how it would end, he wouldn't be interested enough to finish it, mirroring the observation—incorrectly, but understandably, often attributed to Oscar Wilde—that the moment you think you understand a great work of art, it is dead for you.

And even if you think you know what you are making, or being used as the vehicle for, you will find that often others don't understand it the way you do. You must be prepared for your work to be misunderstood, sometimes just in the dismissively insulting "oh, my three-year-old can make art like that" kind of way, but also in the kind of way that holds your work up for ridicule—and worse—on the floor of the Senate, as happened to several photographers during the so-called Culture Wars of the 1990s. If you write *Lolita*—as if any of us possesses that level of genius—you have to be prepared for controversy. Work that invites misinterpretation puts you in the position of asking a cultural commentator to grip your extended forefinger and describe what she is experiencing. It's entirely possible she will say, "Your finger is violently penetrating my fist." You shouldn't be surprised by this perceptual dissonance.

Wallace Stevens, a man given to the study of perspectives within natural phenomena—say, the blackbird, thirteen ways—addressed this in his observation that when twenty people cross a single bridge into a village, they experience the boards of the bridge, the village, and the fruit trees twenty different ways. Devolving into a multiplicity of perspectives, they fragment like a Cubist painting, presenting a kaleidoscopic range of individual experience, while each of them crosses the exact same bridge into the same village. Art is like that; it's up for interpretive grabs, with each reading as slippery as the last.

Whatever art you make, even when you don't screw it up with confidence-shattering mistakes or unnecessary fripperies, when you don't stupidly overlook a great picture or an incandescent poem and your gut is fluttering to say that you've got a keeper (or even an entire body of work, 150 huge prints that you have spent a decade making, hauled up to the attic and covered with plastic for the indefinite future; more on this later), you sometimes must censor your own work.

I have done this almost always out of cowardice and fear. A journalist once reported me as joking that I had pulled an ambiguous photograph of my dog Eva from publication because I didn't want to bring down the ire of the dog lovers, a group in which I place myself at the forefront. It might have been said in a jocular manner, but hell hath no fury like that of us dog lovers when there is an unkindness toward the species, so it was probably true. Parenthetically, I acknowledge I have edited out pictures that I felt went too far, or were gratuitously offensive, and it goes without saying you're not going to see those here. If you have those in your own reject piles, I recommend that you put them away in a box labeled "*Woman's Day Recipes*" or "Condolence Cards," where they will not be opened for the next forty years and your gut will tell you then what to do with them.

In 1995, Edwynn Houk, one of the braver people I know, hung a beautiful show of my Family Pictures series in his gallery on Madison Avenue in New York City. My work had made a brief appearance on the evolving Culture War battlefield maps but had thus far escaped even the most minor skirmish. I was definitely not jonesing for a fight after having watched what happened to Robert Mapplethorpe, Jock Sturges, Andres Serrano, and a few other lesser combatants, and when I walked into the gallery and saw that Edwynn had just snoot-cocked the self-appointed cultural guardians, I quailed. There, smack in the middle of his main wall, he had hung an image taken that same year called *The Three Graces*, a guaranteed gut-flutterer but illegal as hell. At least in Ohio, which was still reeling from the Mapplethorpe trial and busily tightening up the state obscenity laws. Even if it was flying in a plane over Ohio. Or flying anywhere; illegal to ship, as I recall, although the exact legal threat is no longer clear to me. So how odd is it that after all the risky pictures I had taken, this joyous art rip-off of my daughters and me, hands entwined, peeing in front of an ocean backdrop, was the one that was going to get me thrown in the pokey, once and for all.

Any art lover will recognize the Three Graces, the often-painted mythological figures we were portraying, representing the civilizing influence on humanity of joy, elegance, and beauty. Our image was one of many in which we restaged works of art toward the end of the Family Pictures series. It was taken on the island of Bequia, the largest island in the Grenadines, in our last summer of idyllic, uncomplicated family life; in fact, it was the last extended vacation we ever really took all together. This great travel gift came to us as an artist's retreat from a generous benefactor and there has been nothing like it since—without doubt, the happiest months of my life.

In planning the photograph, we followed the long-established pictorial tradition, two Graces facing forward, one facing back, then we stole (yes, flat-out *stole*, we've already talked about this) another idea from Emmet Gowin, that of a standing woman peeing. Having chugged down oceanic amounts of water we were guaranteed to have enough pee for the one-chance-only, perfectly synchronized image capture on the 8 × 10 film. With youthfully obedient bladders, we let go at the count of three and somebody (who will remain nameless since I suppose they could be legally liable) took the picture.

The artist Sam Messer was also on the island that summer and it couldn't have been he whose finger tripped the illegal shutter because he was busily sketching the scene

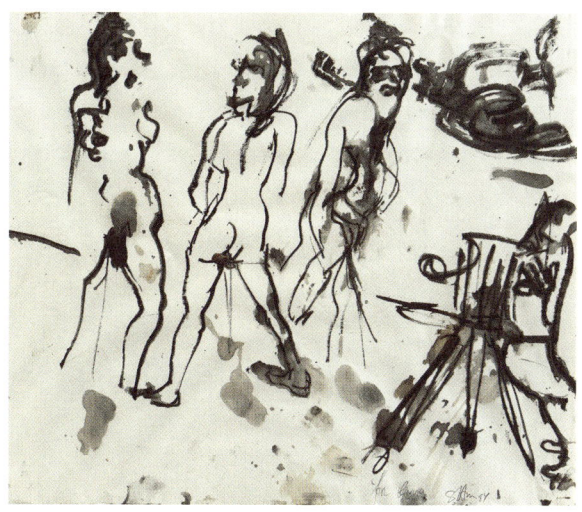

and he later joined me in indictable misdemeanor–hood, by taking his own version there the next year,

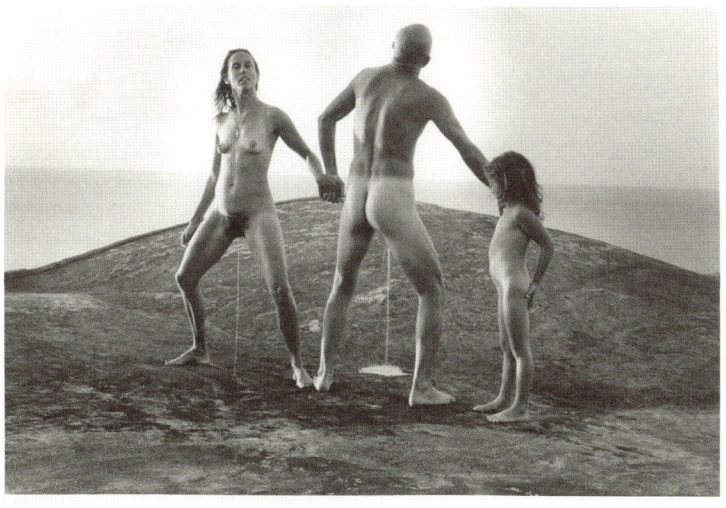

which he titled *Two Idiots, One Grace*. Although I guess since his Grace isn't peeing, he's probably safe.

Because, as I recall, that was the crux of the issue: It was illegal, and spe-cifically statutorily in Ohio (and maybe California?) to take a picture of a child urinating. Never mind that piety-skewering putti are delightedly pee-ing in gardens all over the world. (Although last month, I found this clever work-around, for which somebody *should* have been arrested for portraying the poor putti vomiting water from their mouths like drunken frat boys at a beer-bong party when they all had perfectly serviceable little penises.)

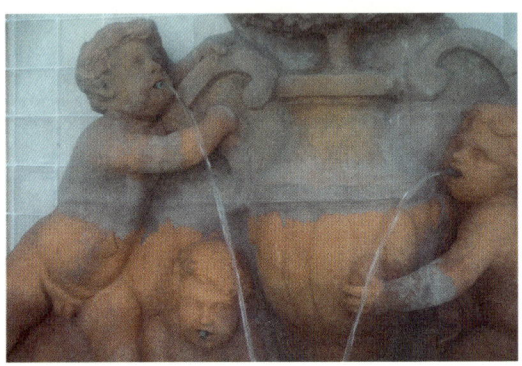

Despite the ubiquity of peeing putti, the law was so clear on the peeing part that even my most dedicated legal defenders hedged a bit when I asked them if it was OK to leave the work on the wall of the gallery. So, there I was, a few hours before the opening, removing the picture, the cynosure of the show, from Edwynn's walls. I was a complete chicken, but what would you do if you got this note on your pillow from one of your children?

I don't wan tyou to be arrestepd because of the three graces. I realy think its worng. I'm worrid

The Three Graces has never been shown on the walls of a museum or gallery in the U.S., to the best of my memory (a near-comical phrase), although of course nobody bats an eye at it in Europe, where they chortle at puritanical American attitudes. I periodically have to remind myself that this country was founded upon Puritan distrust of two aristocratic preoccupations, with art running a close second to the Papacy. I'm puzzled that our culture can easily assimilate the most vulgar slasher movies while expressing indignation about static images containing elegant and occasionally frank treatments of sex and mortality, race, gender, and religion. But the preponderance of our collective ancestry is, after all, British, and as Wilde, who suffered terribly at their hands, supposedly said of the prudishness of the English, "What a price to pay for a few good novels."

One might think that my state of Virginia could have escaped this paradigm because it has always clung to a myth of aristocracy, as noted approvingly by William Faulkner, but it was in Virginia that I ran into just such indignation. Five years after the self-censored exhibition at Houk, I displayed *The Three Graces* in a slide show at the Virginia Museum of Fine Arts in Richmond, and descriptions of it riled the Republican governor, James Gilmore. In a now commonplace Republican strategy (see then-mayor Rudolph Giuliani's threat of freezing $7 million in funding to the Brooklyn Museum if it did not remove from the walls Chris Ofili's *Virgin Mary*), Gilmore garnered headlines, even in the *New York Times*, by not so subtly threatening the state's fiscal support of the museum and in doing so brought down a firestorm of editorial and public criticism. In fact, these attacks on the museum and me were specifically singled out in a national news analysis some years later to explain his subsequent plummet into obscurity.

Gilmore asserted to the press that he had received a letter about the slide show from an anonymous "concerned citizen," later revealed to me by an investigative reporter at the *Washington Post* to have been (allegedly) a member of Gilmore's own staff and written from his own office. The whole thing fizzled out after a while, although at the time it was quite the little tempest, as evidenced by a file in my attic bulging with letters to the editor (remarkably supportive), personal letters (ditto), yellowing newspaper articles, and transcriptions of the few weary and occasionally acerbic statements I gave. To wit:

> I am sorry for the aggravation this has caused the Virginia Museum. I'm sorry for Governor Gilmore whose imagination must have run wild conjuring up the images described in the anonymous letter, and I'm sorry for my family, but most of all I'm sorry for the other artists working in a sincere and honest way, for whom this threat must be chilling.
>
> I want a healthy dialogue between the arts, the museums, and the people of the state. Art, at its best, can provoke that dialogue, and, yes, Governor Gilmore, "challenge the values of our society"— but in a positive and enlightened way. I sincerely hope that the inadvertent dialogue my slide show provoked will not diminish both the governor's office and the artists of this state but will elevate both.

You might note that I am not reproducing *The Three Graces* here. I suppose I am still a yellow-bellied coward, like some sly, cowlicked Mark Twain character who taunts another to jump off the cliff into the water but doesn't do it himself. Here I am telling you to jump in, be brave, put your work out there, take chances, you'll regret it otherwise. Yes. Do those things. And yes, I do. Regret it, I mean: I probably should have left the print on the wall.

But. The note on the pillow.

Self-censorship is one thing, always vexing and fraught. But uninvited, outside censorship is another thing altogether; it is to editing as radical tree-pollarding is to the painstaking pruning of a bonsai. And perhaps ultimately so damaging to your integrity that you will fail like those suburban Bradford pears, cropped down to their core, which struggle for years to send up trifling shoots from their stumpy, amputated limbs. You will have to navigate your own way through complex moments like these.

As an artist, you have an obligation to the viewer to offer up a different sensibility (why otherwise would they bother to explore yours?), to call their closely held belief systems into question (not gratuitously and, to whatever extent you can, with respect and a lagniappe of beauty), and to challenge and subvert. The more effective you are at this, the more agitation, possibly even anger, you may cause. My dear friend the novelist and critic Jim Lewis wrote about the risk and importance of offending the viewer in a letter to a fellow critic, Jerry Saltz. In it, he urges us to push harder, even if people hate our work, suggesting that if nobody hates it, it might not even be art. A great admirer of Samuel Johnson, Lewis bolsters his concept with this winning Johnsonian dropshot: "It is advantageous to an author that his book should be attacked as well as praised. Fame is a shuttlecock . . . To keep it up, it must be struck at both ends."

Lewis is such a brilliant writer that I occasionally experience a stomp-provoking surge of petulance when I read him. Why couldn't I have written that? This happens frequently when I see photographs that I wish I had taken, but as a writer I am humble enough to know there is no way I could improve on Lewis in what he says here: "Those qualities in your work that bother people the most are often precisely the ones that should be cultivated, pushed so far out on the axis of vice that they come around to be virtues."

Axis of vice! How can you top that? It should be the title of a book. Though maybe not this one.

But he's right about the way things often end up coming around. Cynical sophisticates scoff at the belief that if you make your true work with the purest intentions, your sincerity will be rewarded even by the jaded art world, but you know what? I kinda buy that. Do the work of your earnest heart, with all your body and soul, for as long as you breathe and with as much craft and creativity as you can wring from your every filament, and you will have made art. Your art.

If it is tough art, if it is *The Three Graces* kind of tough, if you have listened to Jim Lewis but you don't want to draw attention to it, then give it some temporal insulation, as Wyeth did with the Helga portraits, working on the series privately for years before releasing it. Or just let time's sandpaper take care of it for you, as it did for Stravinsky, whose *Firebird*, initially ridiculed, is now considered a twentieth-century masterpiece. Either way, you press on, regardless. As Flannery O'Connor once wrote: "Be properly scared, and go on doing what you have to do." And hope like hell if it's tough work and you put it out there, it has this kind of reception:

Sally Mann
C/o Houk-Freidman Gallery
851 Madison Avenue
New York, NY 10021

Dear Sally Mann,

After hanging three of your photographs in my home I became a little self-conscious about sharing my peculiar fascination with your art with my house cleaning ladies. They're uncomplicated, conservative, country people, and I wasn't sure what they'd make of, say, "The Three Graces". So I left them a note explaining that I'd hung some pictures that were "a little different", and I hoped it didn't bother them. I thought you might enjoy reading their response, which seems to me to go right to the heart of the matter. You might even want to use the line some day, on a federal prosecutor, say.

I love your art.

Sincerely,

The pictures don't offend us at all Its your home, but thanks for leaving a not on it, we look at it as just art pictures. Have A nice weekend.

That's it in the end: "just art pictures," just somebody making a little something. No big deal. Everybody, calm down. Indeed, these "uncomplicated . . . country people" got right to the heart of the matter.

———◆———

Another instance of self-censorship, or you could euphemistically call it "temporal insulation," is one that I don't second-guess as much as I do withdrawing *The Three Graces* from the Houk show. I don't much like backing down, as anyone who knows me will attest, but I am nevertheless finally mature enough to know when I need to ease off; to listen, for a change, and adapt to what I am hearing. In recent years I've even been able to admit I was wrong a time or two. It's a skill as important as any I have recommended in this book, and I am sure you won't wait until you are my age to acquire it.

Wendell Berry can help us with this—of course he can. He writes that when a loose thread threatens to unravel the whole garment, we must discern when the tug begins and where the thread breaks. Being wrong is part of the unraveling process, making mistakes is the tug. Berry speaks to how we, as creative people, shape the moral imagination of our audience not just by what stories we tell but by how we tell them; "telling the right story" and "telling the story right."

Between 2004 and 2018, I was telling the wrong story, or telling it at the wrong time, even if I told it as right as I could. The work I made over those years, images of Black men, has been given the Wyeth treatment; it will need some time before it can be loosed into the cultural slipstream. If ever it can. This process has caused me to question many of my assumptions, among them whether it matters what an artist was thinking, or what their intentions were when they made their work. I've spent a lot of time explaining my motives and have scaffolded much of my work with conceptual structure, but in the end—the end as in, "Do we really care what Giotto was thinking?"—I don't believe it should, or will, matter. It's either a good picture or it's not. And what decides that is what the viewer is thinking and feeling.

Which means, I reluctantly conclude, that sincerity in art is like truth in art; it doesn't make an iota of difference to anyone but you (but, indeed, it does matter to us). People will take your work and make of it whatever they want. They will, violating all manner of laws, take a picture of your daughter and plaster it on the side of a London bus as an illustration of a battered child in support of some anti-child-abuse ad campaign (this happened with my photograph *Damaged Child*). The truth of it, that the "battered child" had an eye swollen from gnat bites, was completely immaterial to the viewers of the ad. And, similarly, the sincerity of my effort to photographically address questions of race in the American South is probably also immaterial, and another example of that earnest, clueless White-person way we have of messing up everything racial.

From my first roll of film in 1969, and in my earliest poems, so maudlin they could have been optioned for a high school musical, I was drawn artistically to the things that felt emotionally significant. And in that process, I found that the past had unavoidably shoehorned its way into the inquiry and rendered my work occasionally mysterious, even to me. I feel as inextricably connected to the history undergirding my present as the old woman in a Chekhov short story who is caught noisily weeping over a biblical incident as if it had happened yesterday. Her young observer, a theology student, muses: "The past . . . is linked to the present by an unbroken chain of events all flowing from one to the other." When one end of that long chain is disturbed, the other trembles, like a spider's web at the distant, tentative touch of her prey.

Chekhov's young man found this connectedness exhilarating and promising, but I have found that our undeniable connection with the past can also be overwhelming, almost debilitating at times, bringing to mind that line from George Eliot, that if we were truly open to the world, we would hear the grass grow and the squirrel's heart flutter and be destroyed by "that roar which lies on the other side of silence."

I realize that it's a metaphorical and geographic stretch to enlist both Chekhov and Eliot to make a point that might just as easily be accomplished by taking a handful of psychotropic drugs. But even without them, those of us blessed—or cursed—with Eliot-level sensitivity find ourselves vibrating with sensations and perceptions that ineluctably tie the past and present together. Responding to the touch at the end of the chain, and unable to not hear the roar, I have found myself grappling artistically, basically since the beginning, with the influence of race, which has reverberated throughout my life.

I began taking pictures of Black men in June 2004, starting with a college classmate of Jessie's, who, like Jessie, was graduating that week. It was, arguably, a less aware time than now, a time in which much of our country chose not to see what was happening to young Black men, killed with impunity, routinely over-sentenced for commonplace infractions, and packed into our prisons. Having spent the previous decade exploring the American South and, inevitably, the legacy of slavery in that region, I felt I was meeting a personal and political obligation, a deferred rendezvous with destiny. The writer W. G. Sebald suggested that just as we have appointments to keep in the future, we have equally imperative historical appointments, but that sometimes when we show up for those, we discover that the past can be disproportionately and even dangerously close. Indeed, when I kept my own uncomfortable appointment, revisiting my childhood in the 1950s and '60s and photographing these strangers of a different race and sex, the past thrummed inside me like a tuning fork touching an unsheathed nerve.

It's not easy now, in this era of pervasive, instantaneous imagery, to explain how a single black-and-white picture—as I recall reproduced in the pages of *Life* magazine at about smartphone size—can burn an indelible trace on a child's brain. But that happened to me probably in the late 1950s, and the picture I saw was of a man's charred body chained to a tree. In that moment, I took Frost's immortal wound. I have never gotten over it.

Back when I was a child, violence, while possibly just as prevalent, was not as visually ubiquitous as it is now that we have so many forms of dissemination available to us—we see the lives lost to guns, open carry in the grocery store, the nightmare phenomenon of school shootings, war on multiple fronts, and video games in which murder for entertainment is normalized. I grew up in what felt like an innocent time, a willfully ignorant time. Our family had no television, my parents being strenuously opposed to it, so I was not in any way inured to the imagery of violence and suffering. Maybe because of this, I was especially susceptible to feelings of intense empathy when I did encounter it. *The Family of Man*, remember? I damn near wore that book out, the images, and others from that era, seared into my memory and heart.

I had a lonely, rural childhood, and I spent it almost entirely in the company of Virginia Carter, known as Gee-Gee, a smart, stoic, kind Black woman, about whom I wrote in some detail in my first narrative book, *Hold Still*. In the fifty years she worked for us, she almost always presented a positive face to my world, but there were some stories she told that gave me an opening into lives different from mine. Once when we were hanging up laundry, she told me a story that has stuck with me, veering off from our usual conversation about how a wringer washer did a much better job than the new spinny one that my mother had bought. (She was right about that; I had a wringer machine and when it wasn't sucking my fingers into the rollers, it was fantastically efficient. Sometimes in frustration Gee-Gee would carry to her home a pillowcase full of my father's shirts that she felt were unacceptably washed by the modern washing machine so she could run them through the rubber-rollered wringer machine on her back porch and then sneak them back into his bureau drawer, starched and blindingly white.)

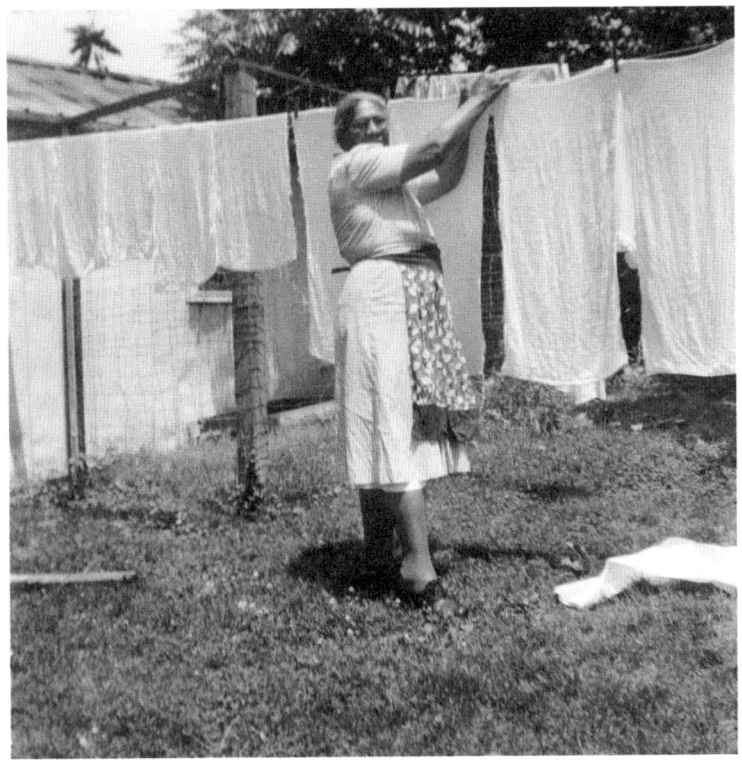

On the day in question, I think I dropped a damp piece of laundry in the dirt below the line, and it brought up the memory for her. With a matter-of-fact tone, clipping the billowing sheets as she spoke, Gee-Gee described an annual event in the lives of the Black community (she would not have used "Black" back then). It was always around the same time, Easter, a season when the ground is typically muddy. The cadets at the local military school would saddle their horses and go "wilding" through the streets and backyards of the Black side of town, Mudtown and Diamond Hill, pulling down laundry and running their horses over it until it was torn and filthy. People tried to anticipate and not do laundry, but the decision to maraud was impulsive, possibly based on the availability of alcohol, and invariably many people lost all the clothes and bedding they had. Almost as an afterthought, she said that one time the cadets tied a protesting man behind a horse and dragged him all the way to the water tower. This was said with a weary "boys will be boys" tone of voice, but I know now that what she meant was "White people will do whatever they fucking want without any fucking justice ever." (And she would never, never, *never* have said it that way.) Imagining what she so stolidly described, I was goggle-eyed and speechless and, obviously, never forgot it.

Because I lived far out in the country with no neighbors or siblings (my much-older brothers were away at school), my most reliable companions were my books. I spent a lot of time imagining what it would be like to be somebody else, somebody I had seen or read about: the dust bowl mother with more runs than stocking, the brutalized child thrown in the river, the pig and the spider, the boy with scarlet fever, the woman leaping between ice floes, the congregant whose work-calloused knees press against the planking of the chapel floor. As I grew up in Gee-Gee's strong arms, I began to wonder how it was that my life was so different from those I read about and imagined, and, indeed, from hers. I began to be uncomfortably aware that I enjoyed great privilege and was fortunate in myriad, unacknowledged ways. I was pretty sure, even when young, that a big part of it was because I was White.

I was also pretty sure that as a child there was little I could do about the pain that I knew existed outside my life, other than being polite, which mostly meant remembering to say Yes, ma'am and thank you. On that point, I was mistaken: at about the same time I was writing Hal Foster, the creator of my favorite comic strip, to ask if its hero, Prince Valiant, had to wear underpants, my friend Drew Faust was herself writing President Eisenhower, petitioning him to put an end to segregation. I wish I could say that I was smart enough to seek out that avenue of protest, but, well . . . who doesn't want to know if Prince Valiant wore underpants? (Foster said he did, deflating one of my primary arguments against having to wear them myself.) The battles I took on were small ones compared to Drew's.

Other members of my family had real-world ways to cope with, and possibly ameliorate, the painful disparities. My physician father cared for many patients, Black and White, for free, but he was also known to be the one White doctor in the area who would always treat Black patients. When a Black doctor, Dr. Alfred Pleasants, came to the community and was denied hospital emergency room access, my father, turning the prohibition on its head, said that if Dr. Pleasants didn't have to do emergency room work, then he wasn't going to either (it was an undesirable rotating position). Dr. Pleasants was soon allowed to admit Black patients and join the hospital staff.

My spirited, Bostonian mother attacked the infamous Virginia poll tax, a blatant attempt, along with the so-called literacy test, to disenfranchise Black voters by charging a then-onerous $1.50 tax to vote in any election—local, state, or national. Over twenty-eight days in October 1963, she amassed enough signatures on a petition (over five hundred) to demonstrate significant opposition to the tax, which was put in place by Governor Albertis Harrison, the man also responsible for the equally odious policy of Virginia's Massive Resistance. Down in North Carolina at college, my brother Chris had joined the civil rights movement, and during numerous sit-ins and marches he was pissed on, struck with a sword, shot at, run over, kicked to the ground, locked up seventeen times, spat upon, ammonia-burned, and ultimately sentenced to five years (most suspended) in jail.

I am well aware that many gave far more, even their lives, for the cause of racial justice. But nonetheless, knowing that my immediate family did something when so many others here didn't is important to me.

Still, the argument could be made that being a White person able to make those defiant gestures without the likelihood of lynching was itself a form of privilege. Deep in the bowels of the Greenville jail, however, Chris might not have felt especially safe or privileged as word reached him about the three civil rights workers found buried in the red clay of a

Mississippi dam. He was my hero in those years, when I believed I was too young to effect any change myself.

Eventually, sent away to the Putney School in Vermont, I experienced what I termed my "awakening," discovering literature, poetry, and then photography, to help me along on my self-guided racial reckoning. Like many other artists, I used my work to help me process my often fluctuating and inchoate emotions and felt protected by art's unspoken but almost Masonic understanding—a secret handshake of latitude and grace, freedom from the threat of undue censure, ridicule, or opprobrium. (Unless of course, the work is truly terrible. Then, have at it.) And like many other artists, I did not feel I had a choice. Rilke posits that a work of art is only good if it has arisen out of necessity and acknowledges the absolute: "I must." But sometimes the way we respond, or even that we respond at all, can bring down a bag of spiders onto our unsuspecting heads, and we have to be prepared to answer for the work we make.

In the case of the photographs I made of the men, I knew my life experiences were not those of my subjects, and that taking on the issues around race was going to be problematic. In hindsight, any of you could have told my naive, earnest (you're right: *dumbass*) self that it was a lot more than just problematic. You would have known that historically marginalized people would rather tell their own stories, not have them interpreted through White eyes and minds. You would have seen far more clearly than I did that my attempt to engage with this issue would bring to the fore centuries of historical White privilege and racism, and that whatever work I made could seem to be both transgressive and trivializing.

You could have directed me all the way back to James Baldwin, who wrote of William Styron's book *The Confessions of Nat Turner*, published in 1967, that Styron was "going to catch it from black and white." "Styron is probing something very dangerous, deep and painful in the national psyche," wrote Baldwin. "I hope it starts a tremendous fight, so that people will learn what they really think about each other." (It did.)

Nowadays it's unlikely that any White author would write Styron's book. A lot has changed since Baldwin's prediction, and even more since Horace asserted in 19 BCE:

pictoribus atque poetis
Quidlibet audendi semper fuit aequa potestas
scimus, et hanc veniam petimusque damusque vicissum.

Painters and poets alike
Have always had license to dare anything.
We know that, and we claim and allow others this indulgence.

(Thank you, Felix Lederer; I might not be able to read Latin like we used to in class, but at least I recognize that "audendi" is the root of audacity, inextricably twinned to art from time immemorial.)

It should be obvious by now how tightly I clutch Horace's permission slip, and how hopeful I am that my artistic output will someday be indulged, but I am also well aware of its potential for pain and confrontation. The response to Dana Schutz's painting of Emmett Till in the 2017 Whitney Biennial is an example of good intentions that were inadvertently hurtful. I followed the story—the protests, the calls for the painting to be destroyed—and found the situation illuminating but also chilling.

For my 2018 show *A Thousand Crossings* at the National Gallery of Art, we had planned to devote one of the biggest rooms to eighteen large prints from the series "Men." But following the Whitney protests, and after many consultations and discussions, the curators and I decided to pull all but four of them from the show. Controversy is a double-edged sword and is often courted by those who have not experienced the suddenness and casual ease with which it can wound. But each of us could imagine, or in my case had experienced, the sharp side of the sword.

So, what was so problematic about these pictures? Don't let your imagination run wild; take Mapplethorpe or Dureau out of your mind. Most were taken on my sunny, vine-covered porch using the wet-plate collodion process, guaranteeing, at least when I am the one doing it, a source of amusement and entertainment for my subjects; indeed, I think some of them were a little embarrassed for me. It is not uncommon for me to peek out from under my dark cloth and see a pitying look directed my way. I am manifestly inexpert, muttering to myself, spilling the chemicals, once even (and this was recorded on video) incorrectly attaching the lens so that it fell from the camera and exploded on the asphalt. For sure, the atmosphere on my studio porch wasn't intimidating and I tried, short of shattering another lens, to put my subjects at ease.

Aside from the technical run-amokery, I kept to a rather stringent conceptual framework in making the pictures. Almost all my models were strangers, responding to ads for paid modeling sessions I tacked up in the local, all-male colleges. Most knew nothing about me as a photographer, and many brought friends, or their girlfriends. My studio is far out in the country, and a little on the peculiar side, so they were guarded at first: Who is this moth-eaten old bird, her clothes covered with silver-nitrate stains, and what kind of pictures does she want? We established that right away: just simple pictures, often of parts of the body, hands, feet, neck, back, with clothes on, unless they felt like taking off a shirt. When it was hot, some did.

Despite the historically weighted and slippery social ground upon which our brief friendships struggled, we often fell into idle, relaxed chat while I coated my glass plates and took the pictures. A few of my models came back several times. One wanted a portrait to send to his family (each model was offered a print after the session). Some fell asleep. Several men invited me to photograph vulnerable physical characteristics—missing digits, scabby, eczema-ridden backs, surgical scars—with no prompting and no embarrassment in the quiet, afternoon light of my studio deck.

In *Hold Still* I wrote at some length about the question of exploitation inherent in the process of making a portrait, positing that even the simplest picture of another person is ethically complex, and that taking a picture can be an invasive act, a one-sided exercise of power. But since then, I have come to believe that the relationship between subject and photographer, while it can be strictly transactional, can also be mutually rewarding, and I like to imagine that these pictures might hold some value for everyone involved. Recently I was heartened when I ran into the mother of one of my subjects, Gary Brown, a stonemason now deceased, who told me that she sees the picture of his work-worn hands every day and prays for him.

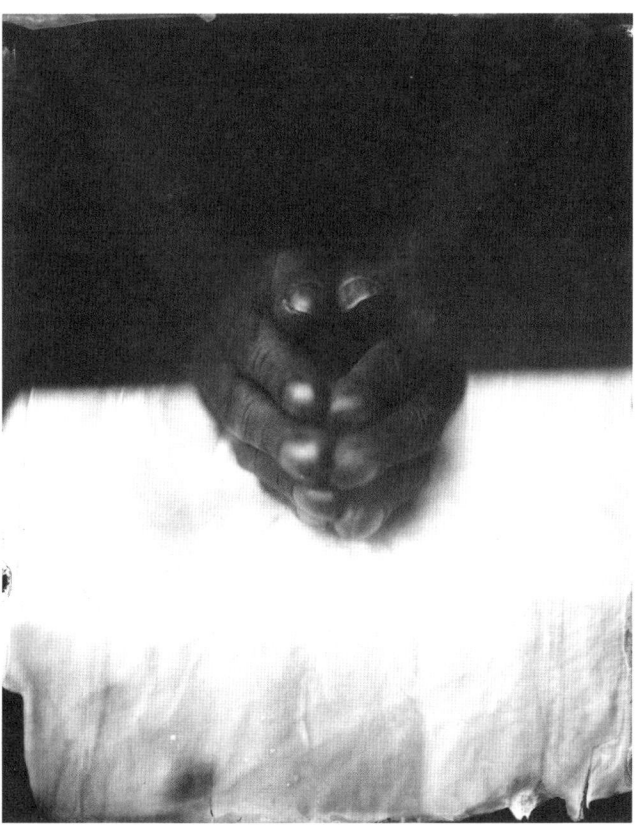

I have at times wondered whether our choice to withhold these photographs from the exhibition diminished an opportunity for dialogue, for the kinds of difficult conversations without which nothing will ever change. If, as I believe, art holds universal truths, then ideally it should be able to illuminate and give access to our collective human experience, reaching across gulfs of difference, racial and historical. So, I had hoped to see the prints on the wall, and possibly serving as a springboard for those conversations, a gesture reaching across the divide, instead of moldering in a plastic-covered pile in my attic.

But ultimately, I concluded that it was not the right moment for this body of work. So, I'll let the tincture of time do its restorative work. If this experience has any value as a cautionary tale, it will perhaps save you from making the kinds of mistakes that I, and others telling stories not their own, have made, however well-intentioned we were. I suspect that most of you can better sense the tenor of the times and are more alert to the evolving social dynamics of the world around you than I was.

Humility (easily mistaken for but distinct from my bottomless insecurity) is not a trait often ascribed to artists, but having taken a big draft of it, I am still on my feet, and the better for it. Styron was correct when he said an open heart and hard work are essential to the art-making process, and in the course of this book I have hammered that belief home with the regularity of a pile driver. But the broody, prayerful, and sometimes isolating process of making art has evolved since 19 BCE, and especially in the last several decades since Styron. New levels of complexity have emerged, and if you're going to make difficult, provocative work you need to extend your antennae beyond their usual range and be willing to course-correct when necessary. The signals you pick up might make you uncomfortable, attracting unexpected geomagnetic disturbances, but they might also bring to your perception of the world an illuminating frequency. As creative people, this is what we live for.

12

Whip, Then Gift

I twang it out and leave it there.
—Wallace Stevens

And now we're there, the place you knew we'd get to eventually. Why else would I have mentioned, right at the beginning, the word I said I was never going to say again in this book? Like Chekhov's loaded gun, you knew it was going to go off, sooner or later, before the final curtain. But not before the strut and fret of the main characters: luck, organization, technique, words (on actual paper), patience, tenacity, risk-taking, moral questioning, and finding your story—or letting it find you—plus, of course, character-building suffering. But all those players have had their moment in the spotlight, and here we are.

Because we're at the end, and because I've kept my promise all the way to this point, I'll break down and again say the unsayable word: talent. But—with a qualifier. I am willing to concede that some among us have . . . let's say, a *weighted sensibility*, a gift, if you insist on thumbing the thesaurus to avoid the unsayable word. When I was a child, my father nicknamed me Bright Eyes. Apparently, I spotted things—and fast. Faster than anyone else at the license-plate game. The basket-burdened winner of Easter egg hunts, the first one to jam a forefinger on the Hidden Pictures in *Highlights*. I was a squinty-eyed sneak, an observer, a watcher; if I saw it, with intention, I usually didn't forget it.

Possessing a slight bright-eyed advantage, I might indeed have had a leg up, to strain the Minimum Appropriateness Requirement for Metaphorical Physical Parallels, but it was not what made me the artist I am today. What made me who I am today, what helped me in every stage of my career, was not this so-called gift. It was not talent. It was passion.

I once read a *New Yorker* article about a Loch Ness Monster hunter, and from it, I typed the following quote on page 83 of my voluminous Quotes list, because it resonated so strongly with me: "I am a mediocre mind, but I have a combination of abilities and possibly a certain force of will which has enabled me to find a niche in life." Having never seen a photograph of the Loch Ness Monster I sense he has been unsuccessful, but I still celebrate his blunt assessment of his abilities, especially the "certain force of will" part. His "force of will" is my passion, although I'm sure almost anyone standing on the shore watching a monster-hunter's diminutive rowboat bobbing on the chill waves of Loch Ness would have to agree that it is not just will: It's passion. Misguided, perhaps. But other than passion, what would send you out there in the mists and rain with only your binoculars to protect you from the massive barnacle-encrusted neck emerging just when you realized you had forgotten your camera?

Perhaps it's a matter of semantics. When does will become passion? On page 61 in my Quotes list, just a few pages before the monster-hunter's quote, is a somewhat embittered, but germane, statement from the inventor of the Post-it note: "In 1931 I won a Carlton Society Award, which is like winning the Nobel Prize. The award reads: 'Arthur Fry, for the novel and creative approaches to the development of products based on his repositionable adhesives and for his tenacious dedication and commitment to the program that resulted in Scotch brand Post-it Notes.' Tenacious, huh? The difference between tenacity and stubbornness, or genius and crackpot, is the difference between success and failure. I was stubborn until I became a success. Then I became tenacious."

I have myriad examples in my own life, not involving a monster hunt or a corporate invention, but for sure they required an unswerving passion, the force of will that catapulted me above the obstacle of my subpar potential and made the difference between success and failure. And there are a thousand examples elsewhere: Who knows if Ted Williams had some unique gift for gauging the speed of a thrown hardball? Did he have some way to chart its probable trajectory based on a deeply intuitive understanding of how the pitcher's body was moving in the windup? He could have possessed that gift and that intuition, or he could have just been a regular guy who turned into Ted Williams by practicing hitting the ball until his hands bled. Day after day: gutting out Malcolm Gladwell's ten thousand hours.

It is unfortunately essential that those hours comprise difficult acts, of increasing miserableness, in order for any of us to improve. We're back to suffering here: If it were easy, then everyone would be doing it. My neuroscientist daughter Jessie (that's *Dr. Mann* to you) once tried to explain this to me in scientific language. She said that what we are feeling as repetitive misery is, on a molecular level, a gradual accretion of myelin wrapping around nerve fibers, sheathing and insulating them so that the electrical impulses transmit more easily. To achieve excellence, this must happen many times, over many years, and usually while the repetitive pain needle lies buried in the critical red zone.

In 1949 a psychologist named Donald Hebb strung together a catchy phrase to make this phenomenon understandable to those of us without a PhD in neuroscience: "Neurons that fire together wire together." When the neurons activate synchronously and repetitively, it becomes easier for them to repeat that action, facilitating the myelin increase and nudging the pain needle back into the midrange. It's the neuro equivalent of muscle memory.

This is exactly what we mean when we speak of the measurable results of repetitive practice, although a distinction must be made here between rote and desire, between mere practice and a burning passion to make each repeated effort just a little better. Ted Williams kept batting until the grip was bloodied because he was convinced that the next time he would hit harder or farther or more accurately. And, the next time, he probably did.

Each time we do better, even if it's incrementally, not only do we improve on a molecular level, but our desire and motivation to try again increases commensurately. Williams's forearm grew stronger, his reflexes quicker, and his inner drive, that indominable, hardheaded conviction, deepened. He likely experienced something approaching the ecstasy I have described at moments in my art-making career, what researchers and philosophers often refer to as "flow"; time slows down and the process, the task at hand, seems almost otherworldly, effortless, sublimely pleasurable. Although once termed by the Boston College psychologist Ellen Winner as "the rage to master," I would substitute the word "passion" for "rage" in my case. A passion for mastery, and the recognition and rewards that follow each improvement, however minor and individual, almost guarantee a greater future investment in the effort; a self-fueling internal combustion engine within each of us.

If Ted Williams was anything like me, somebody had to take a flashlight out onto the field and convince him that it was time to give it up. For decades, I would be annoyed by a knock on my darkroom door and realize that it was way past bedtime and I'd been in there since breakfast. The upshot of those decades of obsessive practice is that I am a pretty good printer, the near-obsolete, darkroom kind of printing. In fact, skipping the false modesty, I'm a damn good printer, maybe one of the best—which is easy to say these days as there are so few of us. In talking about my career as a photographer, I must acknowledge that the quality of the work for which I will be known depends to a great extent on the quality of the printing of that work. I got to be a good printer the Ted Williams way. I printed until I thought it would kill me. I had no printing gift, no printing talent, if there is such a thing. What I had was a passion to make a beautiful object. That is what it meant, to me, to be an artist. The tonality, the darks, the lights, the edges, the balance of the corners, the perfection of the surface, the gasp-inducing-ness of the image on the wall.

Here I am on the first day I pulled what was then a big print for me, 20 × 24, in 1988:

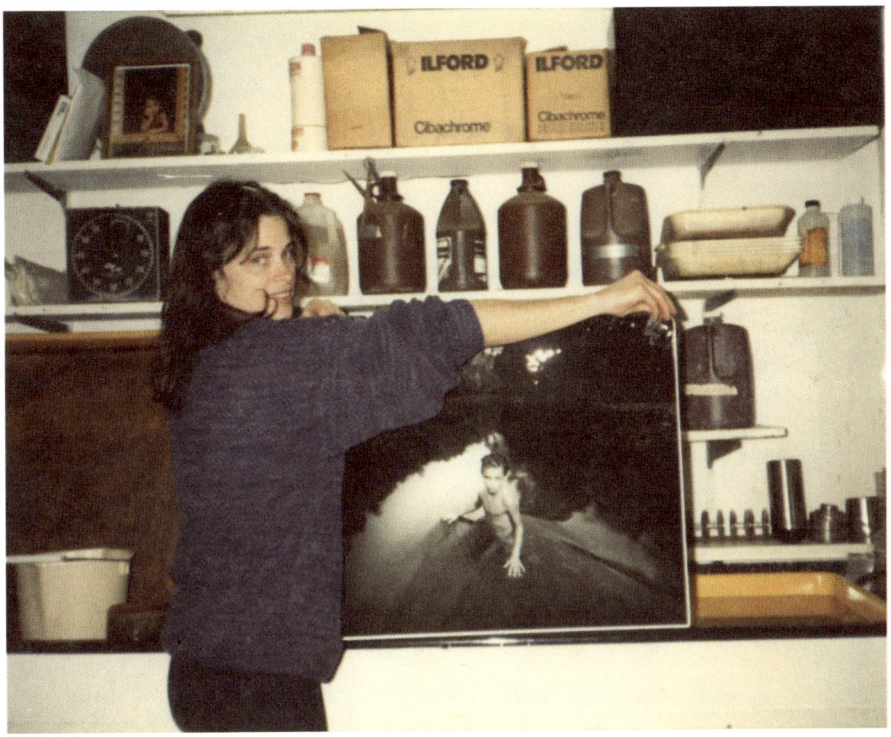

Made with my absurdly archaic Eastman 8 × 10 enlarger—a 1913 model, which puts me in the technophobic company of the fist-shaker on the corner, shouting, "Get a horse!" at a passing Model T. I found this antique in a local attic and getting it down the three flights of stairs, onto a pickup, and thence into my darkroom was nothing compared to the aggravation of cutting a hole in my ceiling to accommodate the reach of its outmoded exposure head. And that, in turn, was nothing compared to teaching myself how to print with the damn thing; retooling my tiny darkroom and sink space, figuring out chemistry, times, patching light leaks in the cracked leather bellows, finding used trays, coping with the disastrous negative melting that occurred until I replaced the condenser head, and devising some archival way to dry the prints in case I ever got a good one. This is just me, mind you: There is assuredly not a population of large-format printers here in Li'l Chickenswitch. I was figuring this out by myself.

But eventually I did, and after months of painful trial and error, while the kids spent their childhoods playing on the darkroom floor, I was finally making prints.

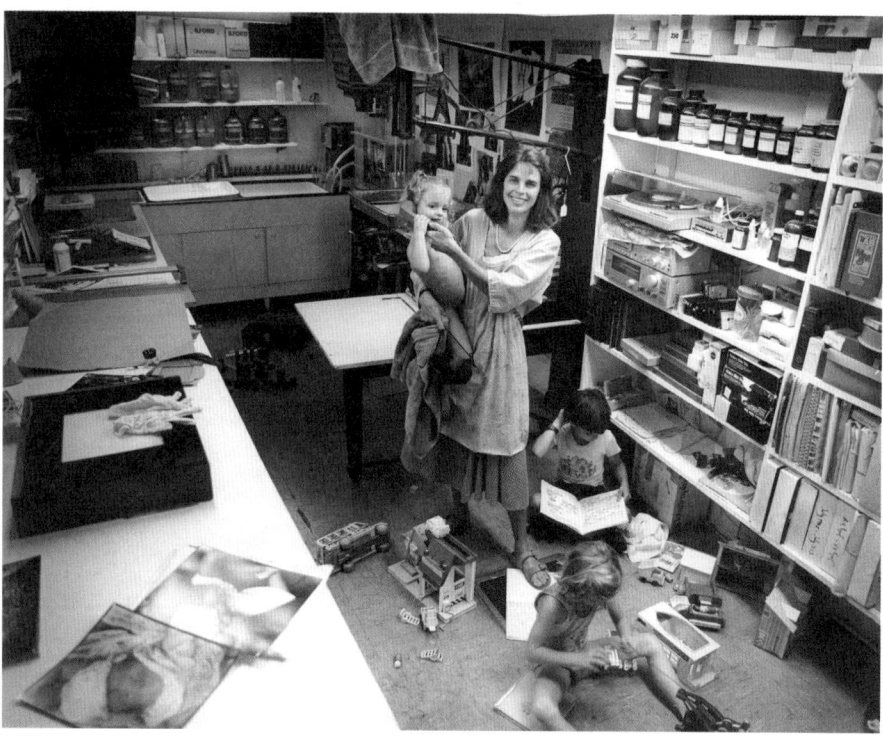

First 20 × 24, then 30 × 40, and finally 40 × 50, as big as photo paper came back then. I printed for decades, with the unbroken regimen of a factory worker. I worked like Trollope, who sat down to his notebook, which he had ruled into segments indicating 250 words, and filled a segment every fifteen minutes. If he didn't achieve that goal, he wrote faster, until by the end of the day he had three thousand words. Trollope began at 6:00 a.m., but I was running my three miles at 6:00 a.m. and didn't make it to the darkroom until 8:00, almost never finishing before 10:00 at night. Like Trollope, I had a goal, which was to fill my twelve-print washer with what I hoped were perfect prints, and I stayed in the darkroom until I had. I did this every day, except Friday, when we assessed prints and decided which ones to reprint. Other than a few 8 × 10s, I made every single print that will ever be so fortunate as to emerge from my storage shelves to be, I hope, hung on the walls of homes or museums.

Instead of making the big prints the way savvy printers do, with pullies and gutter-shaped trays through which the sheets of paper are effortlessly passed, I had two large plexiglass trays made for processing the 40 × 50s. The photo paper came in seventy-pound rolls, over fifty inches wide, which the UPS driver took great pleasure in caber-tossing like a Scottish lumberjack into the yard. Hauling the rolls into the darkroom, I had to razor the easily kinkable paper into sheets for each print. And it didn't get easier after that, what with the endless, boring, repetitive lifting and pouring of three-gallon buckets holding the various chemicals, then filling and dumping the trays for the seven tiresome water rinses.

Each print took an hour to process—and sometimes a quarter hour to expose—and was as fragile as wet tissue. After they dried overnight, I flattened them and compared each print against the next, and against a perfect print, if I had one already from a previous printing. There were viewing days when I tore up every single print from the day before; the average success rate rarely exceeded 50 percent.

The failures were often from misjudgments of mere fractions of seconds in the exposure, or from one of the many burning and dodging maneuvers to lighten or darken areas of the image, or from some damage to the surface—a dog hair, for example, having settled during the exposure, or, once, a fly that landed under the warm light and left a ghostly winged image on the paper. The prints that made the cut, I then dry-mounted (six bites with my old Seal dry-mount press, each bite increasing the risk of a tiny dust-speck wafting down and ruining the whole), then spotted, and—there's still time to screw it up!—signed on the back. Not that I didn't have able and hardworking interns and assistants who helped with all the post-printing chores—I certainly did, and their names and my memories of them are eternally inscribed on my grateful heart—but basically, I made those prints for decades, day and night, as if my life depended on it.

Which, of course, it did. The passion for making my work *exactly right* seemed existentially imperative to me, as I hope it does to you. Truman Capote once said—and he would know—that when God hands you a gift, he also hands you a whip, and if we can please not quibble too much here on the nature of the word "gift," I add a full-throated endorsement to that sentiment. But I can see it the other way, too. You apply the whip, then strain at the harness for decades—batting homers into the record books or practicing Tchaikovsky's violin concerto until your neighbors pack up and leave—and the gift eventually follows.

The gift brings along its own mysterious recipe of essential algorithmic ingredients, including obsession, serendipity, luck, persistence, and epiphany in undisclosed quantities, each of which is as essential as the pinch of baking powder in the cumulous spoon bread Gee-Gee triumphantly served for Wednesday luncheon—and each of which we have touched upon in past chapters. But what we haven't spoken about within that gift is an ingredient perhaps best termed "affection," to borrow again from Wendell Berry. Affection isn't just watered-down love, or flagging passion, at least not in the way Berry uses the term and I understand it. As Berry describes it, affection is more far-reaching and durable, encompassing mercy, forbearance, respect, authentic hope, and sympathy. It is not ecstasy, which almost by definition is short-lived; rather, it is the massive wave beneath the ecstatic froth flecking the curl.

In the late winter of 1972, Larry and I washed up, as travel weary as Odysseus, on the then-un-touristed Greek island of Paros. I had in my backpack a doorstopper edition of Ezra Pound's *Cantos*, having been fascinated by Pound ever since seeing his portrait by Richard Avedon, a classic example of the cross-pollination between imagery and language that has characterized my life. The image is curiously unreadable; at first glance the expression might appear to be anguish or deep grief, and neither is impossible; Pound was a man of oceanically deep sorrows, and he was also batshit crazy.

In this moment captured by Avedon, Pound's expression could be reflecting the exquisite intensity of concentration required as he recited a poem to his friend William Carlos Williams, or it could be the revelatory moment before the camera when he realized he was, in his own words (from Canto 115):

> A blown husk that is finished
> But the light sings eternal

We can never know what this wounded, bitter, and confused man was feeling, and the unknowing, the gift of ambiguity, is what Avedon gave to me early in my seeing life, and which I carried with me to Paros.

In 1958, the year the picture was taken, Pound had just been released from the bughouse, as he called the psych ward at St. Elizabeths Hospital in Washington, D.C. Shortly after this, he adopted his very public vow of total silence, which he steadfastly maintained, breaking it at long last by proclaiming, "I have never made a person happy in my life." Interestingly, Cy Twombly told me that during this famous silence he happened to be sitting behind Pound in his private balcony at the Spoleto festival and clearly heard him speak to his mistress, Olga Rudge; his voice was raspy and weak, but he was lucid. Or as lucid as a man can be who succumbed to a pungent stew of neuroses while locked up outside in a six-by-six-foot wire cage on the barren plains north of Pisa. (In some kind of twisted cosmic irony, the father of Emmett Till was caged next to him until, as Pound notes, "Till was hung yesterday / for murder and rape with trimmings.") There, under the flimsy tar-paper roof, tormented all night by floodlights that did nothing to relieve the cold penetrating the concrete floor, Pound began writing on pieces of toilet paper the uneven but often brilliant *Pisan Cantos*.

It was those cantos that I had chosen to concentrate on in Paros, working through them with all the thoroughness of a forensic accountant, running my finger under each indecipherable line, until in Canto Seventy-Six I encountered something that actually made sense to me.

> nothing matters but the quality
> of the affection—
> in the end—that has carved the trace in the mind
> dove sta memoria

No shit! I said to Ezra, and by Canto Eighty-One we were packed and ready to catch the ferry for our trip back home to Virginia.

The essential, unspoken Poundian preposition is "for"—affection *for*. You by now already know that my own lifelong affection is for place; my ancestral acres here in the Shenandoah Valley. Canto Eighty-One, where I put the final bookmark as I boarded the ferry, contains the most famous of Pound's poetic lines, reproduced many times, including at my family's gravesite. Within all that Pisan derangement, Pound gets one thing unquestionably right: what we love is what remains, our true heritage. Our place on earth is alive with the dead and haunted by the living: where we are is who we are, and who we are, what we do, is defined and enriched by the exigencies of place. It is not a commodity, a resource to be used and discarded, but a beneficent and enduring value—in my view, among the most important.

But whatever your particular place is—it can be a Brooklyn backyard, the mossy spot by the creek where you camped that time, those multifarious earthly places where we make our lives—it is at existential risk. We can make all the art—and it can be great art—and write all the books we want, but as we continue to despoil our landscape with the grotesque extravagance of our waste and greed, we face a catastrophic loss of our fundamental human and artistic (probably the least of it) integrity, and, more to the point, our very existence.

Maybe in other times artists could be free to swan about in their famously louche ways, and indeed I did so myself a time or two, but not anymore. You youngsters have inherited from my wasteful, careless generation a toxic world on fire, and unless you take action, you will lose your air, your water, your land, your democracies. The affection of which I spoke requires of us a selflessness uncharacteristic of our calling, and—I'm risking an eye roll here—I have to reinforce the Berryian formula for good community, which, after all, is the natural habitat of affection: Be kind, be thankful, believe in your work, and, above all, care for your place in the world.

The latter I have been fortunate enough to carry to an extreme, because I have been blessed with a place to love, but Wendell Berry is correct, of course: Find your place, wherever it is, and stay in it; settle for the least and quit that whining about it, try to love your neighbors, even when they put out their right-wing political signs, and, with all the gratitude of thanksgiving, keep working. To paraphrase, indeed mangle, my hero Flaubert, you should be regular and orderly in your life, so you can write like an avenging angel. (And I'm sure if Flaubert were alive right now, he'd also tell you to send any money you can spare to candidates who will keep us from swerving into fascism, to write your congressional representatives, take to the streets, exercise your hard-won right to vote, and, better still, run for office, especially local office.)

It's the lucky artist who can foist off civic obligation to a partner, as I did. Larry Mann did all the righteous heavy lifting for the two of us: He joined the all-volunteer Lexington Fire Department, rising to the level of captain and having some hair-singeing close calls, ran for and won a seat on our city council and served on it in various capacities for four decades, was a stalwart Democratic Party and conservation group member, fought that hard battle for commonwealth's attorney and lost to a country-club Republican by only a handful of votes.

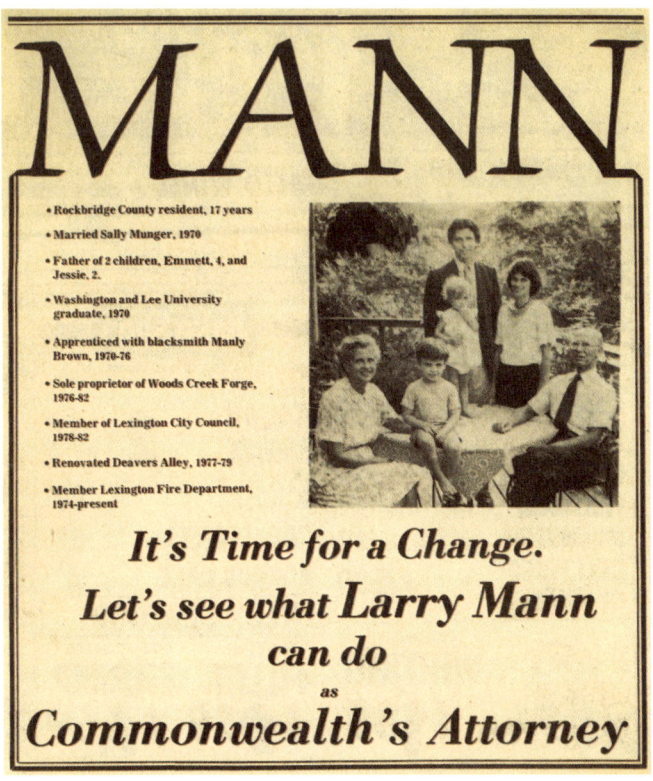

While I was being the artist, and a definite political liability, he was rescuing cats from trees, enduring long meetings about sewer lines, and indulging torrents of fucknuttery while finessing the city's legal policy on the public display of the Confederate flag. He walked the civic walk his entire career and in doing so allowed me to make my work and live with myself and to now sanctimoniously urge you toward an activist stance yourself. I know you're a creative soul and—like me—your tolerance for, say, three-hour committee meetings is probably pretty low, but the situation is dire and if not us, who?

Activism is not antithetical to the practice of your art. Civic responsibilities do not preclude the hard work at which you should be beavering away or dampen the passion that vibrates within you. Ethical and existential issues, moral right and wrong, global turmoil in myriad forms, all operate on a scale of values that is not entirely dissimilar from those you may encounter in your creative life, despite the general misperception that art occupies some rarefied element. In the spirit-rallying, mantra-like words of Henry James's dying character, the novelist Dencombe, "We work in the dark—we do what we can—we give what we have. Our doubt is our passion, and our passion is our task."

That last clause, that our passion is our task, at first perplexed me, but no more. Passion, which is where we started this chapter, is more than just a bacchanal of wanton expression. It is not inherent or intrinsic, something you are born with or not. It is no guarantee of success, nor should you allow your passions to exclude, say, your responsibility to be an involved citizen (*vide supra*), a kind friend, a good spouse and parent. You can have passion but no need for the whole Lord Byron–on–a–windswept–precipice routine; it does not absolve you from the normal activities of a regular working stiff, despite the long and well-parsed history of passionately creative artists so self-absorbed that they leave a wake of emotional destruction behind them.

Passion, however, does allow you to indulge in your task, a seemingly incompatible pairing of verb and predicate; but my argument is that passion can be domesticated—it is manageable and requires both the application of inspirational fuel and a steady hand to alternately stoke it and control the damper. The risk of unfettered passion is that you will flame out and your ashes will mingle with those of so many others before you. You might be remembered for a few conflagrations, but surely you'd rather history spread her metaphorical coattails against a steadily sustaining fireside blaze; a career that you maintained with both passion and deliberately practiced skill in more or less equal measure.

———

It might seem strange that my clever high school boyfriend chose to include the words of that fusty windbag Polonius in a love poem for me in 1968 (and, because I was an idiot, I doubtless thought he had written them himself): *To thine own self be true.* But I never for a moment thought it could be otherwise.

From the beginning, I have dragged my emotions from the back rooms of my heart's rag-and-bone shop, and have given them sincere expression, putting them out onto the street where every asshole with artistic pretensions can poke at them with a stick. Naively, I still subscribe to the belief that the ultimate purpose of art is beauty, within which, in synoptic bedazzlement, we discover a collective harmony and grace. Corny, I know, but before heaping scorn on this, let's bring the Jamesian principle into play, which posits that naivete in art is like the digit zero in math; its value depends on what it's attached to.

In Somerset Maugham's novel *Cakes and Ale*, the narrator, a literary figure, observes that "serious people" tend to laugh at him when he writes from the fullness of his heart, and, indeed, as time passes, he finds he laughs at himself also, despite the sincerity of his emotion. And why not, he muses, for man is but "the ephemeral inhabitant of an insignificant planet," and, despite all his suffering, striving, and ambition, is merely "a jest in an eternal mind."

I encourage you to defy that perception, to attach your zero, which is where we all start, to the limitless integer of your creativity, your drive, your accumulated skills, your tenacity, and your passion. Your sincere emotions matter, and not just to you. It is not sentimental or romantic to want to share your feelings. Or, maybe it is, but do it anyway; the worst that can happen is that you invite the condescension of a supposedly sophisticated audience. *Be true.* Despite the platitudinous precipice on which they tee-ter, embrace without irony or apology the concepts of beauty, hope, joy, honesty, and, always, affection. Leave your fearless trace, *dove sta memo-ria*, because beauty matters. As an artist, you are a sensitive filament pick-ing up unique frequencies and making the work they evoke. And if you are lucky, when that work is released, it will find untingled nerve endings out in the world and lustily tingle them, manifesting indelible truths in which someone will one day find beauty. That is our job.

You know how you go through life seeing massive flaws and terrible fissures and painful lapses and things left undone, and there you are left breathless and gasping in the dust of your life as it stampedes by you...

And so imperfect. I go to bed with my heart breaking in frustration...didn't get as much done as I had hoped and barked at the kids and the laundry was left out in the rain.

But then there are, occasionally, suddenly, those moments of such perfection and enormous grace that all the imperfections seem like slow motes floating in a beam of sun. I find myself at

—from a letter to Ted Orland, 1985

Acknowledgments

Books are bound in signatures, large sheets of paper printed and folded in sets, which determine how many pages a book will have. My adored editor, Michael Sand, and brilliant designer, Laura Lindgren, have just informed me that because of that physical reality, I have exactly one page on which to write my acks, as they say in the biz: 347 words. A strangely specific number. It would seem I am wasting a lot of them explaining the printing process to you, but in this book, as in *Hold Still*, this extraordinary pair has figured out exactly how this complicated book will go together, will read and look, ensuring that it is as carefully written and elegantly designed as we can make it. Thank you, Laura, for cheerfully sorting this all out. And, Michael, as in the last twenty-five years we have worked together, you have been patient, witty, and a wise wielder of the subtle knife.

Many others have helped in dozens of ways, big and small. A friend, the writer Ben Moser, referred to the "polite formula" of the acknowledgments page, but here (185 words already!) I must dispense with that and broad-stroke my way to 347.

I am especially grateful to Ted Orland, for everything; to Putri Tan for everything else; to my friend and agent, Lynn Nesbit; to Eben Ostby and Molly Smith for help with the images; to the people who allowed me to reproduce their images or words; and to friends who have been supportive in various ways: Karen Bailey, Chloe Currens, Paatela Fraga, Leah Green, Sarah Greenough, Renee and John Grisham, Alison Hall, Jenni Holder-Bouafia, Sarah Kennel, Rhea Kosovic, Jim Lewis, Hunter Mohring, Ann Olson, Ann Patchett, and Amy Woolard. I remain forever grateful to the dear friends who traveled to attend the Massey Lectures in 2011, encouraging me on this writing path. And my dogs. We've hit the word limit, but there is no limit to our mutual devotion.

And, as always, with deepest love I thank my family: Larry, Jessie, Virginia, Eyal, Roman, Verus, Adaline, Margot, and Everett.

IMAGE CREDITS

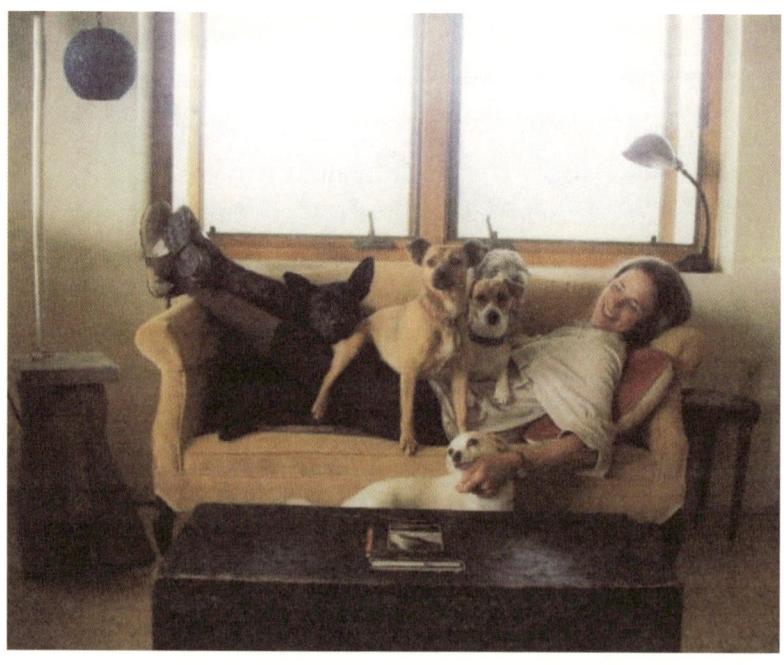